Cisco IOS 12.0 Quality of Service

Cisco Systems, Inc.

CISCO SYSTEMS

CISCO PRESS

Cisco Press
201 West 103rd Street
Indianapolis, IN 46290 USA

Cisco IOS 12.0 Quality of Service

Cisco Systems, Inc.

Copyright© 1999 Cisco Systems, Inc.

Cisco Press logo is a trademark of Cisco Systems, Inc.

Published by:
Cisco Press
201 West 103rd Street
Indianapolis, IN 46290 USA

Printed in the United States of America 1 2 3 4 5 6 7 8 9 0

Library of Congress Cataloging-in-Publication Number 99-60813

ISBN: 1-57870-161-9

Warning and Disclaimer

This book is designed to provide information about **Cisco IOS 12.0 Quality of Service**. Every effort has been made to make this book as complete and as accurate as possible, but no warranty or fitness is implied.

The information is provided on an "as is" basis. The author, Cisco Press, and Cisco Systems, Inc., shall have neither liability nor responsibility to any person or entity with respect to any loss or damages arising from the information contained in this book or from the use of the discs or programs that may accompany it.

The opinions expressed in this book belong to the author and are not necessarily those of Cisco Systems, Inc.

Trademark Acknowledgments

All terms mentioned in this book that are known to be trademarks or service marks have been appropriately capitalized. Cisco Press or Cisco Systems, Inc., cannot attest to the accuracy of this information. Use of a term in this book should not be regarded as affecting the validity of any trademark or service mark.

Feedback Information

At Cisco Press, our goal is to create in-depth technical books of the highest quality and value. Each book is crafted with care and precision, undergoing rigorous development that involves the unique expertise of members from the professional technical community.

Readers' feedback is a natural continuation of this process. If you have any comments regarding how we could improve the quality of this book or otherwise alter it to better suit your needs, you can contact us through e-mail at ciscopress@mcp.com. Please make sure to include the book title and ISBN in your message.

We greatly appreciate your assistance.

Associate Publisher	Jim LeValley
Executive Editor	Alicia Buckley
Cisco Systems Program Manager	H. Kim Lew
Managing Editor	Patrick Kanouse
Acquisitions Editor	Tracy Hughes
Copy Editor	Kitty Jarrett
Team Coordinator	Amy Lewis
Book Designer	Scott Cook
Cover Designer	Karen Ruggles
Production Team	Steve Balle-Gifford
Indexer	Chris Wilcox
Proofreader	Sheri Replin

Acknowledgments

Cisco's IOS software has continually evolved to meet the needs of our customers by the addition and extension of features that comprise the solution set for Cisco IOS software. Quality of service (QoS) is one such area where Cisco has continued to extend and develop new additions to meet the emerging needs of customers as they deploy such value-adding features in their networks. For example, customers need to leverage their existing network infrastructure to offer value-adding services and have the ability to prioritize different types of traffic in their network. In addition, emerging network applications, such as Multimedia and VoIP, present strict requirements on the network behavior. Cisco's IOS QoS feature sets provide the enabling technologies to meet such needs of our customers.

We have been shipping various QoS features in various Cisco IOS software releases such as 11.0, 11.1, 11.1CC, 11.2, and 11.3. The Cisco IOS 12.0 software release has been a good opportunity for us to migrate all the QoS feature sets, which were committed to the afore-mentioned Cisco IOS software releases, into one 12.0 mainline release. This allows more consistency in the Cisco IOS QoS feature offerings, and customers need to run only one release to get these features.

Hence, this book describes the Cisco IOS QoS feature set in 12.0 mainline. These features run on the mainstream router platforms such as the 1600, 1720, 2500, 2600, 3600, 4500, 4700, 7200, 7500-RSP, and derivatives of these platforms. The book also includes descriptions of the VIP QoS features that run on the VIP card in a 7500.

The work presented in this book has been the output of a number of contributors throughout the company who have either contributed directly to or influenced the development of these features, or provided review feedback. Allow me to take this opportunity to thank these folks for their contribution:

- IOS Technical Documentation: Brian Adams, Christy Choate, Ben Jackson, Doug MacBeth, Teresa Oliver Schick, Vicky Payne, Judy Thompson-Melanson, Alliene Turner, Grace Tai, et al.

- IOS Core QoS: Dan Alvarez, Chandrashekhar Appanna, Sandeep Bajaj, Fred Baker, Murali Bashyam, Lisa Birch, Derek Bolton, Claude Cartee, Sanjay Kalra, Dima Khoury, Ted Kuo, Manoj Leelani, Qingming Ma, Rakhi Mahto, Pranav Mehta, Sandeep Nalekonda, Dave Oran, Glenn Reitsma, Dave Rossetti, Arun Sastry, Thesjawi Thimmappa, Alex Tweedly, Pawan Uberoy, et al.

- VIP QoS: Christina Chan, Alan Cheilek, Nathan Chu, Tom Grennan, Atri Indiresan, Darren Kerr, Nick Leavy, Jason Nolet, Bob Olsen, Rob Redford, Dave Rowell, Partha Sarathy, Shu Tai, Andy Teng, Emery Wilkerson, Gang Wu, et al.

- IOS Layer 3 Services: Bruce Davie, Mike Dibiaso, Terry Graf, Carol Ituralde, Francois Le Faucheur, Ashok Narayanan, Tara Posner, et al.

- IOS and Business Unit Marketing: Seenu Banda, Erik Gilbert, Peter Long, Paul McNab, David Powell, et al.

- Other cross-functional folks:

   Frame Relay: Paulina Bettink, Greg Fowler, Dave Langley, et al.
   Consulting Engineering: Bob Allegretti, Clarence Filsfils, et al.
   Policy-Based Routing: Bob Albrightson, Tony Li, Wilber Su, Paul Traina, et al.
   ...Among others.

As we continue to enhance the Cisco IOS QoS feature sets and make the new features available in future IOS releases, we will revise the book to include these new features. We welcome any comments that you have about this book; e-mail qosdocs@cisco.com.

We hope you find this book useful as a one-stop place of technical information for Cisco's IOS QoS and VIP QoS features in 12.0 mainline.

Regards,

Ken Pillay
IOS Core QoS Development Manager
Cisco Systems, Inc.

Contents at a Glance

Table of Contents

Introduction: Quality of Service Overview

This chapter explains quality of service (QoS) and the service models that embody it. It also suggests benefits you can gain from implementing Cisco IOS QoS in your network. Then it trains a closer focus on the Cisco Internetwork Operating System (IOS) QoS features and the technologies that implement them.

What Is QoS?

QoS refers to the ability of a network to provide better service to selected network traffic over various underlying technologies, including Frame Relay, Asynchronous Transfer Mode (ATM), Ethernet and 802.1 networks, SONET, and IP-routed networks. In particular, QoS features provide better and more predictable network service by

- Supporting dedicated bandwidth
- Improving loss characteristics
- Avoiding and managing network congestion
- Shaping network traffic
- Setting traffic priorities across the network

About QoS Architecture

You configure QoS features throughout a network to provide for end-to-end QoS delivery. The following three components are necessary to deliver QoS across a heterogeneous network:

- QoS within a single network element, which includes queuing, scheduling, and traffic shaping features.
- QoS signaling techniques for coordinating QoS from end-to-end between network elements.
- QoS policing and management functions to control and administer end-to-end traffic across a network.

Not all QoS techniques are appropriate for all network routers. Because edge routers and core routers in a network do not necessarily perform the same operations, the QoS tasks they perform might differ. To configure an IP network for real-time voice traffic, for example, you would need to consider the functions of both edge and core routers in the network, then select the appropriate QoS feature or features.

In general, edge routers perform the following QoS functions:

- Packet classification
- Admission control

- Configuration management

In general, core routers perform the following QoS functions:

- Congestion management
- Congestion avoidance

Who Could Benefit from Using Cisco IOS QoS?

All networks can take advantage of aspects of QoS for optimum efficiency, whether the network is for a small corporation, an enterprise, or an Internet service provider (ISP). Different categories of networking users—such as major enterprises, network service providers, and small and medium-sized business networking users—have their own QoS requirements; in many areas, however, these requirements overlap. The Cisco IOS QoS features described in the section "Cisco's QoS Features" later in this introduction address these diverse and common needs.

Enterprise networks, for example, must provide end-to-end QoS solutions across the various platforms comprising the network; providing solutions for heterogeneous platforms often requires taking a different QoS configuration approach for each technology. As enterprise networks carry more complex, mission-critical applications and experience increased traffic from Web multimedia applications, QoS serves to prioritize this traffic to ensure that each application gets the service it requires.

ISPs require assured scalability and performance. For example, ISPs that long have offered best-effort IP connectivity now also transfer voice, video, and other real-time critical application data. QoS answers the scalability and performance needs of these ISPs to distinguish different kinds of traffic, thereby enabling them to offer service differentiation to their customers.

In the small and medium-sized business segment, managers are experiencing firsthand the rapid growth of business on the Internet. These business networks must also handle increasingly complex business applications. QoS lets the network handle the difficult task of utilizing an expensive WAN connection in the most efficient way for business applications.

Why Deploy Cisco IOS QoS?

The Cisco IOS QoS features enable networks to control and predictably service a variety of networked applications and traffic types. Implementing Cisco IOS QoS in your network promotes

- Control over resources. You have control over which resources (bandwidth, equipment, wide-area facilities, and so on) are being used. For example, you can limit bandwidth consumed over a core link by File Transfer Protocol (FTP) transfers or give priority to an important database access.

- Tailored services. If you are an ISP, the control and visibility provided by QoS enables you to offer carefully tailored grades of service differentiation to your customers.

- Coexistence of mission-critical applications. Cisco's QoS features make certain that your WAN is used efficiently by mission-critical applications that are most important to your business; that bandwidth and minimum delays required by time-sensitive multimedia and voice applications are available; and that other applications using the link get their fair service without interfering with mission-critical traffic.

Moreover, in implementing QoS features in your network, you put in place the foundation for a future fully integrated network.

End-to-End QoS Models

A service model, also called a level of service, describes a set of end-to-end QoS capabilities. End-to-end QoS is the ability of the network to deliver service required by specific network traffic from one end of the network to another. Cisco IOS QoS software supports three types of service models: best effort, integrated, and differentiated services.

NOTE QoS service models differ from one another in how they enable applications to send data and in the ways in which the network attempts to deliver that data. For instance, a different service model applies to real-time applications, such as audio and video conferencing and IP telephony, from the one that applies to file transfer and e-mail applications.

Consider the following factors when deciding which type of service to deploy in the network:

- The application or problem you are trying to solve. Each of the three types of service—best effort, integrated, and differentiated—is appropriate for certain applications.

- The kind of ability you want to allocate to your resources.

- Cost-benefit analysis. For example, the cost of implementing and deploying differentiated service is certain to be more expensive than doing so for a best-effort service.

This section describes these service models:

- Best-Effort Service

- Integrated Service

- Differentiated Service

The features in Cisco IOS QoS software address the requirements for these service models.

Best-Effort Service

Best effort is a single service model in which an application sends data whenever it must, in any quantity, and without requesting permission or first informing the network. For best-effort service, the network delivers data if it can, without any assurance of reliability, delay bounds, or throughput.

The Cisco IOS QoS feature that implements best-effort service is first-in, first-out (FIFO) queuing. Best-effort service is suitable for a wide range of networked applications, such as general file transfers or e-mail.

Integrated Service

Integrated service is a multiple service model that can accommodate multiple QoS requirements. In this model, the application requests a specific kind of service from the network before sending data. The request is made by explicit signaling; the application informs the network of its traffic profile and requests a particular kind of service that can encompass its bandwidth and delay requirements. The application is expected to send data only after it gets a confirmation from the network. It is also expected to send data that lies within its described traffic profile.

The network performs admission control, based on information from the application and available network resources. It also commits to meeting the QoS requirements of the application as long as the traffic remains within the profile specifications. The network fulfills its commitment by maintaining per-flow state and then performing packet classification, policing, and intelligent queuing based on that state.

Cisco IOS QoS includes these features that provide controlled load service, which is a kind of integrated service:

- Resource Reservation Protocol (RSVP) can be used by applications to signal their QoS requirements to the router.

- Intelligent queuing mechanisms can be used with RSVP to provide the following kinds of services:

  — Guaranteed Rate Service, which allows applications to reserve bandwidth to meet their requirements. For example, a Voice over IP (VoIP) application can reserve 32 Mbps end to end using this kind of service. Cisco IOS QoS uses weighted fair queuing (WFQ) with RSVP to provide this kind of service.

  — Controlled Load Service, which allows applications to have low delay and high throughput even during times of congestion. For example, adaptive real-time applications, such as playback of a recorded conference, can use this kind of service. Cisco IOS QoS uses RSVP with Weighted Random Early Detection (WRED) to provide this kind of service.

Differentiated Service

Differentiated service is a multiple service model that can satisfy differing QoS requirements. However, unlike the integrated service model, an application using differentiated service does not explicitly signal the router before sending data.

For differentiated service, the network tries to deliver a particular kind of service based on the QoS specified by each packet. This specification can occur in different ways, for example, using the IP precedence bit-settings in IP packets or source and destination addresses. The network uses the QoS specification to classify, shape, and police traffic, and to perform intelligent queuing.

The differentiated service model is used for several mission-critical applications and for providing end-to-end QoS. Typically, this service model is appropriate for aggregate flows because it performs a relatively coarse level of traffic classification.

Cisco IOS QoS includes these features that support the differentiated service model:

- Committed access rate (CAR), which performs packet classification through IP precedence and QoS group settings. CAR performs metering and policing of traffic, providing bandwidth management.

- Intelligent queuing schemes such as WRED and WFQ and their equivalent features on the Versatile Interface Processor (VIP), which are VIP-Distributed WRED and VIP-Distributed WFQ. These features can be used with CAR to deliver differentiated services.

Cisco's QoS Features

The Cisco IOS QoS software provides these major features, some of which have been previously mentioned, and all of which are briefly described in this introduction and then explained more fully in the overview chapters of this book:

- Classification

- Congestion Management

- Congestion Avoidance

- Policing and Shaping

- Signaling

- Link Efficiency Mechanisms

Classification

Packet classification features provide the capability to partition network traffic into multiple priority levels or classes of service. For example, using the three precedence bits in the type of service (ToS) field of the IP packet header—two of the values are reserved for other purposes—you can categorize packets into a limited set of up to six traffic classes. After you classify packets, you can utilize other QoS features to assign the appropriate traffic handling policies, including congestion management, bandwidth allocation, and delay bounds for each traffic class.

Packets can also be classified by external sources, that is, by a customer or by a downstream network provider. You can either allow the network to accept the classification, or override it and reclassify the packet according to a policy that you specify.

Packets can be classified based on policies specified by the network operator. Policies can be set that include classification based on physical port, source or destination IP or MAC address, application port, IP protocol type, and other criteria that you can specify by access lists or extended access lists.

You can use Cisco IOS QoS policy-based routing (PBR) and the classification features of Cisco IOS QoS CAR to classify packets. You can use Border Gateway Protocol (BGP) Policy Propagation to propagate destination-based packet classification policy throughout a large network via BGP routing updates. This section gives a brief description of these features.

For more complete conceptual information on packet classification, see Chapter 1,"Classification Overview."

For information on how to configure the various protocols that implement classification, see the following chapters:

- Chapter 2, "Configuring Policy-Based Routing"

- Chapter 3, "Configuring QoS Policy Propagation via Border Gateway Protocol"

- Chapter 4, "Configuring Committed Access Rate"

IP Precedence

IP precedence allows you to specify a packet's class of service using the three precedence bits in the IPv4 header's ToS field. Other features configured throughout the network can then use these bits to determine how to treat the packet in regard to the type of service to grant it. For example, although IP precedence is not a queuing method, other queuing methods such as WFQ can use the IP precedence setting of the packet to prioritize traffic.

PBR

Cisco IOS QoS PBR allows you to do the following:

- Classify traffic based on extended access list criteria.

- Set IP precedence bits.

- Route specific traffic to engineered paths, which may be required to allow a specific QoS service through the network.

Classification of traffic through PBR allows you to identify traffic for different classes of service at the perimeter of the network and then implement QoS defined for each class of service in the core of the network using priority, custom, or WFQ techniques. This process obviates the need to classify traffic explicitly at each WAN interface in the core network.

Some possible applications for policy routing are to provide equal access, protocol-sensitive routing, source-sensitive routing, routing based on interactive versus batch traffic, or routing based on dedicated links.

CAR (Packet Classification)

CAR is the main feature supporting packet classification. CAR uses the ToS bits in the IP header to classify packets. You can use the CAR classification commands to classify and reclassify a packet.

Here are some example packet classification policies:

- All packets received on a particular T1 line are classified as high priority (port-based classification).

- All HTTP traffic is classified as medium priority (application classification).

- Video traffic from a specified IP address is classified as medium priority.

- Packets bound for particular destinations are classified as high priority traffic (for example, international traffic or traffic bound for a premium customer).

- Some packets are classified for subrate IP services. The network operator delivers a physical T1/E1 or T3/E3 line to the customer, but offers a less expensive subrate service, for example, 1 Mbps on an E1 line or 10 Mbps on a T3 line. The customer pays for the subrate bandwidth and may be upgraded to additional access bandwidth over time based on demand. CAR limits the traffic rate available to the customer and delivered to the network to the agreed upon rate limit (with the ability to temporarily burst over the limit). The network operator may upgrade the service without any physical network arrangement.

- Traffic is classified for exchange point traffic control. An ISP offers transit services to downstream ISPs via exchange point connectivity provided by a Layer 2 switch. The upstream provider utilizes MAC-address rate limits provided by CAR to enforce bandwidth usage limitations on the downstream ISPs.

NOTE	CAR also implements rate-limiting services, which are briefly described later in this chapter.

BGP Policy Propagation

BGP provides a powerful, scalable means of utilizing attributes, such as community values, to propagate destination-based packet classification policy throughout a large network via BGP routing updates. Packet classification policy can be scalably propagated via BGP without writing and deploying complex access lists at each of a large number of routers. BGP ensures that return traffic to customers is handled as premium traffic by the network.

Congestion Management

Congestion management features operate to control congestion once it occurs. One way that network elements handle an overflow of arriving traffic is to use a queuing algorithm to sort the traffic, then determine some method of prioritizing it onto an output link. Each queuing algorithm was designed to solve a specific network traffic problem and has a particular effect on network performance. The Cisco IOS software congestion management, or queuing, features include FIFO, priority queuing (PQ), custom queuing (CQ), and WFQ (and VIP-Distributed WFQ).

For more complete conceptual information on packet classification, see Chapter 5, "Congestion Management Overview."

For information on how to configure the various protocols that implement congestion management, see the following chapters:

- Chapter 6, "Configuring Weighted Fair Queuing"

- Chapter 7, "Configuring Custom Queuing"

- Chapter 8, "Configuring Priority Queuing"

What Is Congestion in Networks?

To give you a more definite sense of congestion in networks, this section briefly describes some of its characteristics, drawing on the explanation presented by V. Paxson and S. Floyd in a paper titled "Wide Area Traffic: The Failure of Poisson Modeling."

What does congestion look like? Consideration of the behavior of congested systems is not simple and cannot be dealt with in a simplistic manner, because traffic rates do not simply rise to a level, stay there a while, and then subside. Periods of traffic congestion can be quite long with losses that are heavily concentrated. In contrast to Poisson traffic models, linear increases in buffer size do not result in large decreases in packet drop rates; a slight increase in the number of active connections can result in a large increase in the packet loss rate. This understanding of the behavior of congested networks suggests that because the level of busy period traffic is not predictable, it would be difficult to efficiently size networks to reduce congestion adequately. Observers of network congestion report that in reality, traffic "spikes," which causes actual losses that ride on longer-term ripples, and they in turn ride on still longer-term swells.

FIFO Queuing

FIFO provides basic store and forward capability. FIFO is the default queuing algorithm in some instances, thus requiring no configuration. See "WFQ and VIP-Distributed WFQ" later in this introduction for a complete explanation of default configuration.

PQ

Designed to give strict priority to important traffic, PQ ensures that important traffic gets the fastest handling at each point where PQ is used. PQ can flexibly prioritize according to network protocol (such as IP, IPX, or AppleTalk), incoming interface, packet size, source/destination address, and so forth.

CQ

CQ reserves a percentage of an interface's available bandwidth for each selected traffic type. If a particular type of traffic is not using the bandwidth reserved for it, then other traffic types may use the remaining reserved bandwidth.

WFQ and VIP-Distributed WFQ

WFQ applies priority (or weights) to identified traffic to classify traffic into conversations and determine how much bandwidth each conversation is allowed relative to other conversations. WFQ classifies traffic into different flows based on such characteristics as source and destination address, protocol, and port and socket of the session.

To provide large-scale support for applications and traffic classes requiring bandwidth allocations and delay bounds over the network infrastructure, Cisco IOS QoS includes a version of WFQ that runs only in distributed mode on VIPs. This version is called VIP-Distributed WFQ. It provides increased flexibility in terms of traffic classification, weight assessment, and discard policy, and delivers Internet-scale performance on the Cisco 7500 series platforms.

For serial interfaces at E1 (2.048 Mbps) and below, WFQ is used by default. When no other queuing strategies are configured, all other interfaces use FIFO by default.

Congestion Avoidance

Congestion avoidance techniques monitor network traffic loads in an effort to anticipate and avoid congestion at common network and internetwork bottlenecks before it becomes a problem. These techniques are designed to provide preferential treatment for premium (priority) class traffic under congestion situations while concurrently maximizing network throughput and capacity utilization and minimizing packet loss and delay. WRED and its counterpart for the VIP, VIP-Distributed WRED, are Cisco's IOS QoS congestion avoidance features.

Router behavior allows output buffers to fill during periods of congestion, using tail drop to resolve the problem when WRED is not configured. During tail drop, a potentially large number of packets from numerous connections are discarded because of lack of buffer capacity. This behavior can result in waves of congestion followed by periods during which the transmission link is not fully used. WRED obviates this situation proactively by providing congestion avoidance. That is, instead of waiting for buffers to fill before dropping packets, the router monitors the buffer depth and performs early discards on selected packets transmitted over selected connections.

WRED is Cisco's implementation of the Random Early Detection (RED) class of congestion avoidance algorithms. When RED is used and the source detects the dropped packet, it slows its transmission. RED is primarily designed to work with TCP in IP internetwork environments.

For more complete conceptual information, see Chapter 9, "Congestion Avoidance Overview."

For information on how to configure WRED and VIP-Distributed WRED, see Chapter 10, "Configuring Weighted Random Early Detection."

WRED

Cisco's implementation of RED, called WRED, combines the capabilities of the RED algorithm with IP precedence to provide preferential traffic handling for higher priority packets. It can selectively discard lower priority traffic when the interface begins to get congested and provide differentiated performance characteristics for different classes of service. WRED is also RSVP-aware. WRED is available on the Cisco 7200 series RSP processors.

VIP-Distributed WRED

VIP-Distributed WRED is Cisco's high-speed version of WRED. The VIP-Distributed WRED algorithm was designed with ISP providers in mind; it allows an ISP to define minimum and maximum queue depth thresholds and drop capabilities for each class of service.

VIP-Distributed WRED, which is available on the Cisco 7500 series VIPs, is analogous in function to WRED, which is available on the 7200 series RSP processors.

Policing and Shaping

Cisco IOS QoS includes traffic policing capabilities implemented through the rate-limiting aspects of CAR and traffic shaping capabilities provided by the Generic Traffic Shaping (GTS) and Frame Relay Traffic Shaping (FRTS) protocols.

For more complete conceptual information, see Chapter 11, "Policing and Shaping Overview."

For information on how to configure these protocols, which implement policing and shaping, see the following chapters:

- Chapter 12, "Configuring Generic Traffic Shaping"

- Chapter 13, "Configuring Frame Relay and Frame Relay Traffic Shaping"

CAR Rate Limiting

The rate-limiting feature of CAR provides the network operator with the means to define Layer 3 aggregate or granular access, or egress bandwidth rate limits, and to specify traffic handling policies when the traffic either conforms to or exceeds the specified rate limits. Aggregate access or egress matches all packets on an interface or subinterface. Granular access or egress matches a particular type of traffic based on precedence. You can designate CAR rate-limiting policies based on physical port, packet classification, IP address, MAC address, application flow, and other criteria specifiable by access lists or extended access lists. CAR rate limits may be implemented either on input or output interfaces or subinterfaces including Frame Relay and ATM subinterfaces.

An example of use of CAR's rate-limiting capability is application-based rates limiting HTTP World Wide Web traffic to 50 percent of link bandwidth, which ensures capacity for non-Web traffic including mission-critical applications.

Shaping

Cisco's IOS QoS software includes these two traffic shaping features, which manage traffic and congestion on the network:

- GTS, which provides a mechanism to control the flow of outbound traffic on a particular interface. It reduces outbound traffic flow to avoid congestion by constraining specified traffic to a particular bit rate. Traffic adhering to a particular profile can be shaped to meet downstream requirements, eliminating bottlenecks in topologies with data rate mismatches.

- FRTS, which provides parameters, such as the following, that are useful for managing network traffic congestion:

    — Committed information rate (CIR)

    — Forward and backward explicit congestion notification (FECN/BECN)

    — The discard eligible (DE) bit

For some time Cisco has provided support for FECN for DECnet and OSI, BECN for SNA traffic using direct LLC2 encapsulation via RFC 1490, and DE bit support. The FRTS feature builds upon this Frame Relay support by providing additional capabilities that improve the scalability and performance of a Frame Relay network by increasing the density of virtual circuits and improving response time.

FRTS applies only to Frame Relay permanent virtual circuits (PVCs) and switched virtual circuits (SVCs).

Signaling

Cisco IOS QoS signaling provides a way for an end station or network node to signal its neighbors to request special handling of certain traffic. QoS signaling is useful for coordinating the traffic handling techniques provided by other QoS features. It plays a key role in configuring successful overall end-to-end QoS service across your network.

Cisco IOS QoS signaling takes advantage of IP. Either in-band (IP precedence, 802.1p) or out-of-band (RSVP) signaling is used to indicate that a particular QoS service is desired for a particular traffic classification. Together, IP precedence and RSVP provide a robust combination for end-to-end QoS signaling: IP precedence signals for differentiated QoS and RSVP for guaranteed QoS.

To achieve the end-to-end benefits of IP precedence and RSVP signaling, Cisco IOS QoS software offers ATM User Network Interface (UNI) signaling and the Frame Relay Local Management Interface (LMI) to provide signaling into their respective core technologies.

For more complete conceptual information, see Chapter 14, "Signaling Overview."

Link Efficiency Mechanisms

Cisco IOS QoS software offers these two link efficiency mechanisms that work in conjunction with queuing and traffic shaping to improve efficiency and predictability of the application services levels: Compressed Real-Time Protocol (CRTP) and Link Fragmentation and Interleaving (LFI).

For more complete conceptual information, see Chapter 16, "Link Efficiency Mechanisms Overview."

For information on how to configure LFI, see Chapter 17, "Configuring Link Fragmentation and Interleaving for Multilink PPP."

For information on how to configure CRTP, see Chapter 18, "Configuring Compressed Real-Time Protocol."

Compressed Real-Time Protocol

Real-Time Protocol (RTP) is a host-to-host protocol used for carrying newer multimedia application traffic, including packetized audio and video, over an IP network. RTP provides end-to-end network transport functions intended for applications transmitting real-time requirements, such as audio, video, or simulation data multicast or unicast network services.

To avoid the unnecessary consumption of available bandwidth, the RTP header compression feature—referred to as CRTP—is used on a link-by-link basis.

Link Fragmentation and Interleaving

Interactive traffic, such as Telnet and Voice over IP, is susceptible to increased latency and jitter when the network processes large packets, such as LAN-to-LAN FTP Telnet transfers traversing a WAN link. This susceptibility increases as the traffic is queued on slower links. Cisco IOS QoS LFI reduces delay and jitter on slower speed links by breaking up large datagrams and interleaving low-delay traffic packets with the resulting smaller packets.

About the Cisco IOS 12.0 Reference Library

The Cisco IOS 12.0 Reference Library books are Cisco documentation that describe the tasks and commands necessary to configure and maintain your Cisco IOS network.

The Cisco IOS software bookset is intended primarily for users who configure and maintain access servers and routers, but are not necessarily familiar with the tasks, the relationship between tasks, or the commands necessary to perform particular tasks.

Cisco IOS Reference Library Organization

The Cisco IOS 12.0 Reference library consists of eleven books. Each book contains technology-specific configuration chapters with corresponding command reference chapters. Each configuration chapter describes Cisco's implementation of protocols and technologies, related configuration tasks, and contains comprehensive configuration examples. Each command reference chapter complements the organization of its corresponding configuration chapter and provides complete command syntax information.

Books Available in the Cisco IOS 12.0 Reference Library

- *Cisco IOS 12.0 Network Protocols*, Volume I, IP, 1-57870-154-6

  This book is a comprehensive guide detailing available IP and IP routing alternatives. It describes how to implement IP addressing and IP services and how to configure support for a wide range of IP routing protocols, including BGP for ISP networks and basic and advanced IP Multicast functionality.

- *Cisco IOS 12.0 Configuration Fundamentals*, 1-57870-155-4

  This comprehensive guide details Cisco IOS software configuration basics. It offers thorough coverage of router and access server configuration and maintenance techniques. In addition to hands-on implementation and task instruction, this book also presents the complete syntax for router and access server commands, and individual examples for each command.

- *Cisco IOS 12.0 Interface Configuration*, 1-57870-156-2

  This book is a comprehensive guide detailing how to configure physical and virtual interfaces—the two types of interfaces supported on Cisco routers. It provides readers with the most current router task and commands information for their network environments and teaches how to effectively implement these techniques and commands on their networks.

- *Cisco IOS 12.0 Wide Area Networking Solutions*, 1-57870-158-9

  This book offers thorough, comprehensive coverage of internetworking technologies, particularly ATM, Frame Relay, SMDS, LAPB, and X.25, teaching the reader how to configure the technologies in a LAN/WAN environment.

- *Cisco IOS 12.0 Switching Services*, 1-57870-157-0

  This book is a comprehensive guide detailing available Cisco IOS switching alternatives. Cisco's switching services range from fast switching and Netflow switching to LAN Emulation. This book describes how to configure routing between virtual LANs (VLANs) and teaches how to effectively configure and implement VLANs on switches.

- *Cisco IOS 12.0 Multiservice Applications*, 1-57870-159-7

  This book shows you how to configure your router or access server to support voice, video, and broadband transmission. Cisco's voice and video support are implemented using voice packet technology. In voice packet technology, voice signals are packetized and transported in compliance with ITU-T specification H.323, which is the ITU-T specification for transmitting multimedia 9voice, video, and data across a local-are network (LAN).

- *Cisco IOS 12.0 Network Security*, 1-57870-160-0

  This book documents security configuration from a remote site and for a central enterprise or service provider network. It describes AAA, Radius, TACACS+, and Kerberos network security features. It also explains how to encrypt data across enterprise networks. The book includes many illustrations that show configurations and functionality, along with a discussion of network security policy choices and some decision-making guidelines.

- *Cisco IOS 12.0 Network Protocols*, Volume II, IPX, AppleTalk and More, 1-57870-164-3

  This book is a comprehensive guide detailing available network protocol alternatives. It describes how to implement various protocols in your network. This book includes documentation of the latest functionality for the IPX and AppleTalk desktop protocols, as well as the following network protocols: Apollo Domain, Banyan VINES, DECNet, ISO CLNS, and XNS.

- *Cisco IOS 12.0 Bridging and IBM Networking Solutions*, 1-57870-162-7

  This book describes Cisco's support for networks in IBM and bridging environments. Support includes: transparent and source-route transparent bridging, source-route bridging (SRB), remote source-route bridging (RSRB), data link switching plus (DLS+), serial tunnel and block serial tunnel, SDLC and LLC2 parameter, IBM network media translation, downstream physical unit and SNA service point, SNA Frame Relay access support, Advanced Peer-to-Peer Networking, and native client interface architecture (NCIA).

- *Cisco IOS 12.0 Dial Solutions*, 1-57870-163-5

  This book provides readers with real-world solutions and how to implement them on a network. Customers interested in implementing dial solutions across their network environment include remote sites dialing in to a central office, Internet Service Providers (ISPs), ISP customers at home offices, and enterprise WAN system administrators implementing dial-on-demand routing (DDR).

Book Conventions

The Cisco IOS documentation set uses the following conventions:

Convention	Description
^ or Ctrl	Represents the Control key. For example, when you read *^D* or *Ctrl-D*, you should hold down the Control key while you press the D key. Keys are indicated in capital letters but are not case sensitive.
string	A string is defined as a nonquoted set of characters. For example, when setting an SNMP community string to public, do not use quotation marks around the string; otherwise, the string will include the quotation marks.

Examples use the following conventions:

Convention	Description
screen	Shows an example of information displayed on the screen.
boldface screen	Shows an example of information that you must enter.
< >	Nonprinting characters, such as passwords, appear in angled brackets.

Convention	Description
!	Exclamation points at the beginning of a line indicate a comment line. They are also displayed by the Cisco IOS software for certain processes.
[ ]	Default responses to system prompts appear in square brackets.

The following conventions are used to attract the reader's attention:

CAUTION	Means *reader be careful*. In this situation, you might do something that could result in equipment damage or loss of data.

NOTE	Means *reader take note*. Notes contain helpful suggestions or references to materials not contained in this manual.

TIMESAVER	Means the *described action saves time*. You can save time by performing the action described in the paragraph.

Within the Cisco IOS 12.0 Reference Library, the term *router* is used to refer to both access servers and routers. When a feature is supported on the access server only, the term *access server* is used.

Within examples, routers and access servers are alternately shown. These products are used only for example purposes; that is, an example that shows one product does not indicate that the other product is not supported.

Command Syntax Conventions

Command descriptions use the following conventions:

Convention	Description
boldface	Indicates commands and keywords that are entered literally as shown.
italics	Indicates arguments for which you supply values; in contexts that do not allow italics, arguments are enclosed in angle brackets (< >).
[**x**]	Keywords or arguments that appear within square brackets are optional.

Convention	Description
{x | y | z}	A choice of required keywords (represented by **x**, **y**, and **z**) appears in braces separated by vertical bars. You must select one.
[x {y | z}]	Braces and vertical bars within square brackets indicate a required choice within an optional element. You do not need to select one. If you do, you have some required choices.

Cisco Connection Online

Cisco Connection Online (CCO) is Cisco Systems' primary, real-time support channel. Maintenance customers and partners can self-register on CCO to obtain additional information and services.

Available 24 hours a day, 7 days a week, CCO provides a wealth of standard and value-added services to Cisco's customers and business partners. CCO services include product information, product documentation, software updates, release notes, technical tips, the Bug Navigator, configuration notes, brochures, descriptions of service offerings, and download access to public and authorized files.

CCO serves a wide variety of users through two interfaces that are updated and enhanced simultaneously: a character-based version and a multimedia version that resides on the World Wide Web (WWW). The character-based CCO supports Zmodem, Kermit, Xmodem, FTP, and Internet e-mail, and it is excellent for quick access to information over lower bandwidths. The WWW version of CCO provides richly formatted documents with photographs, figures, graphics, and video, as well as hyperlinks to related information.

You can access CCO in the following ways:

- WWW: http://www.cisco.com

- WWW: http://www-europe.cisco.com

- WWW: http://www-china.cisco.com

- Telnet: cco.cisco.com

- Modem: From North America, 408-526-8070; from Europe, 33 1 64 46 40 82. Use the following terminal settings: VT100 emulation; databits: 8; parity: none; stop bits: 1; and connection rates up to 28.8 kbps.

Using Cisco IOS Software

This section provides helpful tips for understanding and configuring Cisco IOS software using the command-line interface (CLI).

Getting Help

Entering a question mark (**?**) at the system prompt displays a list of commands available for each command mode. You can also get a list of any command's associated keywords and arguments with the context-sensitive help feature.

To get help specific to a command mode, a command, a keyword, or an argument, use one of the following commands:

Command	Purpose
help	Obtains a brief description of the help system in any command mode.
*abbreviated-command-entry***?**	Obtains a list of commands that begin with a particular character string. (No space between command and question mark.)
abbreviated-command-entry<**Tab**>	Completes a partial command name.
?	Lists all commands available for a particular command mode.
command **?**	Lists a command's associated keywords. (Space between command and question mark.)
command keyword **?**	Lists a keyword's associated arguments. (Space between the keyword and question mark.)

Example: How to Find Command Options

This section provides an example of how to display syntax for a command. The syntax can consist of optional or required keywords. To display keywords for a command, enter a question mark (**?**) at the configuration prompt, or after entering part of a command followed by a space. The Cisco IOS software displays a list of keywords available along with a brief description of the keywords. For example, if you were in global configuration mode, typed the command **arap**, and wanted to see all the keywords for that command, you would type **arap ?**.

Table I-1 shows examples of how you can use the question mark (**?**) to assist you in entering commands. It steps you through entering the following commands:

- **controller t1 1**

- **cas-group 1 timeslots 1-24 type e&m-fgb dtmf**

Table I-1 *How to Find Command Options*

Command	Comment
`Router>` **`enable`** `Password: `*`<password>`* `Router#`	Enter the **enable** command and password to access privileged EXEC commands.
	You have entered privileged EXEC mode when the prompt changes to `Router#`.

Continues

Table I-1 *How to Find Command Options (Continued)*

Command	Comment
Router# **config terminal** Enter configuration commands, one per line. End with Ctrl-Z. Router(config)#	Enter global configuration mode. You have entered global configuration mode when the prompt changes to Router(config)#.
Router(config)# **controller t1 ?** <0-3> Controller unit number Router(config)# **controller t1 1** Router(config-controller)#	Enter controller configuration mode by specifying the T1 controller that you want to configure using the **controller t1** global configuration command. Enter a **?** to display what you must enter next on the command line. In this example, you must enter a controller unit number from 0 to 3. You have entered controller configuration mode when the prompt changes to Router(config-controller)#.

Router(config-controller)# **?**
Controller configuration commands:
  cablelength   Specify the cable length for a DS1 link
  cas-group   Configure the specified timeslots for CAS (Channel Associate Signals)
  channel-group Specify the timeslots to channel-group mapping for an interface
  clock   Specify the clock source for a DS1 link
  default   Set a command to its defaults
  description   Controller specific description
  ds0   ds0 commands
  exit   Exit from controller configuration mode
  fdl   Specify the FDL standard for a DS1 data link
  framing   Specify the type of Framing on a DS1 link
  help   Description of the interactive help system
  linecode   Specify the line encoding method for a DS1 link
  loopback   Put the entire T1 line into loopback
  no   Negate a command or set its defaults
  pri-group   Configure the specified timeslots for PRI
  shutdown   Shut down a DS1 link (send Blue Alarm)
Router(config-controller)#
	Enter a **?** to display a list of all the controller configuration commands available for the T1 controller.

Table I-1 *How to Find Command Options (Continued)*

Command	Comment

`Router(config-controller)# `**`cas-group`**` ?`
 `  <0-23>         ` `Channel number`
`Router(config-controller)# cas-group`
	Enter the command that you want to configure for the controller. In this example, the **cas-group** command is used.

	Enter a **?** to display what you must enter next on the command line. In this example, you must enter a channel number from 0 to 23.
	Because a <cr> is not displayed, it indicates that you must enter more keywords to complete the command.

`Router(config-controller)# `**`cas-group`**` 1 ?`
`  timeslots       ` `List of timeslots in the`
`                    cas-group`
`Router(config-controller)# cas-group 1`
	After you enter the channel number, enter a **?** to display what you must enter next on the command line. In this example, you must enter the **timeslots** keyword.

	Because a <cr> is not displayed, it indicates that you must enter more keywords to complete the command.

`Router(config-controller)# `**`cas-group 1 timeslots`**` ?`
`  <1-24>          ` `List of timeslots which`
`                    comprise the cas-group`
`Router(config-controller)# cas-group 1 timeslots`
	After you enter the **timeslots** keyword, enter a **?** to display what you must enter next on the command line. In this example, you must enter a list of timeslots from 1 to 24.

	You can specify timeslot ranges (for example, 1-24), individual timeslots separated by commas (for example 1, 3, 5), or a combination of the two (for example 1-3, 8, 17-24). The 16th time slot is not specified in the command line, because it is reserved for transmitting the channel signaling.
	Because a <cr> is not displayed, it indicates that you must enter more keywords to complete the command.

`Router(config-controller)# `**`cas-group 1 timeslots 1-24`**` ?`
`  service         ` `Specify the type of`
`                    service`
`  type            ` `Specify the type of`
`                    signaling`
`Router(config-controller)# cas-group 1 timeslots 1-24`
	After you enter the timeslot ranges, enter a **?** to display what you must enter next on the command line. In this example, you must enter the **service** or **type** keyword.

	Because a <cr> is not displayed, it indicates that you must enter more keywords to complete the command.

Continues

Table I-1 *How to Find Command Options (Continued)*

Command	Comment

`Router(config-controller)# `**`cas-group 1 timeslots 1-24`**
`type ?`
` e&m-fgb            E & M Type II FGB`
` e&m-fgd            E & M Type IIFGD`
` e&m-immediate-start  E & M Immediate Start`
` fxs-ground-start   FXS Ground Start`
` fxs-loop-start     FXS Loop Start`
` sas-ground-start   SAS Ground Start`
` sas-loop-start     SAS Loop Start`
`Router(config-controller)# cas-group 1 timeslots 1-24`
`type`
	In this example, the **type** keyword is entered. After you enter the **type** keyword, enter a **?** to display what you must enter next on the command line. In this example, you must enter one of the signaling types.
	
	Because a <cr> is not displayed, it indicates that you must enter more keywords to complete the command.

`Router(config-controller)# `**`cas-group 1 timeslots 1-24`**
`type e&m-fgb ?`
` dtmf               DTMF tone signaling`
` mf                 MF tone signaling`
` service            Specify the type of`
`                    service`
` <cr>`
`Router(config-controller)# cas-group 1 timeslots 1-24`
`type e&m-fgb`
	In this example, the **e&m-fgb** keyword is entered. After you enter the **e&m-fgb** keyword, enter a **?** to display what you must enter next on the command line. In this example, you can enter the **dtmf**, **mf**, or **service** keyword to indicate the type of channel-associated signaling available for the **e&m-fgb** signaling type.
	
	Because a <cr> is displayed, it indicates that you can enter more keywords or press <cr> to complete the command.

`Router(config-controller)# `**`cas-group 1 timeslots 1-24`**
`type e&m-fgb dtmf ?`
` dnis               DNIS addr info provisioned`
` service            Specify the type of`
`                    service`
` <cr>`
`Router(config-controller)# cas-group 1 timeslots 1-24`
`type e&m-fgb dtmf`
	In this example, the **dtmf** keyword is entered. After you enter the **dtmf** keyword, enter a **?** to display what you must enter next on the command line. In this example, you can enter the **dnis** or **service** keyword to indicate the options available for **dtmf** tone signaling.
	
	Because a <cr> is displayed, it indicates that you can enter more keywords or press <cr> to complete the command.

`Router(config-controller)# `**`cas-group 1 timeslots 1-24`** **`type e&m-fgb dtmf`** `Router(config-controller)#`	In this example, enter a <cr> to complete the command.

Understanding Command Modes

The Cisco IOS user interface is divided into many different modes. The commands available to you at any given time depend on which mode you are currently in. Entering a question mark (**?**) at the system prompt allows you to obtain a list of commands available for each command mode.

When you start a session on the router, you begin in user mode, often called EXEC mode. Only a limited subset of the commands are available in EXEC mode. In order to have access to all commands, you must enter privileged EXEC mode. Normally, you must enter a password to enter privileged EXEC mode. From privileged mode, you can enter any EXEC command or enter global configuration mode. Most of the EXEC commands are one-time commands, such as **show** commands, which show the current status of something, and **clear** commands, which clear counters or interfaces. The EXEC commands are not saved across reboots of the router.

The configuration modes allow you to make changes to the running configuration. If you later save the configuration, these commands are stored across router reboots. In order to get to the various configuration modes, you must start at global configuration mode. From global configuration mode, you can enter interface configuration mode, subinterface configuration mode, and a variety of protocol-specific modes.

ROM Monitor mode is a separate mode used when the router cannot boot properly. If your router or access server does not find a valid system image when it is booting, or if its configuration file is corrupted at startup, the system might enter read-only memory (ROM) Monitor mode.

Summary of Main Command Modes

Table I-2 summarizes the main command modes of the Cisco IOS software.

Table I-2 *Summary of Main Command Modes*

Command Mode	Access Method	Prompt	Exit Method
User EXEC	Log in.	`Router>`	Use the **logout** command.
Privileged EXEC	From user EXEC mode, use the **enable** EXEC command.	`Router#`	To exit back to user EXEC mode, use the **disable** command.
			To enter global configuration mode, use the **configure terminal** privileged EXEC command.
Global configuration	From privileged EXEC mode, use the **configure terminal** privileged EXEC command.	`Router(config)#`	To exit to privileged EXEC mode, use the **exit** or **end** command or press **Ctrl-Z**.
			To enter interface configuration mode, enter an **interface** configuration command.

Continues

Table I-2 *Summary of Main Command Modes (Continued)*

Command Mode	Access Method	Prompt	Exit Method
Interface configuration	From global configuration mode, enter by specifying an interface with an **interface** command.	`Router(config-if)#`	To exit to global configuration mode, use the **exit** command. To exit to privileged EXEC mode, use the **exit** command or press **Ctrl-Z**. To enter subinterface configuration mode, specify a subinterface with the **interface** command.
Subinterface configuration	From interface configuration mode, specify a subinterface with an **interface** command.	`Router(config-subif)#`	To exit to global configuration mode, use the **exit** command. To enter privileged EXEC mode, use the **end** command or press **Ctrl-Z**.
ROM Monitor	From privileged EXEC mode, use the **reload** EXEC command. Press the **Break** key during the first 60 seconds while the system is booting.	`>`	To exit to user EXEC mode, type **continue**.

Using the No and Default Forms of Commands

Almost every configuration command also has a **no** form. In general, use the **no** form to disable a function. Use the command without the keyword **no** to reenable a disabled function or to enable a function that is disabled by default. For example, IP routing is enabled by default. To disable IP routing, specify the **no ip routing** command and specify **ip routing** to reenable it. The Cisco IOS software command references provide the complete syntax for the configuration commands and describe what the **no** form of a command does.

Configuration commands can also have a **default** form. The **default** form of a command returns the command setting to its default. Most commands are disabled by default, so the **default** form is the same as the **no** form. However, some commands are enabled by default and have variables set to certain default values. In these cases, the **default** command enables the command and sets variables to their default values. The Cisco IOS software command references describe what the **default** form of a command does if the command is not the same as the **no** form.

Saving Configuration Changes

Enter the **copy system:running-config nvram:startup-config** command to save your configuration changes to your startup configuration so that they will not be lost if there is a system reload or power outage. For example:

```
Router# copy system:running-config nvram:startup-config
Building configuration...
```

It might take a minute or two to save the configuration. After the configuration has been saved, the following output appears:

```
[OK]
Router#
```

On most platforms, this step saves the configuration to nonvolatile random-access memory (NVRAM). On the Class A Flash file system platforms, this step saves the configuration to the location specified by the CONFIG_FILE environment variable. The CONFIG_FILE variable defaults to NVRAM.

Classification

CHAPTER 1

Classification Overview

Classification entails using a traffic descriptor to categorize a packet within a specific group to define that packet and make it accessible for quality of service (QoS) handling on the network. Using packet classification, you can partition network traffic into multiple priority levels or classes of service. When traffic descriptors are used to classify traffic, the source agrees to adhere to the contracted terms and the network promises a QoS. Traffic policers, such as committed access rate's (CAR's) rate-limiting feature, and traffic shapers, such as Frame Relay Traffic Shaping (FRTS) and Generic Traffic Shaping (GTS), use a packet's traffic descriptor—that is, its classification—to ensure adherence to the contract.

Packet classification is pivotal to policy techniques that select packets traversing a network element or a particular interface for different types of QoS service. For example, you can use classification to mark certain packets for IP precedence, and you can identify others as belonging to a Resource Reservation Protocol (RSVP) flow.

Methods of classification were once limited to use of the contents of the packet header. Today's methods of marking a packet with its classification allow you to set information in the Layer 2, 3, or 4 headers, or even by setting information within the packet's payload. Criteria for classification of a group might be as broad as "traffic destined for subnetwork X" or as narrow as a single flow.

This chapter explains IP precedence, then it gives a brief description of the kinds of traffic classification provided by the Cisco IOS QoS features. It discusses the following features:

- Policy-Based Routing
- QoS Policy Propagation via Border Gateway Protocol
- Committed Access Rate

About IP Precedence

Use of IP precedence allows you to specify the class of service (CoS) for a packet. You use the three precedence bits in the IPv4 header's type of service (ToS) field for this purpose. Figure 1-1 shows the ToS field.

Figure 1-1   *IPv4 Packet ToS Field*

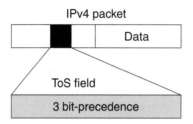

Using the ToS bits, you can define up to six classes of service. Other features configured throughout the network can, then, use these bits to determine how to treat the packet in regard to the type of service to grant it. These other QoS features can assign appropriate traffic-handling policies including congestion management strategy and bandwidth allocation. For example, although IP precedence is not a queuing method, queuing methods such as weighted fair queuing (WFQ) and Weighted Random Early Detection (WRED) can use the IP precedence setting of the packet to prioritize traffic.

By setting precedence levels on incoming traffic and using them in combination with the Cisco IOS QoS queuing features, you can create differentiated service. You can use features such as policy-based routing (PBR) and CAR to set precedence based on extended access list classification. These features afford considerable flexibility for precedence assignment. For example, you can assign precedence based on application or user, or by destination and source subnetwork.

So that each subsequent network element can provide service based on the determined policy, IP precedence is usually deployed as close to the edge of the network or the administrative domain as possible. You can think of IP precedence as an edge function that allows core QoS features, such as WRED, to forward traffic based on CoS. IP precedence can also be set in the host or network client, but this setting can be overridden by policy within the network.

The following QoS features can use the IP precedence field to determine how traffic is treated:

● Distributed WRED

● WFQ

● CAR

How the IP Precedence Bits Are Used to Classify Packets

You use the three IP precedence bits in the ToS field of the IP header to specify CoS assignment for each packet. You can partition traffic into up to six classes—the remaining two are reserved for internal network use—and then use policy maps and extended ACLs to define network policies in terms of congestion handling and bandwidth allocation for each class.

For historical reasons, each precedence corresponds to a name. These names, which continue to evolve, are defined in the RFC 791 document. Table 1-1 lists the numbers and their corresponding names, from least to most important.

Table 1-1 *IP Precedence Values*

Number	Name
0	routine
1	priority
2	immediate
3	flash
4	flash-override
5	critical
6	internet
7	network

However, the IP precedence feature allows you considerable flexibility for precedence assignment. That is, you can define your own classification mechanism. For example, you might want to assign precedence based on application or access router.

NOTE	IP precedence bit settings 6 and 7 are reserved for network control information, such as routing updates.

Setting or Changing the IP Precedence Value

By default, the Cisco IOS software leaves the IP precedence value untouched, preserving the precedence value set in the header, allowing all internal network devices to provide service based on the IP precedence setting. This policy follows the standard approach stipulating that network traffic should be sorted into various types of service at the basic perimeter of the network and that those types of service should be implemented in the core of the network. Routers in the core of the network can then use the precedence bits, for example, to determine the order of transmission, the likelihood of packet drop, and so on.

However, because traffic coming into your network can have precedence set by outside devices, Cisco recommends you reset the precedence for all traffic entering your network. By controlling IP precedence settings, you prohibit users who have already set the IP precedence from acquiring better service for their traffic simply by setting a high precedence for all of their packets.

You can use any of the following features to set the IP precedence in packets:

- Policy-Based Routing (PBR)

- QoS Policy Propagation via Border Gateway Protocol (BGP)

- Committed Access Rate (CAR)

As mentioned previously, after a packet has been classified, you can use other QoS features such as CAR and WRED to specify and enforce business policies to fit your business model.

Policy-Based Routing

PBR gives you a flexible means of routing packets by allowing you to configure a defined policy for traffic flows, which lessens reliance on routes derived from routing protocols. To this end, PBR gives you more control over routing by extending and complementing the existing mechanisms provided by routing protocols. PBR allows you to set the IP precedence. It also allows you to specify a path for certain traffic, such as priority traffic over a high-cost link.

You can set up PBR as a way to route packets based on configured policies. For example, you can implement routing policies to allow or deny paths based on the identity of a particular end system, an application protocol, or the size of packets.

PBR allows you to do the following:

- Classify traffic based on extended ACL criteria. ACLs, then, establish the match criteria.

- Set IP precedence bits, giving the network the ability to enable differentiated CoS.

- Route packets to specific traffic-engineered paths; you might need to route them to allow a specific QoS service through the network.

Policies can be based on IP address, port numbers, protocols, or size of packets. For a simple policy, you can use any one of these descriptors; for a complicated policy, you can use all of them.

For example, classification of traffic through PBR allows you to identify traffic for different classes of service at the edge of the network and then implement QoS defined for each CoS in the core of the network using priority, custom, or WFQ techniques. This process obviates the need to classify traffic explicitly at each WAN interface in the core network.

How It Works

All packets received on an interface with PBR enabled are passed through enhanced packet filters known as route maps. The route maps used by PBR dictate the policy, which determines where the packets are forwarded.

Route maps are composed of statements. The route map statements can be marked as permit or deny, and they are interpreted in the following way:

- If the packets do not match any route map statements, then all the set clauses are applied.

- If a statement is marked as deny, the packets meeting the match criteria are sent back through the normal forwarding channels and destination-based routing is performed.

- If the statement is marked as permit and the packets do not match any route map statements, the packets are sent back through the normal forwarding channels and destination-based routing is performed.

You specify PBR on the interface that receives the packet, not on the interface from which the packet is sent.

When Should You Use PBR?

You might enable PBR if you want certain packets to be routed some way other than the obvious shortest path. Some possible applications for PBR are to provide equal access, protocol-sensitive routing, source-sensitive routing, routing based on interactive versus batch traffic, or routing based on dedicated links.

Some applications or traffic can benefit from QoS-specific routing; for example, you could transfer stock records to a corporate office on a higher-bandwidth, higher-cost link for a short time while transmitting routine application data such as e-mail over a lower-bandwidth, lower-cost link.

QoS Policy Propagation via Border Gateway Protocol

BGP is an interdomain routing protocol that exchanges reachability information with other BGP systems. It is defined by RFC 1163.

QoS policy propagation via BGP allows you to classify packets based on the following:

- Access lists.

- BGP community lists. A community is a group of destinations that share some common attribute. You use community lists to create groups of communities to use in a match clause of a route map. As with access lists, a series of community lists can be created.

- BGP autonomous system paths. An autonomous system path is a collection of networks under a common administration sharing a common routing strategy. BGP carries the autonomous system path in its routing updates. You can filter routing updates by specifying an access list on both incoming and outbound updates based on the BGP autonomous system path.

- IP precedence. See the section "About IP Precedence" earlier in this chapter.

- Source and destination address lookup. You can specify whether the IP precedence level is obtained from the source (input) address or destination (output) address entry in the route table.

After a packet has been classified using BGP, you can use other QoS features such as CAR and WRED to specify and enforce business policies to fit your business model.

BGP policy propagation leverages BGP to distribute QoS policy to remote routers in your network. It allows ingress routers to prioritize incoming traffic.

QoS policy propagation via BGP is supported on these platforms:

● Cisco 7000 series routers with the RSP7000 and RSP7000CI

● Cisco 7200 series

● Cisco 7500 series

For the QoS policy propagation via BGP feature to work, you must enable BGP and Cisco Express Forwarding (CEF)/Distributed CEF (DCEF) on the router.

Subinterfaces on an ATM interface that has the **bgp-policy** command enabled must use CEF mode because Distributed CEF is not supported. (Note that DCEF uses the VIP rather than the RSP to perform forwarding functions.)

Committed Access Rate

CAR is a multifaceted feature that implements both classification services and policing through rate limiting. This section describes its classification capability. For information on its rate limiting features, see Chapter 11, "Policing and Shaping Overview."

You can use CAR's classification services to set the IP precedence for packets entering the network. This capability of CAR allows you to partition your network into multiple priority levels or CoS. Networking devices within your network can then use the adjusted IP precedence to determine how to treat the traffic. For example, VIP-Distributed WRED uses the IP precedence to determine the probability of whether a packet will be dropped.

As discussed in the section "About IP Precedence," you can use the three precedence bits in the ToS field of the IP header to define up to six classes of service.

You can classify packets using policies based on physical port, source or destination IP or MAC address, application port, IP protocol type, or other criteria specifiable by access lists or extended access lists. You can even classify packets by categories external to the network (for example, by customer). After a packet has been classified, a network can either accept or override the packet and reclassify it according to a specified policy. CAR includes commands you can use to classify and reclassify packets.

CAR is supported on these routers:

● Cisco 2600 series

● Cisco 3600 series

● Cisco 4500 series

- Cisco 4700 series

- Cisco 7200 series

VIP-Distributed CAR is a version of CAR that runs on the Versatile Interface Processor (VIP). It is supported on the following routers with a VIP2-40 or greater interface processor:

- Cisco 7000 series with RSP7000

- Cisco 7500 series

CHAPTER 2

Configuring Policy-Based Routing

This chapter describes the tasks for configuring policy-based routing (PBR) on a router. To locate documentation of related commands, you can search online at www.cisco.com.

PBR Configuration Task List

To configure PBR, perform the tasks in the following sections:

- Enable PBR
- Enable Fast-Switched PBR
- Enable Local PBR

The section "PBR Configuration Examples" later in this chapter provides examples of configuring PBR.

Enable PBR

To enable PBR, you must create a route map that specifies the match criteria and the resulting action if all of the match clauses are met. Then you must enable PBR for that route map on a particular interface. All packets arriving on the specified interface matching the match clauses will be subject to PBR.

To enable PBR on an interface, use the following commands beginning in global configuration mode:

Step	Command	Purpose
1	**route-map** *map-tag* [**permit** | **deny**] [*sequence-number*]	Defines a route map to control where packets are output. This command puts the router into route-map configuration mode.
2		Specifies the match criteria. You can specify one or both of the following:
	match length *min max* and/or	• Match the Level 3 length of the packet. and/or
	match ip address {*access-list-number* | *name*} [*...access-list-number* | *name*]	• Match the source and destination IP address that is permitted by one or more standard or extended access lists.
		If you do not specify a **match** command, the route map applies to all packets.

Continues

Step	Command	Purpose
3		Specifies the action or actions to take on the packets that match the criteria. You can specify any or all of the following:
	set ip precedence [*number* | *name*]	• Set precedence value in the IP header. You can specify either the precedence number or name.
	set ip next-hop *ip-address* [*... ip-address*]	• Set next hop to route the packet. (It need not be adjacent.)
	set interface *interface-type interface-number* [*... type number*]	• Set output interface for the packet.
	set ip default next-hop *ip-address* [*... ip-address*]	• Set next hop to which to route the packet if there is no explicit route for this destination.
	set default interface *interface-type interface-number* [*... type ...number*]	• Set output interface for the packet if there is no explicit route for this destination.
4	**interface** *interface-type interface-number*	Specifies the interface. This command puts the router into interface configuration mode.
5	**ip policy route-map** *map-tag*	Identifies the route map to use for PBR. One interface can have only one route-map tag, but you can have multiple route map entries with different sequence numbers. These entries are evaluated in sequence number order until the first match. If there is no match, the packets will be routed as usual.

The **set** commands can be used in conjunction with each other. They are evaluated in the order shown in the previous table. A usable next hop implies an interface. Once the local router finds a next hop and a usable interface, it routes the packet.

NOTE   Enabling PBR disables fast switching of all packets arriving on this interface.

If you want PBR to be fast-switched, see the section "Enable Fast-Switched PBR" that follows.

Enable Fast-Switched PBR

IP PBR can now be fast-switched. Prior to Cisco IOS Release 12.0, PBR could only be process-switched, which meant that on most platforms the switching rate was approximately 1000 to

10,000 packets per second. This speed was not fast enough for many applications. Users who need PBR to occur at faster speeds can now implement PBR without slowing down the router.

Fast-switched PBR supports all of the **match** commands and most of the **set** commands with the following restrictions:

● The **set ip default next-hop** and **set default interface** commands are not supported.

● The **set interface** command is supported only over point-to-point links, unless a route-cache entry exists using the same interface specified in the **set interface** command in the route map. Also, at the process level, the routing table is consulted to determine if the interface is on a reasonable path to the destination. During fast switching, the software does not make this check. Instead, if the packet matches, the software blindly forwards the packet to the specified interface.

PBR must be configured before you configure fast-switched PBR. Fast switching of PBR is disabled by default. To enable fast-switched PBR, use the following command in interface configuration mode:

Command	Purpose
ip route-cache policy	Enables fast switching of PBR.

To display the cache entries in the policy route cache, use the **show ip cache policy** command. Use the **show ip policy** command to display which route map is associated with which interface.

Enable Local PBR

Packets that are generated by the router are not normally policy-routed. To enable local PBR for such packets, indicate which route map the router should use by using the following command in global configuration mode:

Command	Purpose
ip local policy route-map *map-tag*	Identifies the route map to use for local PBR.

All packets originating on the router will then be subject to local PBR.

Use the **show ip local policy** command to display the route map used for local PBR if one exists.

PBR Configuration Examples

This section provides the following examples of PBR configurations:

● Equal Access Example

● Differing Next Hops Example

Equal Access Example

The following example provides two sources with equal access to two different service providers. Packets arriving on asynchronous interface 1 from the source 1.1.1.1 are sent to the router at 6.6.6.6 if the router has no explicit route for the packet's destination. Packets arriving from the source 2.2.2.2 are sent to the router at 7.7.7.7 if the router has no explicit route for the packet's destination. All other packets for which the router has no explicit route to the destination are discarded.

```
access-list 1 permit ip 1.1.1.1
access-list 2 permit ip 2.2.2.2
!
interface async 1
 ip policy route-map equal-access
!
route-map equal-access permit 10
 match ip address 1
 set ip default next-hop 6.6.6.6
route-map equal-access permit 20
 match ip address 2
 set ip default next-hop 7.7.7.7
route-map equal-access permit 30
 set default interface null0
```

Differing Next Hops Example

The following example illustrates how to route traffic from different sources to different places (next hops) and how to set the precedence bit in the IP header. Packets arriving from source 1.1.1.1 are sent to the next hop at 3.3.3.3 with the precedence bit set to priority; packets arriving from source 2.2.2.2 are sent to the next hop at 3.3.3.5 with the precedence bit set to critical.

```
access-list 1 permit ip 1.1.1.1
access-list 2 permit ip 2.2.2.2
!
interface ethernet 1
   ip policy route-map Texas
!
route-map Texas permit 10
   match ip address 1
   set ip precedence priority
   set ip next-hop 3.3.3.3
!
route-map Texas permit 20
   match ip address 2
   set ip precedence critical
   set ip next-hop 3.3.3.5
```

CHAPTER 3

Configuring QoS Policy Propagation via Border Gateway Protocol

This chapter describes the tasks for configuring quality of service (QoS) policy propagation via Border Gateway Protocol (BGP) on a router. To locate documentation of related commands, you can search online at www.cisco.com.

This feature is supported on these platforms:

- Cisco 7000 series routers with RSP7000 and RSP7000CI interface processors
- Cisco 7200 series
- Cisco 7500 series

QoS Policy Propagation via BGP Configuration Task List

The QoS policy propagation via BGP feature allows you to classify packets by IP precedence based on BGP community lists, BGP autonomous system (AS) paths, and access lists. After a packet has been classified, you can use other QoS features such as committed access rate (CAR) and Weighted Random Early Detection (WRED) to specify and enforce policies to fit your business model.

Overview of Tasks

To configure QoS policy propagation via BGP, perform the following basic tasks:

- Configure BGP and Cisco Express Forwarding (CEF) or Distributed CEF (DCEF).
- Define the policy.
- Apply the policy through BGP.
- Configure the BGP community list, BGP autonomous system path, or access list, and enable the policy on an interface.
- Enable CAR or WRED to use the policy. To enable CAR, refer to Chapter 4, "Configuring Committed Access Rate." To configure WRED, refer to Chapter 10, "Configuring Weighted Random Early Detection."

This chapter describes how to configure QoS policy propagation based on BGP community lists, the BGP AS path, or an access list. It assumes you have already configured BGP and CEF or DCEF. See the next section for the list of tasks covered in this chapter.

Configuration Task List

The tasks required to configure QoS policy propagation via BGP and verify that the information is correct are described in the following sections in this chapter:

● Configure Policy Propagation Based on Community Lists

● Configure Policy Propagation Based on the AS Path Attribute

● Configure Policy Propagation Based on an Access List

● Monitor QoS Policy Propagation via BGP

NOTE   For the QoS policy propagation via BGP feature to work, you must enable BGP and CEF/DCEF on the router. Subinterfaces on an ATM interface that have the **bgp-policy** command enabled must use CEF mode because DCEF is not supported. DCEF uses the Versatile Interface Processor (VIP) rather than the Route Switch Processor (RSP) to perform forwarding functions.

For examples of propagating policy using access lists, BGP community lists, and BGP autonomous system paths, see the section "QoS Policy Propagation via BGP Configuration Examples" later in this chapter.

Configure Policy Propagation Based on Community Lists

This section describes how to configure QoS policy propagation via BGP using community lists. The tasks listed in this section are required unless noted as optional. This section assumes you have already configured CEF/DCEF and BGP on your router.

To configure the router to propagate the IP precedence based on the community lists, use the following commands beginning in global configuration mode:

Step	Command	Purpose
1	**route-map** *route-map-name* [**permit**	**deny** [*sequence-number*]]	Defines a route map to control redistribution, and enters route-map configuration mode.

Step	Command	Purpose
2	**match community-list** *community-list-number* [**exact**]	Matches a BGP community list.
3	**set ip precedence** [*number* | *name*]	Sets the IP precedence field when the community list matches. You can specify either a precedence number or name.
4	**router bgp** *autonomous-system*	Enters router configuration mode.
5	**table-map** *route-map-name*	Modifies the metric and tag values when the IP routing table is updated with BGP learned routes.
6	**ip community-list** *community-list-number* {**permit** | **deny**} *community-number*	Creates a community list for BGP, and controls access to it.
7	**interface** *interface-type interface-number*	Specifies the interfaces (or subinterface), and enters interface configuration mode.
8	**bgp-policy ip-prec-map**	Classifies packets using IP precedence.
9	**ip bgp-community new-format**	(Optional) Configures a new community format so that the community number is displayed in the short form.
10	**end**	Exits configuration mode.

Configure Policy Propagation Based on the AS Path Attribute

This section describes how to configure QoS policy propagation via BGP based on the AS path. The tasks listed in this section are required unless noted as optional. This section assumes you have already configured CEF/DCEF and BGP on your router.

To configure the router to propagate the IP precedence based on the AS path attribute, use the following commands beginning in global configuration mode:

Step	Command	Purpose
1	**route-map** *route-map-name* [**permit** | **deny** [*sequence-number*]]	Defines a route map to control redistribution, and enters route-map configuration mode.
2	**match as-path** *path-list-number*	Matches a BGP AS path access list.
3	**set ip precedence** [*number* | *name*]	Sets the IP precedence field when the autonomous system path matches. Specifies either a precedence number or name.
4	**router bgp** *autonomous-system*	Enters router configuration mode.

Continues

Step	Command	Purpose
5	**table-map** *route-map-name*	Modifies the metric and tag values when the IP routing table is updated with BGP learned routes.
6	**ip as-path access-list** *access-list-number* {**permit**	**deny**} *as-regular-expression*	Defines an AS path access list.
7	**interface** *interface-type interface-number*	Specifies the interfaces (or subinterface), and enters interface configuration mode.
8	**bgp-policy ip-prec-map**	Classifies packets using IP precedence.
9	**end**	Exits configuration mode.

Configure Policy Propagation Based on an Access List

This section describes how to configure QoS policy propagation via BGP based on an access list. The tasks listed in this section are required unless noted as optional. This section assumes you have already configured CEF/DCEF and BGP on your router.

To configure the router to propagate the IP precedence based on an access list, use the following commands beginning in global configuration mode:

Step	Command	Purpose
1	**route-map** *route-map-name* [**permit**	**deny** [*sequence-number*]]	Defines a route map to control redistribution, and enters route-map configuration mode.
2	**match ip address** *access-list-number*	Matches an access list.
3	**set ip precedence** [*number*	*name*]	Sets the IP precedence field when the AS path matches.
4	**router bgp** *autonomous-system*	Enters router configuration mode.
5	**table-map** *route-map-name*	Modifies the metric and tag values when the IP routing table is updated with BGP learned routes.
6	**access-list** *access-list-number* {**permit**	**deny**} *source*	Defines an access list.
7	**interface** *interface-type interface-number*	Specifies the interfaces (or subinterface), and enters interface configuration mode.
8	**bgp-policy ip-prec-map**	Classifies packets using IP precedence.
9	**end**	Exits configuration mode.

Monitor QoS Policy Propagation via BGP

To monitor the QoS policy propagation via BGP configuration, use any of the following commands in EXEC mode. The commands listed in this section are optional.

Command	Purpose
show ip bgp	Shows entries in the BGP routing table to verify that the correct community is set on the prefixes.
show ip bgp community-list *community-list-number*	Shows routes permitted by the BGP community list to verify that the correct prefixes are selected.
show ip cef *network*	Shows entries in the FIB table based on the IP address to verify that CEF has the correct precedence value for the prefix.
show ip interface	Shows information about the interface.
show ip route *prefix*	Shows the current status of the routing table to verify that the correct precedence values are set on the prefixes.

QoS Policy Propagation via BGP Configuration Examples

The following example shows how to create route maps to match access lists, BGP community lists, and BGP AS paths, and apply IP precedence to routes learned from neighbors.

As shown in Figure 3-1, Router A learns routes from AS 10 and AS 60. QoS policy is applied to all packets that match the defined route maps. Any packets from Router A to AS 10 or AS 60 are sent the appropriate QoS policy.

Figure 3-1   *Router Learns Routes and Applies QoS Policy*

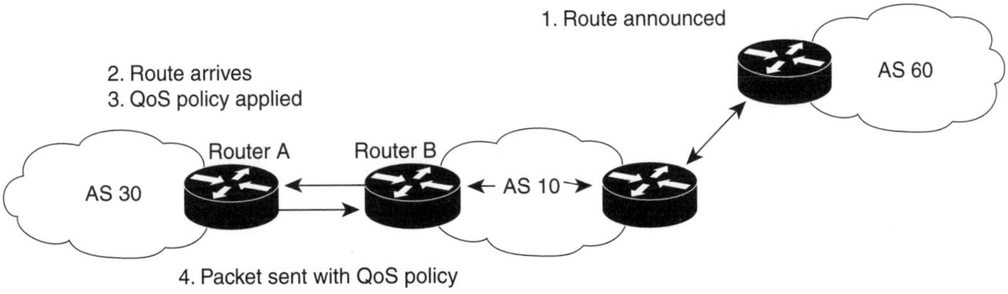

Router A's Configuration

```
router bgp 30
 table-map precedence-map
 neighbor 20.20.20.1 remote-as 10
 neighbor 20.20.20.1 send-community
 neighbor 20.20.20.1 route-map precedence-map out
!
ip bgp-community new-format
!
! Match community 1 and set the IP precedence to priority
route-map precedence-map permit 10
 match community 1
 set ip precedence priority
!
! Match community 2 and set the IP precedence to immediate
route-map precedence-map permit 20
 match community 2
 set ip precedence immediate
!
! Match community 3 and set the IP precedence to flash
route-map precedence-map permit 30
 match community 3
 set ip precedence flash
!
! Match community 4 and set the IP precedence to flash-override
route-map precedence-map permit 40
 match community 4
 set ip precedence flash-override
!
! Match community 5 and set the IP precedence to critical
route-map precedence-map permit 50
 match community 5
 set ip precedence critical
!
! Match community 6 and set the IP precedence to Internet
route-map precedence-map permit 60
 match community 6
 set ip precedence Internet
!
! Match community 7 and set the IP precedence to network
route-map precedence-map permit 70
 match community 7
 set ip precedence network
!
! Match ip address access list 69 or match as path 1
! and set the IP precedence to critical
route-map precedence-map permit 75
 match ip address 69
 match as-path 1
 set ip precedence critical
!
! For everything else, set the IP precedence to routine
route-map precedence-map permit 80
 set ip precedence routine
```

```
!
! Define the community lists
ip community-list 1 permit 60:1
ip community-list 2 permit 60:2
ip community-list 3 permit 60:3
ip community-list 4 permit 60:4
ip community-list 5 permit 60:5
ip community-list 6 permit 60:6
ip community-list 7 permit 60:7
!
! Define the as path
ip as-path access-list 1 permit ^10_60
!
! Define the access list
access-list 69 permit 69.0.0.0
```

Router B's Configuration

```
router bgp 10
 neighbor 30.30.30.1 remote-as 30
 neighbor 30.30.30.1 send-community
 neighbor 30.30.30.1 route-map send_community out
!
ip bgp-community new-format
!
! Match prefix 10 and set community to 60:1
route-map send_community permit 10
 match ip address 10
 set community 60:1
!
! Match prefix 20 and set community to 60:2
route-map send_community permit 20
 match ip address 20
 set community 60:2
!
! Match prefix 30 and set community to 60:3
route-map send_community permit 30
 match ip address 30
 set community 60:3
!
! Match prefix 40 and set community to 60:4
route-map send_community permit 40
 match ip address 40
 set community 60:4
!
! Match prefix 50 and set community to 60:5
route-map send_community permit 50
 match ip address 50
 set community 60:5
!
! Match prefix 60 and set community to 60:6
route-map send_community permit 60
 match ip address 60
 set community 60:6
```

```
!
! Match prefix 70 and set community to 60:7
route-map send_community permit 70
 match ip address 70
 set community 60:7
!
! For all others, set community to 60:8
route-map send_community permit 80
 set community 60:8
!
! Define the access lists
access-list 10 permit 61.0.0.0
access-list 20 permit 62.0.0.0
access-list 30 permit 63.0.0.0
access-list 40 permit 64.0.0.0
access-list 50 permit 65.0.0.0
access-list 60 permit 66.0.0.0
access-list 70 permit 67.0.0.0
```

CHAPTER 4

Configuring Committed Access Rate

This chapter describes how to configure committed access rate (CAR) and Distributed CAR (DCAR). To locate documentation of related commands, you can search online at www.cisco.com.

CAR is supported on these platforms:

- Cisco 2600 series
- Cisco 3600 series
- Cisco 4500 series
- Cisco 4700 series
- Cisco 7200 series

DCAR is supported on Cisco 7000 series routers with either a Route Switch Processor-based RSP7000 interface processor, or Cisco 7500 series routers with a Versatile Interface Processor-based VIP2-40 or greater interface processor. A VIP2-50 interface processor is strongly recommended when the aggregate line rate of the port adapters on the VIP is greater than DS3. A VIP2-50 interface processor is required for OC-3 rates.

NOTE   CAR and DCAR can only be used with IP traffic. Non-IP traffic is not rate limited. CAR and DCAR can be configured on an interface or subinterface. However, CAR and DCAR are not supported on the Fast EtherChannel, tunnel, or PRI interfaces, nor on any interface that does not support Cisco Express Forwarding (CEF).

DCAR is not supported on ATM subinterfaces, nor with the ATM encapsulations AAL5-MUX and AAL5-NLPID.

CEF must be enabled on the interface before configuring CAR or DCAR.

CAR Configuration Task List

The CAR and DCAR services limit the input or output transmission rate on an interface or subinterface based on a flexible set of criteria. CAR is often configured on interfaces at the edge of a network to limit traffic into or out of the network.

CAR can rate limit traffic based on certain matching criteria, such as incoming interface, IP precedence, or IP access list. You configure the actions CAR will take when traffic conforms to or exceeds the rate limit.

You can set CAR rate policies that are associated with one of the following:

- All IP traffic

- IP precedence

- MAC address

- IP access list, both standard and extended (Matching to IP access lists is more processor-intensive than matching based on other criteria.)

Each interface can have multiple CAR policies, corresponding to different types of traffic. For example, low priority traffic may be limited to a lower rate than high priority traffic. With multiple rate policies, the router examines each policy in the order entered until the packet matches. If a match is not found, the default action is to transmit.

The rate policies can be independent; each rate policy deals with a different type of traffic. Alternatively, rate policies can be cascading; a packet can be compared to multiple different rate policies in succession. You can configure up to 20 rate policies on a subinterface.

To configure CAR, perform the tasks in the following sections:

- Configure CAR and DCAR for All IP Traffic

- Configure CAR and DCAR Policies

- Configure a Class-Based DCAR Policy

- Monitor CAR and DCAR

See the section "CAR and DCAR Configuration Examples" later in this chapter for ideas of how to configure CAR and DCAR on your network.

Configure CAR and DCAR for All IP Traffic

To configure CAR (or DCAR on Cisco 7000 series with RSP7000, or Cisco 7500 series routers with a VIP2-40 or greater interface processor) for all IP traffic, use the following commands beginning in global configuration mode:

Step	Command	Purpose
1	**interface** *interface-type interface-number*	Specifies the interface or subinterface. This command puts the router in interface configuration mode.

Step	Command	Purpose
2	**rate-limit** {**input**	**output**} *bps burst-normal burst-max* **conform-action** *action* **exceed-action** *action*	Specifies a basic CAR policy for all IP traffic. See Table 4-1 for a description of conform and exceed *action* keywords.
3	**end**	Exits interface configuration mode.

Basic CAR and DCAR functionality requires the following criteria to be defined:

● Packet direction, incoming or outgoing.

● An average rate, determined by a long-term average of the transmission rate. Traffic that falls under this rate will always conform.

● A normal burst size, which determines how large traffic bursts can be before some traffic is considered to exceed the rate limit.

● An excess burst size.

  Traffic that falls between the normal burst size and the excess burst size exceeds the rate limit with a probability that increases as the burst size increases. CAR propagates bursts. It does no smoothing or shaping of traffic.

Conform and exceed actions are described in Table 4-1.

Table 4-1 *Rate-Limit Command Action Keywords*

Keyword	Description
continue	Evaluates the next **rate-limit** command.
drop	Drops the packet.
set-prec-continue *new-prec*	Sets the IP precedence and evaluates the next **rate-limit** command.
set-prec-transmit *new-prec*	Sets the IP precedence and transmits the packet.
transmit	Transmits the packet.

See the sections "Configure CAR and DCAR Policies" and "Configure a Class-Based DCAR Policy" to understand how to configure other CAR and DCAR policy options. See the sections "Subrate IP Services Example" and "Input and Output Rate Limiting on an Interface Example" for examples of how to configure CAR for all IP traffic.

Configure CAR and DCAR Policies

To configure CAR (or DCAR on Cisco 7000 series with the RSP7000, or Cisco 7500 series routers with a VIP2-40 or greater interface processor), use the following commands beginning in interface configuration mode (only the first two commands are required):

Step	Command	Purpose
1	**interface** *interface-type interface-number*	Specifies the interface or subinterface. This command puts the router in interface configuration mode.
2	**rate-limit** {**input** | **output**} [**access-group** [**rate-limit**] *acl-index*] *bps burst-normal burst-max* **conform-action** *action* **exceed-action** *action*	Specifies the rate policy for each particular class of traffic. Refer to Table 4-1 for a description of conform and exceed *action* keywords. Repeat this command for each different class of traffic.
3	**access-list rate-limit** *acl-index* {*precedence* | *mac-address* | **mask** *prec-mask*}	(Optional) Specifies a rate-limited access list. Repeat this command if you wish to specify a new access list.
4	**access-list** *acl-index* {**deny** | **permit**} *source* [*source-wildcard*] or **access-list** *acl-index* {**deny** | **permit**} *protocol source source-wildcard destination destination-wildcard* [**precedence** *precedence*] [**tos** *tos*] [**log**]	(Optional) Specifies a standard or extended access list. Repeat this command to further configure the access list or specify a new access list.
5	**end**	Exits interface configuration mode.

The following sections describe requirements for specific policies.

IP Precedence or MAC Address

Use the **access-list rate-limit** command to classify packets using either IP precedence or MAC addresses. You can then apply CAR policies using the **rate-limit** command to individual rate-limited access lists. Packets with different IP precedences or MAC addresses are treated differently by the CAR service. See the section "Rate Limiting in an IXP Example" for an example of how to configure a CAR policy using MAC addresses.

IP Access List

Use the **access-list** command to define CAR policy based on access list. The *acl-index* argument is an access list number. Use a number from 1 to 99 to classify packets by precedence or precedence mask. Use a number from 100 to 199 to classify by MAC address.

NOTE	If an access list is not present, the **rate-limit** command will act as if no access list is defined and all traffic will be rate limited accordingly.

See the section "Rate Limiting by Access List Example" for an example of how to configure a CAR policy using IP access lists.

Configure a Class-Based DCAR Policy

When you configure DCAR on Cisco 7000 series with RSP7000, or Cisco 7500 series routers with a VIP2-40 or greater interface processor, you can classify packets by group to allow you to partition your network into multiple priority levels or classes of service. This classification is done by setting IP precedences based on different criteria for use by other QoS features such as Weighted Random Early Detection (WRED) or weighted fair queuing (WFQ).

To configure a class-based DCAR policy, use the following commands beginning in interface configuration mode (the **access-list** command is optional):

Step	Command	Purpose
1	**interface** *interface-type interface-number*	Specifies the interface or subinterface. This command puts the router in interface configuration mode.
2	**rate-limit** {**input** | **output**} [**access-group** [**rate-limit**] *acl-index*] *bps burst-normal burst-max* **conform-action** *action* **exceed-action** *action*	Specifies the rate policy for each particular class of traffic. Repeat this command for each different class of traffic. Refer to Table 4-1 for policy conform and exceed *action* keywords.
3	**random-detect precedence** *precedence min-threshold max-threshold mark-prob-denominator*	Configures WRED and specifies parameters for packets with specific IP precedence.

Continues

Step	Command	Purpose
4	**access-list** *acl-index* {**deny** | **permit**} *source* [*source-wildcard*] or **access-list** *acl-index* {**deny** | **permit**} *protocol source source-wildcard destination destination-wildcard* [**precedence** *precedence*] [**tos** *tos*] [**log**]	(Optional) Specifies a standard or extended access list. Repeat this command to further configure the access list or specify a new access list.
5	**end**	Exits interface configuration mode.

Monitor CAR and DCAR

To monitor CAR and DCAR services in your network, use any the following commands in EXEC mode:

Command	Purpose
show access-lists	Shows the contents of current IP and rate-limited access lists.
show access-lists rate-limit [*access-list-number*]	Shows information about rate-limited access lists.
show interfaces [*interface-type interface-number*] **rate-limit**	Shows information about an interface configured for CAR.

CAR and DCAR Configuration Examples

The following sections provide examples of ways you might use CAR and DCAR to control traffic into and out of your network:

- Subrate IP Services Example

- Input and Output Rate Limiting on an Interface Example

- Rate Limiting in an IXP Example

- Rate Limiting by Access List Example

Subrate IP Services Example

The following example illustrates how to configure a basic CAR policy that allows all IP traffic. In the example, the network operator delivers a physical T3 link to the customer but offers a less expensive 20 Mbps subrate service. The customer pays only for the subrate bandwidth, which can be upgraded with additional access bandwidth based on demand. The CAR policy limits the traffic rate available to the customer and delivered to the network to the agreed upon rate limit, plus the ability to temporarily burst over the limit.

```
interface hssi 0/0/0
rate-limit output 20000000 24000 32000 conform-action transmit exceed-action drop
ip address 10.1.0.9 255.255.255.0
```

Input and Output Rate Limiting on an Interface Example

In this example, a customer is connected to an Internet service provider (ISP) by a T3 link. The ISP wants to rate limit the customer's transmissions to 20 Mbps of the 45 Mbps. In addition, the customer is allowed to transmit bursts of 24000 bytes. All exceeding packets are dropped. The following commands are configured on the ISP's High-Speed Serial Interface (HSSI) connected to the customer:

```
interface Hssi0/0/0
 description 45Mbps to R1
 rate-limit input 20000000 24000 24000 conform-action transmit exceed-action drop
 ip address 200.200.14.250 255.255.255.252
 rate-limit output 20000000 24000 24000 conform-action transmit exceed-action drop
```

To verify the configuration and monitor CAR statistics, use the **show interfaces rate-limit** command:

```
Router# show interfaces hssi 0/0/0 rate-limit

Hssi0/0/0 45Mbps to R1
 Input
  matches: all traffic
   params: 20000000 bps, 24000 limit, 24000 extended limit
   conformed 8 packets, 428 bytes; action: transmit
   exceeded 0 packets, 0 bytes; action: drop
   last packet: 8680ms ago, current burst: 0 bytes
   last cleared 00:03:59 ago, conformed 0 bps, exceeded 0 bps
 Output
  matches: all traffic
   params: 20000000 bps, 24000 limit, 24000 extended limit
   conformed 0 packets, 0 bytes; action: transmit
   exceeded 0 packets, 0 bytes; action: drop
   last packet: 8680ms ago, current burst: 0 bytes
   last cleared 00:03:59 ago, conformed 0 bps, exceeded 0 bps
```

Rate Limiting in an IXP Example

The following example uses rate limiting to control traffic in an Internet Exchange Point (IXP). Because an IXP comprises many neighbors around an FDDI ring, MAC address rate-limited access lists are used to control traffic from a particular ISP. Traffic from one ISP (at MAC address 00e0.34b0.7777) is compared to a rate limit of 80 Mbps of the 100 Mbps available on the FDDI connection. Traffic that conforms to this rate is transmitted. Nonconforming traffic is dropped.

```
interface Fddi2/1/0
 rate-limit input access-group rate-limit 100 800000000 64000 80000 conform-action
  transmit exceed-action drop
 ip address 200.200.6.1 255.255.255.0
!
access-list rate-limit 100 00e0.34b0.7777
```

To verify the configuration and monitor the CAR statistics, use the **show interfaces rate-limit** command:

```
Router# show interfaces fddi2/1/0 rate-limit

Fddi2/1/0
 Input
  matches: access-group rate-limit 100
   params: 800000000 bps, 64000 limit, 80000 extended limit
   conformed 0 packets, 0 bytes; action: transmit
   exceeded 0 packets, 0 bytes; action: drop
   last packet: 4737508ms ago, current burst: 0 bytes
   last cleared 01:05:47 ago, conformed 0 bps, exceeded 0 bps
```

Rate Limiting by Access List Example

The following example shows how CAR can be used to limit the rate by application to ensure capacity for other traffic including mission-critical applications. In the example:

● All World Wide Web traffic is transmitted. However, the IP precedence for Web traffic that conforms to the first rate policy is set to 5. For nonconforming Web traffic, the IP precedence is set to 0 (best effort).

● FTP traffic is transmitted with an IP precedence of 5 if it conforms to the second rate policy. If the FTP traffic exceeds the rate policy, it is dropped.

● Any remaining traffic is limited to 8 Mbps with a normal burst size of 16000 bytes and an excess burst size of 24000 bytes. Traffic that conforms is transmitted with an IP precedence of 5. Traffic that does not conform is dropped.

Figure 4-1 illustrates the configuration. Notice that two access lists are created to classify the Web and FTP traffic so that they can be handled separately by CAR.

Figure 4-1   *Rate Limiting by Access List*

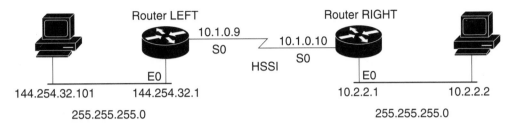

Router LEFT   Router RIGHT

10.1.0.9   10.1.0.10
S0   S0
HSSI
E0   E0
144.254.32.101   144.254.32.1   10.2.2.1   10.2.2.2
255.255.255.0   255.255.255.0

Configuration Commands for Router LEFT

```
interface Hssi0/0/0
description 45Mbps to R2
rate-limit output access-group 101 20000000 24000 32000 conform-action set-prec-
transmit 5 exceed-action set-prec-transmit 0
rate-limit output access-group 102 10000000 24000 32000 conform-action
set-prec-transmit 5 exceed-action drop
rate-limit output 8000000 16000 24000 conform-action set-prec-transmit 5
exceed-action drop
ip address 10.1.0.9 255.255.255.0
!
access-list 101 permit tcp any any eq www
access-list 102 permit tcp any any eq ftp
```

To verify the configuration and monitor CAR statistics, use the **show interfaces rate-limit** command:

```
Router# show interfaces hssi 0/0/0 rate-limit

Hssi0/0/0 45Mbps to R2
 Input
  matches: access-group 101
   params: 20000000 bps, 24000 limit, 32000 extended limit
   conformed 3 packets, 189 bytes; action: set-prec-transmit 5
   exceeded 0 packets, 0 bytes; action: set-prec-transmit 0
   last packet: 309100ms ago, current burst: 0 bytes
   last cleared 00:08:00 ago, conformed 0 bps, exceeded 0 bps
  matches: access-group 102
   params: 10000000 bps, 24000 limit, 32000 extended limit
   conformed 0 packets, 0 bytes; action: set-prec-transmit 5
   exceeded 0 packets, 0 bytes; action: drop
   last packet: 19522612ms ago, current burst: 0 bytes
   last cleared 00:07:18 ago, conformed 0 bps, exceeded 0 bps
  matches: all traffic
   params: 8000000 bps, 16000 limit, 24000 extended limit
   conformed 5 packets, 315 bytes; action: set-prec-transmit 5
   exceeded 0 packets, 0 bytes; action: drop
   last packet: 9632ms ago, current burst: 0 bytes
   last cleared 00:05:43 ago, conformed 0 bps, exceeded 0 bps
```

PART II

Congestion Management

CHAPTER 5

Congestion Management Overview

Congestion management features allow you to control congestion by determining the order in which packets are transmitted out an interface based on priorities assigned to those packets. Congestion management entails the creation of queues, assignment of packets to those queues based on the packet's classification, and scheduling of the packets in a queue for transmission. The congestion management QoS feature offers four types of queuing protocols, each allowing you to specify creation of a different number of queues, which affords greater or lesser degrees of differentiation of traffic and the order in which that traffic is transmitted.

During periods with light traffic, that is, when no congestion exists, packets are transmitted out the interface as soon as they arrive. During periods of transmit congestion at the outgoing interface, packets arrive faster than the interface can transmit them. If you use congestion management features, packets accumulating at an interface are queued until the interface is free to transmit them; they are then scheduled for transmission according to their assigned priority and the queuing mechanism configured for the interface. The router determines the order of packet transmission by controlling which packets are placed in which queue and how queues are serviced with respect to each other.

This chapter discusses these four types of queuing, which constitute the congestion management QoS feature:

- **First-In, First-Out Queuing (FIFO)**—FIFO entails no concept of priority or classes of traffic. With FIFO, transmission of packets out the interface occurs in the order the packets arrive.

- **Weighted Fair Queuing (WFQ)**—WFQ offers dynamic, fair queuing that divides bandwidth across queues of traffic based on weights. WFQ ensures that all traffic is treated fairly, given its weight. To help understand how WFQ works, consider the queue for a train of File Transfer Protocol (FTP) packets as a queue for the collective and the queue for discrete interactive traffic packets as a queue for the individual. Given the weight of the queues, WFQ ensures that for all FTP packets transmitted as a collective an equal number of individual interactive traffic packets are transmitted.

  Given this handling, WFQ ensures satisfactory response time to critical applications, such as interactive, transaction-based applications, that are intolerant of performance degradation. For serial interfaces at E1 (2.048 Mbps) and below, WFQ is used by default. When no other queuing strategies are configured, all other interfaces use FIFO by default.

- **Custom Queuing (CQ)**—With CQ, bandwidth is allocated proportionally for each different class of traffic. CQ allows you to specify the number of bytes or packets to be drawn from the queue, which is especially useful on slow interfaces.

- **Priority Queuing (PQ)**—With PQ, packets belonging to one priority class of traffic are transmitted before all lower priority traffic to ensure timely delivery of those packets.

NOTE   You can assign only one queuing mechanism type to an interface.

Why Use Congestion Management?

Today's heterogeneous networks include many different protocols used by applications, giving rise to the need to prioritize traffic in order to satisfy time-critical applications while still addressing the needs of less time-dependent applications, such as file transfer. Different types of traffic sharing a data path through the network can interact with one another in ways that affect their application performance. If your network is designed to support different traffic types that share a single data path between routers, you should consider using congestion management techniques to ensure fairness of treatment across the various traffic types.

Here are some broad ideas to consider in determining if you need to configure congestion management QoS:

- Traffic prioritization is especially important for delay-sensitive, interactive transaction-based applications—for instance, desktop video conferencing—that require higher priority than file transfer applications. However, use of WFQ ensures that all traffic is treated fairly, given its weight, and in a dynamic manner. For example, WFQ addresses the requirements of the interactive application without penalizing the FTP application.

- Prioritization is most effective on WAN links where the combination of bursty traffic and relatively lower data rates can cause temporary congestion.

- Depending on the average packet size, prioritization is most effective when applied to links at T1/E1 bandwidth speeds or lower.

- If users of applications running across your network notice poor response time, you should consider using congestion management features. Congestion management features are dynamic, tailoring themselves to the existing network conditions. However, if a WAN link is constantly congested, traffic prioritization may *not* resolve the problem. Adding bandwidth might be the appropriate solution.

- If there is no congestion on the WAN link, there is no reason to implement traffic prioritization.

Here are some steps that summarize aspects to consider in determining whether you should establish and implement a queuing policy for your network:

Step 1   Determine if the WAN is congested—that is, whether users of certain applications perceive a performance degradation.

Step 2   Determine your goals and objectives based on the mix of traffic you need to manage and your network topology and design. In identifying what you want to achieve, consider whether your goal is among the following:

- To establish fair distribution of bandwidth allocation across all of the types of traffic you identify.

- To grant strict priority to traffic from special kinds of applications you service—for example, interactive multimedia applications—possibly at the expense of less critical traffic you also support.

- To customize bandwidth allocation so that network resources are shared among all of the applications you service, each having the specific bandwidth requirements you have identified.

To effectively configure queuing, you must analyze the types of traffic using the interface and determine how to distinguish them. See Chapter 1, "Classification Overview," for a description of how packets are classified.

After you assess your needs, review the available congestion management queuing mechanisms described in this chapter and determine which approach best addresses your requirements and goals.

Step 3   Configure the interface for the kind of queuing strategy you have chosen, and observe the results.

Traffic patterns change over time, so you should repeat the analysis process described in Step 2 periodically and adapt the queuing configuration accordingly.

See the section "Deciding Which Queuing Policy to Use" for elaboration of the differences between the various queuing mechanisms.

Deciding Which Queuing Policy to Use

This section looks briefly at some of the differences between the types of queuing and includes a table that compares the three main queuing strategies.

FIFO queuing performs no prioritization of data packets on user data traffic. It entails no concept of priority or classes of traffic. When FIFO is used, ill-behaved sources can consume available bandwidth, bursty sources can cause delays in time-sensitive or important traffic, and important traffic may be dropped because less important traffic fills the queue.

Consider these differences in deciding whether to use CQ or PQ:

- CQ guarantees some level of service to all traffic, because you can allocate bandwidth to all classes of traffic. You can define the size of the queue by determining its configured packet-count capacity, thereby controlling bandwidth access.

- PQ guarantees strict priority because it ensures that one type of traffic will be transmitted, possibly at the expense of all others. For PQ, a low priority queue can be detrimentally affected and, in the worst case, never allowed to transmit its packets either if there is a limited amount of available bandwidth, or if the transmission frequency of critical traffic is high.

In deciding whether to use WFQ or one of the other two queuing types, consider these differences in WFQ and PQ and CQ:

- WFQ does not require configuration of access lists to determine the preferred traffic on a serial interface. Rather, the fair queue algorithm dynamically sorts traffic into messages that are part of a conversation.

- Low-volume, interactive traffic gets fair allocation of bandwidth with WFQ, as does high-volume traffic such as file transfers.

Table 5-1 compares the salient features of WFQ, CQ, and PQ.

Table 5-1 *Queuing Comparison*

	WFQ	CQ	PQ
Number of Queues	Configurable number of queues (256 user queues, by default)	16 user queues	4 queues
Kind of Service	Ensures fairness among all traffic flows based on weights	Round-robin service Proportional allocation of bandwidth for different classes of service	High priority queues serviced first Absolute prioritization; ensures critical traffic of highest priority
Configuration	No configuration required	Requires configuration	Requires configuration

First-In, First-Out Queuing

In its simplest form, FIFO queuing—also known as first-come, first-served (FCFS) queuing—involves storing packets when the network is congested and forwarding them in order of arrival when the network is no longer congested.

FIFO embodies no concept of priority or classes of traffic and consequently makes no decision about packet priority. There is only one queue, and all packets are treated equally. Packets are sent out an interface in the order in which they arrive. Higher priority packets are not transmitted faster than lower priority packets.

When FIFO is used, ill-behaved sources can consume all the bandwidth, bursty sources can cause delays in time-sensitive or important traffic, and important traffic can be dropped because less important traffic fills the queue.

When no other queuing strategies are configured, all interfaces excepting serial interfaces at E1 (2.048 Mbps) and below use FIFO by default. (Serial interfaces at E1—2.048 Mbps—and below use WFQ by default.)

FIFO, which is the fastest method of queuing, is effective for large links that have little delay and minimal congestion. If your link has very little congestion, FIFO queuing may be the only queuing you need to use.

Weighted Fair Queuing

This section discusses the following:

- About WFQ
- VIP-Distributed WFQ

Table 5-2 summarizes the differences between WFQ and VIP-Distributed WFQ (DWFQ).

Table 5-2 *WFQ and DWFQ Comparison*

WFQ	VIP-Distributed WFQ
Flow-based WFQ	Flow-based WFQ
• Weighted, when packets are classified	• FQ, not weighted
• FQ, when packets are not classified	
Runs on all standard IOS platforms	Runs on Versatile Interface Processor (faster performance)

All queuing is transacted by the Versatile Interface Processor (VIP). On the VIP, all packets are transmitted directly out the interface. An RSP resides on the same platform as the VIP. The RSP handles all tasks associated with system maintenance and routing. The VIP and the RSP each handle some scheduling. The dual-processor supports accounts for the faster speed of VIP-Distributed WFQ over WFQ running on standard IOS platforms.

About WFQ

WFQ is an automated scheduling method that provides fair bandwidth allocation to all network traffic. WFQ applies priority, or weights, to identified traffic to classify traffic into conversations and determine how much bandwidth each conversation is allowed relative to other conversations. WFQ is a flow-based algorithm that simultaneously schedules interactive traffic to the front of a queue to reduce response time and fairly shares the remaining bandwidth among high-bandwidth flows. In other words, WFQ gives low-volume traffic, such as Telnet sessions, priority over high-volume traffic, such as FTP sessions. WFQ gives concurrent file transfers balanced use of link capacity; that is, when multiple file transfers occur, the transfers are given comparable bandwidth. Figure 5-1 shows how WFQ works.

Figure 5-1   *WFQ*

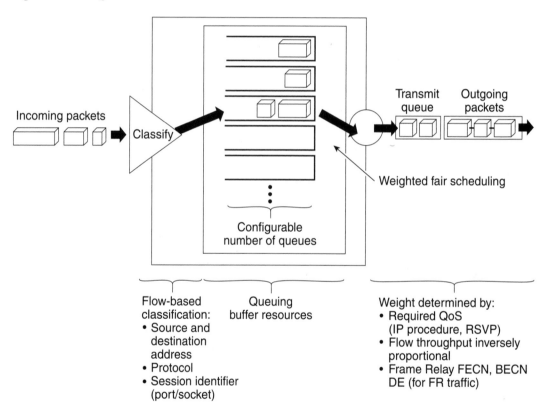

WFQ overcomes a serious limitation of FIFO queuing. When FIFO is in effect, traffic is transmitted in the order received without regard for bandwidth consumption or the associated delays. As a result, file transfers and other high-volume network applications often generate series of packets of associated data. These related packets are known as packet trains. Packet trains are groups of packets that tend to move together through the network. These packet trains can consume all available bandwidth, depriving other traffic of it.

WFQ provides traffic priority management that dynamically sorts traffic into messages that make up a conversation. WFQ breaks up the train of packets within a conversation to ensure that bandwidth is shared fairly between individual conversations and that low-volume traffic is transferred in a timely fashion.

WFQ classifies traffic into different flows based on packet header addressing, including such characteristics as source and destination network or MAC address, protocol, source and destination port and socket numbers of the session, Frame Relay data-link connection identifier (DLCI) value, and type of service (ToS) value. There are two categories of flows: high-bandwidth sessions and low-bandwidth sessions. Low-bandwidth traffic has effective priority over high-bandwidth traffic, and high-bandwidth traffic shares the transmission service proportionally according to assigned weights. Low-bandwidth traffic streams, which comprise the majority of traffic, receive preferential service, transmitting their entire offered loads in a timely fashion. High-volume traffic streams share the remaining capacity proportionally among themselves.

WFQ places packets of the various conversations in the fair queues before transmission. The order of removal from the fair queues is determined by the virtual time of the delivery of the last bit of each arriving packet.

New messages for high-bandwidth flows are discarded after the congestive-messages threshold has been met. However, low-bandwidth flows, which include control-message conversations, continue to enqueue data. As a result, the fair queue may occasionally contain more messages than specified by the threshold number.

WFQ can manage duplex data streams, such as those between pairs of applications, and simplex data streams such as voice or video.

The WFQ algorithm also addresses the problem of round-trip delay variability. If multiple high-volume conversations are active, their transfer rates and interarrival periods are made much more predictable. WFQ greatly enhances algorithms such as SNA Logical Link Control (LLC) and Transmission Control Protocol (TCP) congestion control and slow start features.

WFQ is used as the default queuing mode on most serial interfaces configured to run at or below E1 speeds (2.048 Mbps).

WFQ provides the solution for situations in which it is desirable to provide consistent response time to heavy and light network users alike without adding excessive bandwidth. WFQ automatically adapts to changing network traffic conditions.

WFQ and IP Precedence

WFQ is IP precedence-aware. That is, it is able to detect higher priority packets marked with precedence by the IP Forwarder and can schedule them faster, providing superior response time for this traffic. Thus, as the precedence increases, WFQ allocates more bandwidth to the conversation during periods of congestion.

WFQ assigns a weight to each flow, which determines the transmit order for queued packets. In this scheme, lower weights are served first. For standard IOS WFQ, the IP precedence serves as a divisor to this weighting factor.

Like CQ, WFQ transmits a certain number of bytes from each queue. With WFQ, each queue corresponds to a different flow. For each cycle through all the flows, WFQ effectively transmits a number of bytes equal to the precedence of the flow plus one.

Actually, this number is only used as a ratio to determine how many bytes/packets to transmit. However, for the purposes of understanding WFQ, using this number as the byte count is sufficient. For instance, traffic with an IP precedence field value of 7 gets a lower weight than traffic with an IP precedence field value of 3. Thus, the priority is in transmit order.

To determine the bandwidth allocation for each queue, divide the byte count for the flow by the total byte count for all flows.

For example, if you have one flow at each precedence level, each flow will get precedence+1 parts of the link:

$$1+2+3+4+5+6+7+8 = 36$$

Thus, precedence 0 traffic will get 1/36 of the bandwidth, precedence 1 traffic will get 2/36, and precedence 7 traffic will get 8/36.

However, if you have 18 precedence 1 flows and one of each of the rest, the total is now:

$$1+2(18)+3+4+5+6+7+8 = 70$$

Precedence 0 traffic will get 1/70, each of the precedence 1 flows will get 2/70, and so on.

As flows are added or ended, the actual allocated bandwidth will continuously change. Thus, WFQ adapts to changing network conditions by allocating traffic.

WFQ and Resource Reservation Protocol

Resource Reservation Protocol (RSVP) uses WFQ to allocate buffer space and schedule packets and guarantee bandwidth for reserved flows. WFQ works with RSVP to help provide differentiated and guaranteed QoS services.

RSVP is the IETF Internet Standard (RFC 2205) protocol for allowing an application to dynamically reserve network bandwidth. RSVP enables applications to request a specific QoS for a data flow. Cisco's implementation allows RSVP to be initiated within the network using configured proxy RSVP.

RSVP is the only standard signaling protocol designed to guarantee network bandwidth from end to end for IP networks. Hosts and routers use RSVP to deliver QoS requests to the routers along the paths of the data stream and to maintain router and host state to provide the requested service, usually bandwidth and latency. RSVP uses a mean data rate, the largest amount of data the router will keep in queue, and minimum QoS to determine bandwidth reservation.

WFQ or WRED acts as the preparator for RSVP, setting up the packet classification and scheduling required for the reserved flows. Using WFQ, RSVP can deliver an Integrated Services Guaranteed Service.

WFQ and Frame Relay

WFQ weights are affected by Frame Relay discard eligible (DE), forward explicit congestion notification (FECN), and backward explicit congestion notification (BECN) bits when traffic is switched by the Frame Relay switching module. Once congestion is flagged, the weights used by the algorithm are altered so that the conversation encountering the congestion transmits less frequently.

Considerations

Although WFQ automatically adapts to changing network traffic conditions, it does not offer the degree of precise control over bandwidth allocation that CQ does.

VIP-Distributed WFQ

VIP-Distributed WFQ is a special high-speed version of WFQ that runs on the VIP. It is supported on the following routers with a VIP2-40 or greater interface processor:

- Cisco 7000 series with RSP7000

- Cisco 7500 series

A VIP2-50 interface processor is recommended when the aggregate line rate of the port adapters on the VIP is greater than DS3. A VIP2-50 card is required for OC-3 rates.

To use VIP-Distributed WFQ, Distributed Cisco Express Forwarding (DCEF) switching must be enabled on the interface.

This section describes flow-based VIP-Distributed WFQ. This section also includes a discussion that describes the drop policy used by both types of VIP-Distributed WFQ.

NOTE   The VIP-Distributed WFQ implementation differs from WFQ that runs on all other platforms. For a comparison of features, refer to Table 5-1.

Flow-Based VIP-Distributed WFQ

With flow-based VIP-Distributed WFQ, packets are classified by flow. Packets with the same source IP address, destination IP address, source TCP or UDP port, destination TCP or UDP port, protocol, and ToS field belong to the same flow. (All non-IP packets are treated as flow 0.)

Each flow corresponds to a separate output queue. When a packet is assigned to a flow, it is placed in the queue for that flow. During periods of congestion, VIP-Distributed WFQ allocates an equal share of the bandwidth to each active queue.

Flow-based VIP-Distributed WFQ is also called fair queuing, because all flows are equally weighted and allocated equal bandwidth. In the current implementation of VIP-Distributed WFQ, weights are not assigned to flows. With VIP-Distributed WFQ, well-behaved hosts are protected from badly behaved hosts.

Restrictions

Use VIP-Distributed WFQ with IP traffic. All non-IP traffic is treated as a single flow and, therefore, placed in the same queue.

VIP-Distributed WFQ has the following restrictions:

● Can be configured on interfaces, but not subinterfaces

● Is not supported on Fast EtherChannel or tunnel interfaces

● Cannot be configured on the same interface as RSP-based PQ

Drop Policy

VIP-Distributed WFQ keeps track of the number of packets in each queue and the total number of packets in all queues.

When the total number of packets is below the aggregate limit, queues can buffer more packets than the individual queue limit.

When the total number of packets reaches the aggregate limit, the interface starts enforcing the individual queue limits. Any new packets that arrive for a queue that has exceeded its individual queue limit are dropped. Packets that are already in the queue will not be dropped, even if the queue is over the individual limit.

In some cases, the total number of packets in all queues put together may exceed the aggregate limit.

Custom Queuing

CQ allows you to specify a number of bytes to forward from a queue each time the queue is serviced, thereby allowing you to share the network resources among applications with specific minimum bandwidth or latency requirements. You can also specify a maximum number of packets in each queue.

How It Works

CQ handles traffic by specifying the number of packets or bytes to be serviced for each class of traffic. It services the queues by cycling through them in round-robin fashion, sending the portion of allocated bandwidth for each queue before moving to the next queue. If one queue is empty, the router will send packets from the next queue that has packets ready to send.

When CQ is enabled on an interface, the system maintains 17 output queues for that interface. You can specify queues 1 through 16. Associated with each output queue is a configurable byte count, which specifies how many bytes of data the system should deliver from the current queue before it moves on to the next queue.

Queue number 0 is a system queue; it is emptied before any of the queues numbered 1 through 16 are processed. The system queues high priority packets, such as keepalive packets and signaling packets, to this queue. Other traffic cannot be configured to use this queue.

For queue numbers 1 through 16, the system cycles through the queues sequentially (in a round-robin fashion), dequeuing the configured byte count from each queue in each cycle, delivering packets in the current queue before moving on to the next one. When a particular queue is being processed, packets are sent until the number of bytes sent either exceeds the queue byte count, or the queue is empty. Bandwidth used by a particular queue can only be indirectly specified in terms of byte count and queue length.

Figure 5-2 shows how CQ behaves.

Figure 5-2   *CQ*

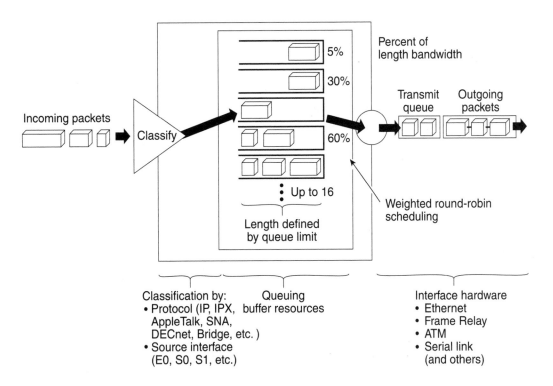

CQ ensures that no application, or specified group of applications, achieves more than a predetermined proportion of overall capacity when the line is under stress. Like PQ, CQ is statically configured and does not automatically adapt to changing network conditions.

On most platforms, all protocols are classified in the fast switching path.

Determining Byte Count Values for Queues

In order to allocate bandwidth to different queues, you must specify the byte count for each queue.

How the Byte Count Is Used

The router sends packets from a particular queue until the byte count is exceeded. Once the byte count value is exceeded, the packet that is currently being transmitted will be completely sent. Therefore, if you set the byte count to 100 bytes and the packet size of your protocol is 1024 bytes, then every time this queue is serviced, 1024 bytes will be sent, not 100 bytes.

For example, suppose one protocol has 500-byte packets, another has 300-byte packets, and a third has 100-byte packets. If you want to split the bandwidth evenly across all three protocols, you might choose to specify byte counts of 200, 200, and 200 for each queue. However, this configuration does not result in 33/33/33 ratio. When the router services the first queue, it sends a single 500-byte packet; when it services the second queue, it sends a 300-byte packet; and when it services the third queue, it sends two 100-byte packets. The effective ratio is 50/30/20.

Thus, setting the byte count too low can result in an unintended bandwidth allocation.

However, very large byte counts will produce a "jerky" distribution. That is, if you assign 10 KB, 10 KB, and 10 KB to three queues in the example given, each protocol is serviced promptly when its queue is the one being serviced, but it may be a long time before the queue is serviced again. A better solution is to specify 500-byte, 600-byte, and 500-byte counts for the queue. This configuration results in a ratio of 31/38/31, which may be acceptable.

In order to service queues in a timely manner and ensure that the configured bandwidth allocation is as close as possible to the required bandwidth allocation, you must determine the byte count based on each protocol's packet size. Otherwise, your percentages may not match what you configure.

NOTE   Some protocols, such as IPX, will negotiate the frame size at session startup time.

Determining the Byte Count

To determine the correct byte counts, perform the following tasks:

Step 1   For each queue, divide the percentage of bandwidth you want to allocate to the queue by the packet size, in bytes. For example, assume the packet size for protocol A is 1086 bytes, protocol B is 291 bytes, and protocol C is 831 bytes. You want to allocate 20 percent for A, 60 percent for B, and 20 percent for C. The ratios would be:

20/1086, 60/291, 20/831 or

0.01842, 0.20619, 0.02407

Step 2 Normalize the numbers by dividing by the lowest number:

1, 11.2, 1.3

The result is the ratio of the number of packets that must be sent so that the percentage of bandwidth that each protocol uses is approximately 20, 60, and 20 percent.

Step 3 A fraction in any of the ratio values means that an additional packet will be sent. Round up the numbers to the next whole number to obtain the actual packet count.

In this example, the actual ratio will be 1 packet, 12 packets, and 2 packets.

Step 4 Convert the packet number ratio into byte counts by multiplying each packet count by the corresponding packet size.

In this example, the number of packets sent is one 1086-byte packet, twelve 291-byte packets, and two 831-byte packets or 1086, 3492, and 1662 bytes, respectively, from each queue. These are the byte counts you would specify in your custom queuing configuration.

Step 5 To determine the bandwidth distribution this ratio represents, first determine the total number of bytes sent after all three queues are serviced:

(1 x 1086) + (12 x 291) +(2 x 831) = 1086 + 3492 + 1662 = 6240

Step 6 Then determine the percentage of the total number of bytes sent from each queue:

1086/6240, 3492/6240, 1662/6240 = 17.4, 56, and 26.6 percent

As you can see, this is close to the desired ratio of 20/60/20.

Step 7 If the actual bandwidth is not close enough to the desired bandwidth, multiply the original ratio of 1:11.2:1.3 by the best value and try to get as close to three integer values as possible. Note that the multiplier you use need not be an integer. For example, if you multiply the ratio by two, you get 2:22.4:2.6. You would now send two 1086-byte packets, twenty-three 291-byte packets, and three 831-byte packets, or 2172/6693/2493, for a total of 11,358 bytes. The resulting ratio is 19/59/22 percent, which is much closer to the desired ratio that you achieved.

Window Size

Window size also affects the bandwidth distribution. If the window size of a particular protocol is set to one, then that protocol will not place another packet into the queue until it receives an acknowledgment. The custom queuing algorithm moves to the next queue either if the byte count is exceeded, or there are no packets in that queue.

Therefore, with a window size of one, only one frame will be sent each time. If your frame count is set to 2 KB, and your frame size is 256 bytes, then only 256 bytes will be sent each time this queue is serviced.

Why Use CQ?

You can use the Cisco IOS QoS CQ feature to provide specific traffic guaranteed bandwidth at a potential congestion point, assuring the traffic a fixed portion of available bandwidth and leaving the remaining bandwidth to other traffic. For example, you could reserve half of the bandwidth for SNA data, allowing the remaining half to be used by other protocols.

If a particular type of traffic is not using the bandwidth reserved for it, then unused bandwidth can be dynamically allocated to other traffic types.

Considerations

CQ is statically configured and does not adapt to changing network conditions. With CQ enabled, the system takes longer to switch packets than FIFO because the packets are classified by the processor card.

Priority Queuing

PQ allows you to define how traffic is prioritized in the network. You configure four traffic priorities. You can define a series of filters based on packet characteristics to cause the router to place traffic into these four queues; the queue with the highest priority is serviced first until it is empty, then the lower queues are serviced in sequence.

How It Works

During transmission, PQ gives priority queues absolute preferential treatment over low priority queues; important traffic, given the highest priority, always takes precedence over less important traffic. Packets are classified based on user-specified criteria and placed into one of the four output queues—high, medium, normal, and low—based on the assigned priority. Packets that are not classified by priority fall into the normal queue. Figure 5-3 illustrates this process.

Figure 5-3 *PQ*

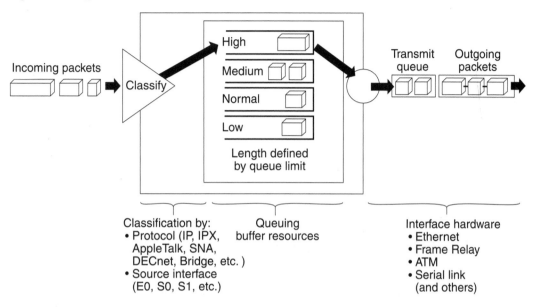

When a packet is to be sent out an interface, the priority queues on that interface are scanned for packets in descending order of priority. The high priority queue is scanned first, then the medium priority queue, and so on. The packet at the head of the highest queue is chosen for transmission. This procedure is repeated every time a packet is to be transmitted.

The maximum length of a queue is defined by the length limit. When a queue is longer than the queue limit, all additional packets are dropped.

NOTE   The priority output queuing mechanism can be used to manage traffic from all networking protocols. Additional fine-tuning is available for IP and for setting boundaries on the packet size.

How Packets Are Classified for PQ

A priority list is a set of rules that describe how packets should be assigned to priority queues. A priority list might also describe a default priority or the queue size limits of the various priority queues.

Packets can be classified by the following:

● Protocol or subprotocol type

● Incoming interface

● Packet size

● Fragments

● Access list

Keepalives sourced by the network server are always assigned to the high priority queue; all other management traffic (such as IGRP updates) must be configured. Packets that are not classified by the priority list mechanism are assigned to the normal queue.

Why Use PQ?

PQ provides absolute preferential treatment to high priority traffic, ensuring that mission-critical traffic traversing various WAN links gets priority treatment. In addition, PQ provides a faster response time than other methods of queuing.

Although you can enable priority output queuing for any interface, it is best used for low-bandwidth, congested serial interfaces.

Considerations

When choosing to use PQ, consider that because lower priority traffic is often denied bandwidth in favor of higher priority traffic, use of PQ could, in the worst case, result in lower priority traffic never being transmitted. To avoid inflicting these conditions on lower priority traffic, you can use traffic shaping or CAR to rate-limit the higher priority traffic.

PQ introduces extra overhead that is acceptable for slow interfaces, but may not be acceptable for higher speed interfaces such as Ethernet. With PQ enabled, the system takes longer to switch packets because the packets are classified by the processor card.

PQ uses a static configuration and does not adapt to changing network conditions.

Restrictions

PQ is not supported on any tunnels.

CHAPTER 6

Configuring Weighted Fair Queuing

This chapter describes the tasks for configuring QoS weighted fair queuing (WFQ) and Distributed WFQ (DWFQ) on a router. To locate documentation of related commands, you can search online at www.cisco.com.

WFQ Configuration Task List

WFQ provides traffic priority management that automatically sorts among individual traffic streams without requiring that you first define access lists. WFQ can also manage duplex data streams such as those between pairs of applications and simplex data streams such as voice or video. There are two categories of WFQ sessions: high bandwidth and low bandwidth. Low-bandwidth traffic has effective priority over high-bandwidth traffic, and high-bandwidth traffic shares the transmission service proportionally according to assigned weights.

When WFQ is enabled for an interface, new messages for high-bandwidth traffic streams are discarded after the configured or default congestive messages threshold has been met. However, low-bandwidth conversations, which include control message conversations, continue to enqueue data. As a result, the fair queue may occasionally contain more messages than its configured threshold number specifies.

With standard WFQ, packets are classified by flow. Packets with the same source IP address, destination IP address, source Transmission Control Protocol (TCP) or User Datagram Protocol (UDP) port, or destination TCP or UDP port belong to the same flow. WFQ allocates an equal share of the bandwidth to each flow. Flow-based WFQ is also called fair queuing because all flows are equally weighted.

The Cisco IOS software provides two forms of WFQ:

- Standard WFQ, which is enabled by default on all serial interfaces that run at or below 2 Mbps and can run on all Cisco serial interfaces.

- DWFQ, which runs only on Cisco 7000 series routers with a Route Switch Processor-based RSP7000 interface processor, or Cisco 7500 series routers with a Versatile Interface Processor-based VIP2-40 or greater interface processor. (A VIP2-50 interface processor is strongly recommended when the aggregate line rate of the port adapters on the VIP is greater than DS3. A VIP2-50 interface processor is required for OC-3 rates.)

To configure WFQ and DWFQ, perform the tasks in the following sections:

- Configure WFQ and DWFQ

- Monitor Fair Queuing

See the section "Fair Queuing Configuration Examples" later in this chapter for examples of how to configure fair queuing in your network.

Configure WFQ and DWFQ

To configure fair queuing on an interface, use one of the following commands in interface configuration mode after specifying the interface:

Command	Purpose
fair-queue [*congestive-discard-threshold* [*dynamic-queues* [*reservable-queues*]]]	Configures an interface to use fair queuing.
or	or
fair-queue	Configures an interface to use fair queuing on a Cisco router using a VIP-based interface.

WFQ uses a traffic data stream discrimination registry service to determine to which traffic stream a message belongs. Defaults are provided for the congestion threshold after messages for high-bandwidth conversations are dropped and for the number of dynamic and reservable queues; however, you can fine-tune your network operation by changing these defaults.

For DWFQ, packets are classified by flow. Packets with the same source IP address, destination IP address, source TCP or UDP port, destination TCP or UDP port, protocol, and type of service (ToS) field belong to the same flow.

NOTE	WFQ is the default queuing mode on interfaces that run at or below E1 speeds (2.048 Mbps or less). It is enabled by default for physical interfaces that do not use Link Access Procedure, Balanced (LAPB), X.25, or Synchronous Data Link Control (SDLC) encapsulations. WFQ is not an option for these protocols. WFQ is also enabled by default on interfaces configured for Multilink Point-to-Point Protocol (MLP). However, if custom queuing or priority queuing is enabled for a qualifying link, it overrides fair queuing, effectively disabling it. Additionally, WFQ is automatically disabled if you enable autonomous or SSE switching.
	DWFQ can be configured on interfaces but not subinterfaces. It is not supported on Fast EtherChannel, tunnel, or other logical or virtual interfaces such as MLP.

Monitor Fair Queuing

To monitor fair queuing services in your network, use the following commands in EXEC mode:

Command	Purpose
show interfaces [*interface*] **fair-queue**	Shows information about an interface configured for WFQ and DWFQ.
show queuing fair	Shows status of the fair queuing configuration.

Fair Queuing Configuration Examples

This section provides the following examples of QoS fair queuing configurations:

- WFQ Example
- DWFQ Example

WFQ Example

The following example requests a fair queue with a congestive discard threshold of 64 messages, 512 dynamic queues, and 18 RSVP queues:

```
interface Serial 3/0
 ip unnumbered Ethernet 0/0
 fair-queue 64 512 18
```

DWFQ Example

The following example enables DWFQ on the HSSI 0/0/0 interface:

```
interface Hssi0/0/0
 description 45Mbps to R2
 ip address 200.200.14.250 255.255.255.252
 fair-queue
```

The following is sample output from the **show interfaces fair-queue** command for this configuration:

```
Router# show interfaces hssi 0/0/0 fair-queue

Hssi0/0/0 queue size 0
    packets output 35, drops 0
WFQ: global queue limit 401, local queue limit 200
```

CHAPTER 7

Configuring Custom Queuing

This chapter describes the tasks for configuring QoS custom queuing on a router. To locate documentation of related commands, you can search online at www.cisco.com.

NOTE Custom queuing is not supported on any tunnels.

Custom Queuing Configuration Task List

You must follow certain required, basic steps to enable custom queuing for your network. In addition, you can choose to assign packets to custom queues based on protocol type, the interface where the packets enter the router, or other criteria you specify. The following sections outline these tasks:

- Define the Custom Queue List

- Specify the Maximum Size of the Custom Queues

- Assign Packets to Custom Queues

- Monitor Custom Queue Lists

See the section "Custom Queuing Configuration Examples" later in this chapter for ideas of how to configure custom queuing on your network.

Define the Custom Queue List

To assign a custom queue list to an interface, use the following commands:

Step	Command	Purpose
1	**interface** *interface-type interface-number*	Specifies the interface, and then enters interface configuration mode.
2	**custom-queue-list** *list*	Assigns a custom queue list to the interface. The list argument is any number from 1 to 16. There is no default assignment.

NOTE Use the **custom-queue-list** command in place of the **priority-list** command. Only one queue list can be assigned per interface.

Custom queuing allows a fairness not provided with priority queuing. With custom queuing, you can control the interface's available bandwidth when it is unable to accommodate the aggregate traffic enqueued. Associated with each output queue is a configurable byte count, which specifies how many bytes of data should be delivered from the current queue by the system before the system moves on to the next queue. When a particular queue is being processed, packets are sent either until the number of bytes sent exceeds the queue byte count defined by the **queue-list queue byte-count** command (see the section "Specify the Maximum Size of the Custom Queues"), or until the queue is empty.

Specify the Maximum Size of the Custom Queues

You can specify the maximum number of packets allowed in each of the custom queues or the maximum queue size in bytes. The default is 20 entries.

To do so, for each queue, use one of the following commands in global configuration mode:

Command	Purpose
queue-list *list-number* **queue** *queue-number* **limit** *limit-number*	Specifies the maximum number of packets allowed in each of the custom queues. The *limit-number* argument specifies the number of packets that can be enqueued at any one time. The range is 0 to 32,767.
queue-list *list-number* **queue** *queue-number* **byte-count** *byte-count-number*	Designates the byte size allowed per queue. The *byte-count-number* argument specifies the lowest number of bytes the system allows to be delivered from a given queue during a particular cycle.

Assign Packets to Custom Queues

You can assign packets to custom queues based on the protocol type or interface where the packets enter the router. Additionally, you can set the default queue for packets that do not match other assignment rules. You can also specify multiple rules.

To define the custom queuing lists, use one of the following commands in global configuration mode:

Command	Purpose
queue-list *list-number* **protocol** *protocol-name* *queue-number queue-keyword keyword-value*	Establishes queuing priorities based upon the protocol type.
queue-list *list-number* **interface** *interface-type interface-number queue-number*	Establishes custom queuing based on packets entering from a given interface.
queue-list *list-number* **default** *queue-number*	Assigns a queue number for those packets that do not match any other rule in the custom queue list.

All protocols supported by Cisco are allowed. The *queue-keyword* variable provides additional options, including byte count, Transmission Control Protocol (TCP) service and port number assignments, and AppleTalk, IP, IPX, VINES, or XNS access list assignments.

When you use multiple rules, remember that the system reads the **queue-list** commands in order of appearance. When classifying a packet, the system searches the list of rules specified by **queue-list** commands for a matching protocol or interface type. When a match is found, the packet is assigned to the appropriate queue. The list is searched in the order it is specified, and the first matching rule terminates the search.

Monitor Custom Queue Lists

To show information about the input and output queues when custom queuing is enabled on an interface, use one of the following commands in EXEC mode:

Command	Purpose
show queuing custom	Shows the status of the custom queuing lists.
s**how interface** *interface-type interface-number*	Shows the current status of the custom output queues when custom queuing is enabled.

Custom Queuing Configuration Examples

The following sections provide examples of ways you might configure QoS custom queuing to control traffic in your network:

- Define the Custom Queue List Example

- Specify Maximum Number of Packets Allowed in Each Custom Queue Example

- Specify Maximum Queue Size in Bytes Example

- Assign by Protocol Type Examples

- Assign by Interface Type Example

- Assign by Default Queue Example

Define the Custom Queue List Example

This example illustrates how to assign custom queue list number 3 to serial interface 0:

```
interface serial 0
custom-queue-list 3
```

Specify Maximum Number of Packets Allowed in Each Custom Queue Example

In the following example, the queue length of queue 10 is increased from the default 20 packets to 40 packets:

```
queue-list 3 queue 10 limit 40
```

The queue length limit is the maximum number of packets that can be enqueued at any time, with the range being 0 to 32,767 queue entries.

Specify Maximum Queue Size in Bytes Example

The following example decreases queue list 9 from the default byte count of 1500 to 1400 for queue number 10:

```
queue-list 9 queue 10 byte-count 1400
```

The byte count establishes the lowest number of bytes the system allows to be delivered from a given queue during a particular cycle.

Assign by Protocol Type Examples

This example assigns traffic that matches IP access list 10 to queue number 1:

```
queue-list 1 protocol ip 1 list 10
```

This example assigns Telnet packets to queue number 2:

```
queue-list 4 protocol ip 2 tcp 23
```

This example assigns UDP Domain Name Service packets to queue number 3:

```
queue-list 4 protocol ip 3 udp 53
```

Assign by Interface Type Example

In this example, queue list 4 establishes queuing priorities for packets entering on serial interface 0. The queue number assigned is 10.

```
queue-list 4 interface serial 0 10
```

You can define multiple rules; the system reads the priority settings in order of appearance. The system searches the list in the order it is specified, and the first matching rule terminates the search. When a match is found, the packet is assigned to the appropriate queue.

Assign by Default Queue Example

You can specify a default queue for packets that do not match other assignment rules. In this example, the default queue for list 10 is set to queue number 2.

```
queue-list 10 default 2
```

CHAPTER 8

Configuring Priority Queuing

This chapter describes the tasks for configuring priority queuing on a router. To locate documentation of related commands, you can search online at www.cisco.com.

Priority Queuing Configuration Task List

You must follow certain required, basic steps to enable priority queuing in your network. The following sections outline these tasks:

- Define the Priority List
- Assign the Priority List to an Interface
- Monitor Priority Queuing Lists

See the section "Priority Queuing Configuration Examples" later in this chapter for ideas of how to configure priority queuing on your network.

Define the Priority List

A priority list contains the definitions for a set of priority queues. The priority list specifies which queue a packet will be placed in and, optionally, the maximum length of the different queues.

In order to perform queuing using a priority list, you must assign the list to an interface. The same priority list can be applied to multiple interfaces. Alternatively, you can create many different priority policies to apply to different interfaces.

To define a priority list, perform the tasks in the following sections. The second task is optional.

- Assign Packets to Priority Queues
- Specify the Maximum Size of the Priority Queues

Assign Packets to Priority Queues

Assign packets to priority queues based on the following:

- Protocol type
- Interface where the packets enter the router

You can specify multiple assignment rules. The **priority-list** commands are read in order of appearance until a matching protocol or interface type is found. When a match is found, the packet is assigned to the appropriate queue and the search ends. Packets that do not match other assignment rules are assigned to the default queue.

To specify which queue to place a packet in, use the following commands in global configuration mode:

Step	Command	Purpose
1	**priority-list** *list-number* **protocol** *protocol-name* {**high**	**medium**	**normal**	**low**} *queue-keyword keyword-value*	Establishes queuing priorities based upon the protocol type.
2	**priority-list** *list-number* **interface** *interface-type interface-number* {**high**	**medium**	**normal**	**low**}	Establishes queuing priorities for packets entering from a given interface.
3	**priority-list** *list-number* **default** {**high**	**medium**	**normal**	**low**}	Assigns a priority queue for those packets that do not match any other rule in the priority list.

All protocols supported by Cisco are allowed. The *queue-keyword* variable provides additional options including byte count, Transmission Control Protocol (TCP) service and port number assignments, and AppleTalk, IP, IPX, VINES, or XNS access list assignments.

Specify the Maximum Size of the Priority Queues

You can specify the maximum number of packets allowed in each of the priority queues. Perform this task for each priority list.

To do so, use the following command in global configuration mode:

Command	Purpose
priority-list *list-number* **queue-limit** [*high-limit* [*medium-limit* [*normal-limit* [*low-limit*]]]]	Specifies the maximum number of packets allowed in each of the priority queues.

The default queue limit arguments are listed in Table 8-1.

Table 8-1 *Default Priority Queue Packet Limits*

Priority Queue Argument	Packet Limits
high-limit	20
medium-limit	40
normal-limit	60
low-limit	80

Assign the Priority List to an Interface

You can assign a priority list number to an interface. Only one list can be assigned per interface. To assign a priority group to an interface, use the following commands:

Step	Command	Purpose
1	**interface** *interface-type interface-number*	Specifies the interface, and then enters interface configuration mode.
2	**priority-group** *list-number*	Assigns a priority list number to the interface.

Monitor Priority Queuing Lists

To display information about the input and output queues, use the following command in EXEC mode:

Command	Purpose
show queuing priority	Shows the status of the priority queuing lists.

Priority Queuing Configuration Examples

This section provides examples of priority queuing configurations. It includes the following examples:

- Priority Queuing Based on Protocol Type Example
- Priority Queuing Based on Interface Example
- Specify the Maximum Size of the Priority Queue Example
- Assign Priority List to an Interface Example
- Priority Queuing Using Multiple Rules Example

Priority Queuing Based on Protocol Type Example

This example establishes queuing based on protocol type. The example assigns 1 as the arbitrary priority list number, specifies IP as the protocol type, and assigns a high priority level to traffic that matches IP access list 10.

```
access-list 10 permit 239.1.1.0 0.0.0.255
priority-list 1 protocol ip high list 10
```

Priority Queuing Based on Interface Example

This example establishes queuing based on interface. The example sets any packet type entering on Ethernet interface 0 to a medium priority.

```
priority-list 3 interface ethernet 0 medium
```

Specify the Maximum Size of the Priority Queue Example

This example changes the maximum number of packets in the high priority queue to 10. The medium, normal, and low limit queue sizes remain at their default 40-, 60-, and 80-packet limits.

```
priority-list 4 queue-limit 10 40 60 80
```

Assign Priority List to an Interface Example

This example assigns priority group list 4 to serial interface 0:

```
interface serial 0
  priority-group 4
```

Priority Queuing Using Multiple Rules Example

When classifying a packet, the system searches the list of rules specified by **priority-list** commands for a matching protocol type. The following example specifies four rules:

● DECnet packets with a byte count less than 200 are assigned a medium priority queue level.

● IP packets originating or destined to TCP port 23 are assigned a medium priority queue level.

● IP packets originating or destined to User Datagram Protocol (UDP) port 53 are assigned a medium priority queue level.

● All IP packets are assigned a high priority queue level.

Remember that when using multiple rules for a single protocol, the system reads the priority settings in the order of appearance.

```
priority-list 4 protocol decnet medium lt 200
priority-list 4 protocol ip medium tcp 23
priority-list 4 protocol ip medium udp 53
priority-list 4 protocol ip high
```

Congestion Avoidance

CHAPTER 9

Congestion Avoidance Overview

Congestion avoidance techniques monitor network traffic loads in an effort to anticipate and avoid congestion at common network bottlenecks. Congestion avoidance is achieved through packet dropping. Among the more commonly used congestion avoidance mechanisms is Random Early Detection (RED), which is optimum for high-speed transit networks. Cisco IOS quality of service (QoS) includes an implementation of RED that, when configured, controls when the router drops packets. If you do not configure Weighted Random Early Detection (WRED), the router uses the cruder default packet drop mechanism called tail drop.

NOTE	For an explanation of network congestion, see the Introduction, "Quality of Service Overview."

This chapter gives a brief description of the kinds of congestion avoidance features provided by the Cisco IOS QoS features. It discusses the following features:

- Tail Drop. This is the default congestion avoidance behavior when WRED is not configured.
- Weighted Random Early Detection. WRED and VIP-Distributed WRED—both of which are Cisco's implementations of RED—combine the capabilities of the RED algorithm with IP precedence.

Tail Drop

Tail drop treats all traffic equally and does not differentiate between classes of service. Queues fill during periods of congestion. When the output queue is full and tail drop is in effect, packets are dropped until the congestion is eliminated and the queue is no longer full.

Weighted Random Early Detection

This section gives a brief introduction to RED concepts and addresses WRED, Cisco's implementation of RED for standard IOS platforms.

WRED avoids the globalization problems that occur when tail drop is used as the congestion avoidance mechanism on the router. Global synchronization occurs as waves of congestion crest only to be followed by troughs during which the transmission link is not fully utilized. Global synchronization of Transmission Control Protocol (TCP) hosts, for example, can occur because packets are dropped all at once. Global synchronization manifests when multiple TCP hosts reduce their transmission rates in response to packet dropping, then increase their transmission rates once again when the congestion is reduced.

This section comprises:

- About RED
- About WRED
- VIP-Distributed WRED

About RED

The RED mechanism was proposed by Sally Floyd and Van Jacobson in the early 1990s to address network congestion in a responsive rather than reactive manner. Underlying the RED mechanism is the premise that most traffic runs on data transport implementations which are sensitive to loss and will temporarily slow down when some of their traffic is dropped. TCP, which responds appropriately—even robustly—to traffic drop by slowing down its traffic transmission, effectively allows RED's traffic-drop behavior to work as a congestion-avoidance signaling mechanism.

TCP constitutes the most heavily used network transport. Given the ubiquitous presence of TCP, RED offers a widespread, effective congestion-avoidance mechanism.

In considering RED's usefulness when robust transports such as TCP are pervasive, it is important to consider also the seriously negative implications of employing RED when a significant percentage of the traffic is not robust in response to packet loss. Neither Novell NetWare nor AppleTalk are appropriately robust in response to packet loss; therefore, you should not use RED for them.

How It Works

RED aims to control the average queue size by indicating to the end hosts when they should temporarily slow down transmission of packets.

RED takes advantage of TCP's congestion control mechanism. By randomly dropping packets prior to periods of high congestion, RED tells the packet source to decrease its transmission rate. Assuming the packet source is using TCP, it will decrease its transmission rate until all the packets reach their destination, indicating that the congestion is cleared. You can use RED as a way to cause TCP to slow down transmission of packets. TCP not only pauses, but it also restarts quickly and adapts its transmission rate to the rate that the network can support.

RED distributes losses in time and maintains normally low queue depth while absorbing spikes. When enabled on an interface, RED begins dropping packets when congestion occurs at a rate you select during configuration.

For explication of how Cisco's WRED implementation determines parameters to use in the WRED queue size calculations and how to determine optimum values to use for the weight factor, see the section "Average Queue Size" later in this chapter.

Packet Drop Probability

The packet drop probability is based on the minimum threshold, maximum threshold, and mark probability denominator.

When the average queue depth is above the minimum threshold, RED starts dropping packets. The rate of packet drop increases linearly as the average queue size increases until the average queue size reaches the maximum threshold.

The mark probability denominator is the fraction of packets dropped when the average queue depth is at the maximum threshold. For example, if the denominator is 512, one out of every 512 packets is dropped when the average queue is at the maximum threshold.

When the average queue size is above the maximum threshold, all packets are dropped. Figure 9-1 summarizes the packet drop probability.

Figure 9-1   *RED Packet Drop Probability*

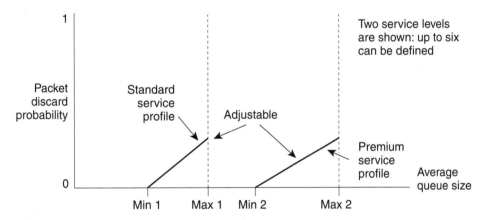

The minimum threshold value should be set high enough to maximize the link utilization. If the minimum threshold is too low, packets may be dropped unnecessarily, and the transmission link will not be fully used.

The difference between the maximum threshold and the minimum threshold should be large enough to avoid global synchronization. If the difference is too small, many packets may be dropped at once, resulting in global synchronization.

How TCP Handles Traffic Loss

NOTE	The sections "How TCP Handles Traffic Loss" and "How the Router Interacts with TCP" contain detailed information that you need not read in order to use WRED or to have a general sense of RED's capabilities. If you want to understand why problems of global synchronization occur in response to congestion when tail drop is used by default and how RED addresses them, read these sections.

When the recipient of TCP traffic—called the receiver—receives a data segment, it checks that data segment's four octet (32-bit) sequence number against the number the receiver expected, which would indicate that the data segment was received in order. If the numbers match, the receiver delivers all of the data that it holds to the target application, then it updates the sequence number to reflect the next number in order, and finally it either immediately transmits an acknowledgment (ACK) packet to the sender or it schedules an ACK to be transmitted to the sender after a short delay. The ACK notifies the sender that the receiver received all data segments up to but not including the one marked with the new sequence number.

Receivers usually try to send an ACK in response to alternating data segments they receive; they send the ACK because for many applications, if the receiver waits out a small delay, it can efficiently piggyback its reply acknowledgment on a normal response to the sender. However, when the receiver receives a data segment out of order, it immediately responds with an ACK to direct the sender to retransmit the lost data segment.

When the sender receives an ACK, it determines if any data is outstanding. If not, the sender determines that the ACK is a keepalive, meant to keep the line active, and it does nothing. If data is outstanding, the sender determines whether the ACK indicates that the receiver has received some or none of the data. If the ACK acknowledges receipt of some data sent, the sender determines if new credit has been granted to allow it to send more data. When the ACK acknowledges receipt of none of the data sent and there is outstanding data, the sender interprets the ACK to be a repeatedly sent ACK. This condition indicates that some data was received out of order, forcing the receiver to remit the first ACK, and that a second data segment was received out of order, forcing the receiver to remit the second ACK. In most cases, the receiver would receive two segments out of order because one of the data segments had been dropped.

When a TCP sender detects a dropped data segment, it retransmits the segment. Then it adjusts its transmission rate so that it is half of what is was before the drop was detected. This is the TCP back-off or slow down behavior. Although this behavior is appropriately responsive to congestion, problems can arise when multiple TCP sessions are carried on concurrently with the same router and all TCP senders slow down transmission of packets at the same time.

How the Router Interacts with TCP

NOTE	The sections "How TCP Handles Traffic Loss" and "How the Router Interacts with TCP" contain detailed information that you need not read in order to use WRED or to have a general sense of RED's capabilities. If you want to understand why problems of global synchronization occur in response to congestion when tail drop is used by default and how RED addresses them, read these sections.

For example, on average, the router receives traffic from one particular TCP stream every other, every 10th, and every 100th or 200th message in the interface in MAE-EAST or FIX-WEST. A router can handle multiple concurrent TCP sessions. Because network flows are additive, there is a high probability that when traffic exceeds the Transmit Queue Limit (TQL) at all, it will vastly exceed the limit. However, there is also a high probability that the excessive traffic depth is temporary and that traffic will not stay excessively deep except at points where traffic flows merge or at edge routers.

If the router drops all traffic that exceeds the TQL, as is done when tail drop is used by default, many TCP sessions will simultaneously go into slow start. Consequently, traffic temporarily slows down to the extreme and then all flows slow-start up again; this activity creates a condition of global synchronization.

However, if the router drops no traffic, as is the case when queuing features such as fair queuing (FQ) or custom queuing (CQ) are used, then the data is likely to be stored in main memory, drastically degrading router performance.

By directing one TCP session at a time to slow down, RED solves the problems described, allowing for full utilization of the bandwidth rather than utilization manifesting as crests and troughs of traffic.

About WRED

WRED combines the capabilities of the RED algorithm with IP precedence to provide for preferential traffic handling of higher priority packets. WRED can selectively discard lower priority traffic when the interface begins to get congested and provide differentiated performance characteristics for different classes of service.

You can configure WRED to ignore IP precedence when making drop decisions so that nonweighted RED behavior is achieved.

For interfaces configured to use the Resource Reservation Protocol (RSVP), WRED chooses packets from other flows to drop rather than the RSVP flows. Also, IP precedence governs which packets are dropped—traffic that is at a lower precedence has a higher drop rate and therefore is more likely to be throttled back.

WRED differs from other congestion avoidance techniques such as queuing strategies because it attempts to anticipate and avoid congestion rather than control congestion once it occurs. WRED is available on the Cisco 7200 series RSP processors. Figure 9-2 illustrates how WRED works.

Figure 9-2 *WRED*

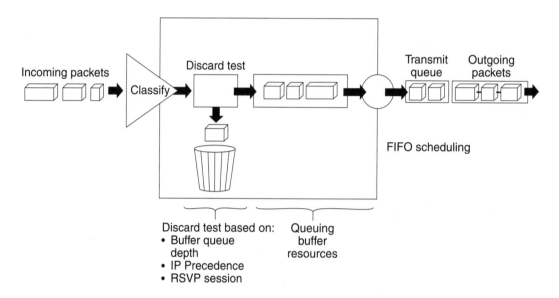

Why Use WRED?

WRED makes early detection of congestion possible and provides for multiple classes of traffic. It also protects against global synchronization. For these reasons, WRED is useful on any output interface where you expect congestion to occur.

However, WRED is usually used in the core routers of a network, rather than the nework's edge. Edge routers assign IP precedences to packets as they enter the network. WRED uses these precedences to determine how to treat different types of traffic.

WRED provides separate thresholds and weights for different IP precedences, allowing you to provide different qualities of service in regard to packet dropping for different traffic types. Standard traffic may be dropped more frequently than premium traffic during periods of congestion.

WRED is also RSVP-aware, and it can provide integrated services controlled-load QoS service.

How It Works

By randomly dropping packets prior to periods of high congestion, WRED tells the packet source to decrease its transmission rate. If the packet source is using TCP, it will decrease its transmission rate until all the packets reach their destination, which indicates that the congestion is cleared.

WRED generally drops packets selectively based on IP precedence. Packets with a higher IP precedence are less likely to be dropped than packets with a lower precedence. Thus, the higher the priority of a packet, the higher the probability that the packet will be delivered.

WRED reduces the chances of tail drop by selectively dropping packets when the output interface begins to show signs of congestion. By dropping some packets early rather than waiting until the queue is full, WRED avoids dropping large numbers of packets at once and minimizes the chances of global synchronization. Thus, WRED allows the transmission line to be used fully at all times.

In addition, WRED statistically drops more packets from large users than small. Therefore, traffic sources that generate the most traffic are more likely to be slowed down than traffic sources that generate little traffic.

WRED avoids the globalization problems that occur when tail drop is used as the congestion avoidance mechanism. Global synchronization manifests when multiple TCP hosts reduce their transmission rates in response to packet dropping, then increase their transmission rates once again when the congestion is reduced.

WRED is only useful when the bulk of the traffic is TCP/IP traffic. With TCP, dropped packets indicate congestion, so the packet source will reduce its transmission rate. With other protocols, packet sources may not respond or may resend dropped packets at the same rate. Thus, dropping packets does not decrease congestion.

WRED treats non-IP traffic as precedence 0, the lowest precedence. Therefore, non-IP traffic, in general, is more likely to be dropped than IP traffic.

Average Queue Size

The router automatically determines parameters to use in the WRED calculations. The average queue size is based on the previous average and the current size of the queue. The formula is

$$\text{average} = (\text{old\_average} * (1\text{-}2\text{ -n})) + (\text{current\_queue\_size} * 2\text{ -n})$$

where n is the exponential weight factor, a user-configurable value.

Cisco recommends using the default value for the exponential weight factor. Change this value from the default only if you have determined that your situation would benefit from using a different value.

For high values of n, the previous average becomes more important. A large factor smooths out the peaks and lows in queue length. The average queue size is unlikely to change very quickly, avoiding drastic swings in size. The WRED process will be slow to start dropping packets, but it may continue dropping packets for a time after the actual queue size has fallen below the minimum threshold. The slow-moving average will accommodate temporary bursts in traffic.

> **NOTE**   If the value of n gets too high, WRED will not react to congestion. Packets will be transmitted or dropped as if WRED were not in effect.

For low values of n, the average queue size closely tracks the current queue size. The resulting average may fluctuate with changes in the traffic levels. In this case, the WRED process responds quickly to long queues. Once the queue falls below the minimum threshold, the process will stop dropping packets.

If the value of n gets too low, WRED will overreact to temporary traffic bursts and drop traffic unnecessarily.

VIP-Distributed WRED

VIP-Distributed WRED is an implementation of WRED for the Versatile Interface Processor (VIP). VIP-Distributed WRED provides the complete set of functions for the VIP that WRED provides on standard IOS platforms. VIP-Distributed WRED is supported on the following routers with a VIP2-40 or greater interface processor:

● Cisco 7000 series with RSP7000

● Cisco 7500 series

> **NOTE**   As its name implies, the VIP-Distributed WRED feature uses the VIP rather than the Route Switch Processor (RSP) to perform queuing, which is why it requires a Cisco 7500 series router or Cisco 7000 series router with RSP7000.

A VIP2-50 interface processor is strongly recommended when the aggregate line rate of the port adapters on the VIP is greater than DS3. A VIP2-50 interface processor is required for OC-3 rates.

VIP-Distributed WRED is configured the same way as WRED. If you enable WRED on a suitable VIP interface, such as a VIP2-40 or greater with at least 2 MB of SRAM, VIP-Distributed WRED will be enabled instead.

In order to use VIP-Distributed WRED, Distributed Cisco Express Forwarding (DCEF) switching must be enabled on the interface.

You can configure both VIP-Distributed WRED and Distributed weighted fair queuing (DWFQ) on the same interface, but you cannot configure VIP-Distributed WRED on an interface for which RSP-based CQ, priority queuing (PQ), or WFQ are configured.

Why Use VIP-Distributed WRED?

VIP-Distributed WRED provides faster performance than does RSP-based WRED. You should run WRED on the VIP if you want to achieve very high speed on the Cisco 7500 series platform—for example, you can achieve speed at the OC-3 rates by running WRED on a VIP2-50 interface processor.

Additionally, the same reasons you would use WRED on standard IOS platforms apply to using VIP-Distributed WRED on the VIP. (See the section "Why Use WRED?" earlier in this chapter.) For instance, when WRED or VIP Distributed-WRED are not configured, tail drop is enacted during periods of congestion. Enabling VIP-Distributed WRED on the VIP obviates the global synchronization problems that result when tail drop is used to avoid congestion.

Restrictions

The following restrictions apply to VIP-Distributed WRED:

- VIP-Distributed WRED is only available on a per-interface basis. You cannot configure VIP-Distributed WRED on a subinterface. (A subinterface is one of a number of virtual interfaces on a single physical interface.)

- VIP-Distributed WRED is not supported on Fast EtherChannel and tunnel interfaces.

- RSVP is not supported on VIP-Distributed WRED.

CHAPTER 10

Configuring Weighted Random Early Detection

This chapter describes the tasks for configuring Weighted Random Early Detection (WRED) and Distributed WRED (DWRED) on a router. To locate documentation of related commands, you can search online at www.cisco.com.

The WRED feature is supported on these Cisco router platforms:

- Cisco 1600 series

- Cisco 2500 series

- Cisco 3600 series

- Cisco 4000 series (including 4500 and 4700 series)

- Cisco 7200 series

- Cisco 7500 series with RSP interface card

The DWRED feature is only supported on Cisco 7000 series routers with a Route Switch Processor-based RSP7000 interface processor and Cisco 7500 series routers with a Versatile Interface Processor-based VIP2-40 or greater interface processor. A VIP2-50 interface processor is strongly recommended when the aggregate line rate of the port adapters on the VIP is greater than DS3. A VIP2-50 interface processor is required for OC-3 rates. To use DWRED, Distributed Cisco Express Forwarding (DCEF) switching must first be enabled on the interface.

NOTE WRED is useful with adaptive traffic such as Transmission Control Protocol/Internet Protocol (TCP/IP). With TCP, dropped packets indicate congestion, so the packet source will reduce its transmission rate. With other protocols, packet sources may not respond or may resend dropped packets at the same rate. Thus, dropping packets does not decrease congestion.

WRED treats non-IP traffic as precedence 0, the lowest precedence. Therefore, non-IP traffic is more likely to be dropped than IP traffic.

You cannot configure WRED on the same interface as Route Switch Processor (RSP)-based custom queuing, priority queuing, or weighted fair queuing (WFQ). However, you can configure both DWRED and DWFQ on the same interface.

WRED Configuration Task List

Random Early Detection (RED) is a congestion avoidance mechanism that takes advantage of TCP's congestion control mechanism. By randomly dropping packets prior to periods of high congestion, RED tells the packet source to decrease its transmission rate. WRED drops packets selectively based on IP precedence. Edge routers assign IP precedences to packets as they enter the network. WRED is useful on any output interface where you expect to have congestion. However, WRED is usually used in the core routers of a network, rather than the edge. WRED uses these precedences to determine how it treats different types of traffic.

When a packet arrives, the following events occur:

● The average queue size is calculated.

● If the average is less than the minimum queue threshold, the arriving packet is queued.

● If the average is between the minimum queue threshold for that type of traffic and the maximum threshold for the interface, the packet is either dropped or queued, depending on the packet drop probability for that type of traffic.

● If the average queue size is greater than the maximum threshold, the packet is dropped.

See the section "About WRED" in Chapter 9, "Congestion Avoidance Overview," for more details on the queue calculations and how WRED works.

To configure WRED or DWRED on an interface, perform the tasks described in the following sections:

● Enable WRED

● Change WRED Parameters

● Monitor WRED and DWRED

The section "WRED and DWRED Configuration Examples" later in this chapter provides examples of configuring WRED.

Enable WRED

To enable WRED, use the following command in interface configuration mode:

Command	Purpose
random-detect	Enables WRED. If you configure this command on a VIP interface, DWRED is enabled.

You need not specify any other commands or parameters in order to configure WRED on the interface. WRED will use the default parameter values.

Change WRED Parameters

To change WRED parameters, use one of the following commands in interface configuration mode:

Command	Purpose
random-detect exponential-weighting-constant *exponent*	Configures the weight factor used in calculating the average queue length.
random-detect precedence *precedence* *min-threshold max-threshold mark-prob-denominator*	Configures parameters for packets with a specific IP precedence. The minimum threshold for IP precedence 0 corresponds to half the maximum threshold for the interface. Repeat this command for each precedence. To configure RED, rather than WRED, use the same parameters for each precedence.

When you enable WRED with the **random-detect** command, the parameters are set to their default values. The weight factor is 9. For all precedences, the mark probability denominator is 10, and maximum threshold is based on the output buffering capacity and the transmission speed for the interface.

The default minimum threshold depends on the precedence. The minimum threshold for IP precedence 0 corresponds to half of the maximum threshold. The values for the remaining precedences fall between half the maximum threshold and the maximum threshold at evenly spaced intervals.

NOTE	The default WRED parameter values are based on the best available data. Cisco recommends that you do not change the parameters from their default values unless you have determined that your applications will benefit from the changed values.

Monitor WRED and DWRED

To monitor WRED services in your network, use any of the following commands in EXEC mode:

Command	Purpose
show interfaces [*interface-type interface-number*] **random-detect**	Shows information about WRED for an interface.
show queue *interface-type interface-number*	Shows WRED configuration and statistics for a particular interface.
show queuing [**red**]	Shows the queuing configuration for WRED.
show interfaces [*type slot*	*port-adapter*	*port*]	Shows DWRED statistics for Cisco 7500 series routers.

WRED and DWRED Configuration Examples

The following sections provide these examples:

- WRED and DWRED Configuration Example

- Parameter-Setting DWRED Example

- Parameter-Setting WRED Example

WRED and DWRED Configuration Example

The following example enables WRED or DWRED with default parameter values:

```
router(config)# interface Serial5/0
router(config-if)# description to qos1-75a
router(config-if)# ip address 200.200.14.250 255.255.255.252
router(config-if)# random-detect
```

Use the **show interfaces** command output to verify the configuration and view the default settings for the different precedences. Notice that the "Queuing strategy" report lists "random early detection (RED)." Also notice that the default minimum thresholds are spaced evenly between half and the entire maximum threshold. Thresholds are specified in terms of packet count.

```
router# show interfaces serial 5/0

Serial5/0 is up, line protocol is up
  Hardware is M4T
  Description: to qos1-75a
  Internet address is 200.200.14.250/30
  MTU 1500 bytes, BW 128 Kbit, DLY 20000 usec,
     reliability 255/255, txload 1/255, rxload 237/255
  Encapsulation HDLC, crc 16, loopback not set
  Keepalive not set
  Last input 00:00:15, output 00:00:00, output hang never
  Last clearing of "show interface" counters 00:05:08
  Input queue: 0/75/0 (size/max/drops); Total output drops: 1036
  Queuing strategy: random early detection(RED)
    mean queue depth: 28
    drops: class  random   tail    min-th   max-th   mark-prob
           0      330      0       20       40       1/10
           1      267      0       22       40       1/10
           2      217      0       24       40       1/10
           3      156      0       26       40       1/10
           4      61       0       28       40       1/10
           5      6        0       31       40       1/10
           6      0        0       33       40       1/10
           7      0        0       35       40       1/10
           rsvp   0        0       37       40       1/10
  30 second input rate 0 bits/sec, 2 packets/sec
  30 second output rate 119000 bits/sec, 126 packets/sec
     594 packets input, 37115 bytes, 0 no buffer
     Received 5 broadcasts, 0 runts, 0 giants, 0 throttles
```

```
      0 input errors, 0 CRC, 0 frame, 0 overrun, 0 ignored, 0 abort
      37525 packets output, 4428684 bytes, 0 underruns
      0 output errors, 0 collisions, 0 interface resets
      0 output buffer failures, 0 output buffers swapped out
      0 carrier transitions      DCD=up  DSR=up  DTR=up  RTS=up  CTS=up
```

Use the **show queue** command output to view the current contents of the interface queue. Notice that there is only a single queue into which packets from all IP precedences are placed after dropping has taken place.

```
router# show queue serial 5/0

Output queue for Serial5/0 is 5/0

Packet 1, linktype: ip, length: 118, flags: 0x288
  source: 190.1.3.4, destination: 190.1.2.2, id: 0x0001, ttl: 254,
  TOS: 128 prot: 17, source port 11111, destination port 22222
    data: 0x2B67 0x56CE 0x005E 0xE89A 0xCBA9 0x8765 0x4321
        0x0FED 0xCBA9 0x8765 0x4321 0x0FED 0xCBA9 0x8765

Packet 2, linktype: ip, length: 118, flags: 0x288
  source: 190.1.3.5, destination: 190.1.2.2, id: 0x0001, ttl: 254,
  TOS: 160 prot: 17, source port 11111, destination port 22222
    data: 0x2B67 0x56CE 0x005E 0xE89A 0xCBA9 0x8765 0x4321
        0x0FED 0xCBA9 0x8765 0x4321 0x0FED 0xCBA9 0x8765

Packet 3, linktype: ip, length: 118, flags: 0x280
  source: 190.1.3.6, destination: 190.1.2.2, id: 0x0001, ttl: 254,
  TOS: 192 prot: 17, source port 11111, destination port 22222
    data: 0x2B67 0x56CE 0x005E 0xE89A 0xCBA9 0x8765 0x4321
        0x0FED 0xCBA9 0x8765 0x4321 0x0FED 0xCBA9 0x8765

Packet 4, linktype: ip, length: 118, flags: 0x280
  source: 190.1.3.7, destination: 190.1.2.2, id: 0x0001, ttl: 254,
  TOS: 224 prot: 17, source port 11111, destination port 22222
    data: 0x2B67 0x56CE 0x005E 0xE89A 0xCBA9 0x8765 0x4321
        0x0FED 0xCBA9 0x8765 0x4321 0x0FED 0xCBA9 0x8765

Packet 5, linktype: ip, length: 118, flags: 0x280
  source: 190.1.3.8, destination: 190.1.2.2, id: 0x0001, ttl: 254,
  TOS: 0 prot: 17, source port 11111, destination port 22222
    data: 0x2B67 0x56CE 0x005E 0xE89A 0xCBA9 0x8765 0x4321
        0x0FED 0xCBA9 0x8765 0x4321 0x0FED 0xCBA9 0x8765
```

Use the **show queuing** command output to view the current settings for each of the precedences.

```
router# show queuing

Current RED queue configuration:
  Interface: Serial5/0   Exp-weight-constant: 9
    Class   Min-th   Max-th   Mark-prob
    0       20       40       1/10
    1       22       40       1/10
    2       24       40       1/10
```

```
3        26        40        1/10
4        28        40        1/10
5        31        40        1/10
6        33        40        1/10
7        35        40        1/10
rsvp     37        40        1/10
```

Parameter-Setting DWRED Example

The following example specifies the same parameters for each IP precedence. Thus, all IP precedences receive the same treatment. Start by enabling DWRED.

```
router(config)# interface FastEthernet1/0/0
router(config-if)# ip address 200.200.14.250 255.255.255.252
router(config-if)# random-detect
```

Next, use the **show interfaces random-detect** command to determine reasonable values to use for the precedence-specific parameters:

```
router# show interfaces random-detect

 FastEthernet1/0/0 queue size 0
        packets output 29692, drops 0
WRED: queue average 0
       weight 1/512
    Precedence 0: 109 min threshold, 218 max threshold, 1/10 mark weight
       1 packets output, drops: 0 random, 0 threshold
    Precedence 1: 122 min threshold, 218 max threshold, 1/10 mark weight
       (no traffic)
    Precedence 2: 135 min threshold, 218 max threshold, 1/10 mark weight
       14845 packets output, drops: 0 random, 0 threshold
    Precedence 3: 148 min threshold, 218 max threshold, 1/10 mark weight
       (no traffic)
    Precedence 4: 161 min threshold, 218 max threshold, 1/10 mark weight
       (no traffic)
    Precedence 5: 174 min threshold, 218 max threshold, 1/10 mark weight
       (no traffic)
    Precedence 6: 187 min threshold, 218 max threshold, 1/10 mark weight
       14846 packets output, drops: 0 random, 0 threshold
    Precedence 7: 200 min threshold, 218 max threshold, 1/10 mark weight
       (no traffic)
```

Complete the configuration by assigning the same parameter values to each precedence. Use the values obtained from the **show interfaces random-detect** command output to choose reasonable parameter values.

```
router(config)# interface FastEthernet1/0/0
router(config-if)# random-detect precedence 0 100 218 10
router(config-if)# random-detect precedence 1 100 218 10
router(config-if)# random-detect precedence 2 100 218 10
router(config-if)# random-detect precedence 3 100 218 10
```

```
router(config-if)# random-detect precedence 4 100 218 10
router(config-if)# random-detect precedence 5 100 218 10
router(config-if)# random-detect precedence 6 100 218 10
router(config-if)# random-detect precedence 7 100 218 10
```

Parameter-Setting WRED Example

The following example enables WRED on the interface and specifies parameters for the different IP precedences:

```
router(config)# interface Hssi0/0/0
router(config-if)# description 45Mbps to R1
router(config-if)# ip address 200.200.14.250 255.255.255.252
router(config-if)# random-detect
router(config-if)# random-detect precedence 0 32 256 100
router(config-if)# random-detect precedence 1 64 256 100
router(config-if)# random-detect precedence 2 96 256 100
router(config-if)# random-detect precedence 3 120 256 100
router(config-if)# random-detect precedence 4 140 256 100
router(config-if)# random-detect precedence 5 170 256 100
router(config-if)# random-detect precedence 6 290 256 100
router(config-if)# random-detect precedence 7 210 256 100
router(config-if)# random-detect precedence rsvp 230 256 100
```

PART IV

Policing and Shaping

CHAPTER 11

Policing and Shaping Overview

Cisco IOS QoS offers two kinds of traffic regulation mechanisms: the rate-limiting feature of committed access rate (CAR) for policing traffic, and Generic Traffic Shaping (GTS) and Frame Relay Traffic Shaping (FRTS) for shaping traffic. You can deploy these features throughout your network to ensure that a packet, or data source, adheres to a stipulated contract and to determine the QoS to render the packet. Both policing and shaping mechanisms use the traffic descriptor for a packet—indicated by the packet's classification—to ensure adherence and service. (See Chapter 1, "Classification Overview," for a description of a traffic descriptor.)

Policers and shapers usually identify traffic descriptor violations in an identical manner. They usually differ, however, in the way they respond to violations, for example:

- A policer typically drops traffic. (For example, CAR's rate-limiting policer will either drop the packet or rewrite its IP precedence, resetting the packet header's type of service bits.)

- A shaper typically delays excess traffic using a buffer, or queuing mechanism, to hold packets and shape the flow when the data rate of the source is higher than expected. (For example, GTS uses a weighted fair queue to delay packets in order to shape the flow, and FRTS uses either a priority queue [PQ], a custom queue [CQ], or a first-in, first-out [FIFO] queue for the same, depending on how you configure it.)

Traffic shaping and policing can work in tandem. For example, a good traffic shaping scheme should make it easy for nodes inside the network to detect misbehaving flows. This activity is sometimes called policing the flow's traffic.

This chapter gives a brief description of the Cisco IOS QoS traffic policing and shaping mechanisms. Because policing with CAR and shaping with FRTS and GTS all use the token bucket mechanism, this chapter first explains how a token bucket works. This chapter includes the following sections:

- What Is a Token Bucket?
- Policing with CAR
- Traffic Shaping

What Is a Token Bucket?

A token bucket is a formal definition of a rate of transfer. It has three components: a burst size, a mean rate, and a time interval (Tc). Although the mean rate is generally represented as bits per second, any two values may be derived from the third by the relation shown as follows:

$$\text{mean rate} = \frac{\text{(burst size)}}{\text{(time interval)}}$$

Here are some definitions of these terms:

- Mean rate—Also called the committed information rate (CIR), it specifies how much data can be sent or forwarded per unit time on average.

- Burst size—Also called the Committed Burst (Bc) size, it specifies in bits per burst how much can be sent within a given unit of time to not create scheduling concerns.

- Time interval—Also called the measurement interval, it specifies the time quantum in seconds per burst.

By definition, over any integral multiple of the interval, the bit rate of the interface will not exceed the mean rate. The bit rate, may, however, be arbitrarily fast within the interval.

A token bucket is used to manage a device that regulates the flow's data. For example, the regulator might be a traffic policer, such as CAR, or a traffic shaper, such as FRTS or GTS. A token bucket itself has no discard or priority policy. Rather, a token bucket discards tokens and leaves to the flow the problem of managing its transmission queue if the flow overdrives the regulator. (Neither CAR nor FRTS and GTS implement either a true token bucket or true leaky bucket.)

In the token bucket metaphor, tokens are put into the bucket at a certain rate. The bucket itself has a specified capacity. If the bucket fills to capacity, newly arriving tokens are discarded. Each token is permission for the source to send a certain number of bits into the network. To transmit a packet, the regulator must remove from the bucket a number of tokens equal in representation to the packet size.

If not enough tokens are in the bucket to send a packet, the packet either waits until the bucket has enough tokens or the packet is discarded. If the bucket is already full of tokens, incoming tokens overflow and are not available to future packets. Thus, at any time, the largest burst a source can send into the network is roughly proportional to the size of the bucket.

Note that the token bucket mechanism used for traffic shaping has both a token bucket and a data buffer, or queue; if it did not have a data buffer, it would be a policer. For traffic shaping, packets that arrive that cannot be sent immediately are delayed in the data buffer.

For traffic shaping, a token bucket permits burstiness but bounds it. It guarantees that the burstiness is bounded so that the flow will never send faster than the token bucket's capacity plus the time interval divided by the established rate at which tokens are placed in the bucket. It also guarantees that the long-term transmission rate will not exceed the established rate at which tokens are placed in the bucket.

Policing with CAR

CAR embodies a rate-limiting feature for policing traffic, in addition to its packet classification feature discussed in Chapter 1, "Classification Overview." CAR's rate-limiting feature manages a network's access bandwidth policy by ensuring that traffic falling within specified rate parameters is transmitted, while dropping packets that exceed the acceptable amount of traffic or transmitting them with a different priority. CAR's exceed action is to drop packets.

The rate-limiting function of CAR does the following:

● Allows you to control the maximum rate of traffic transmitted or received on an interface.

● Gives you the ability to define Layer 3 aggregate or granular incoming or outgoing (ingress or egress) bandwidth rate limits and to specify traffic handling policies when the traffic either conforms to or exceeds the specified rate limits.

   Aggregate bandwidth rate limits match all of the packets on an interface or subinterface. Granular bandwidth rate limits match a particular type of traffic based on precedence, MAC address, or other parameters.

CAR is often configured on interfaces at the edge of a network to limit traffic into or out of the network.

CAR is supported on these routers:

● Cisco 2600 series

● Cisco 3600 series

● Cisco 4500 series

● Cisco 4700 series

● Cisco 7200 series

VIP-Distributed CAR is a version of CAR that runs on the Versatile Interface Processor (VIP). It is supported on the following routers with a VIP2-40 or greater interface processor:

● Cisco 7000 series with RSP7000

● Cisco 7500 series

Distributed Cisco Express Forwarding (DCEF) switching must be enabled on any interface that uses VIP-Distributed CAR, even when only output CAR is configured. A VIP2-50 interface processor is strongly recommended when the aggregate line rate of the port adapters on the VIP is greater than DS3. A VIP2-50 interface processor is required for OC-3 rate PAs.

How It Works

CAR examines traffic received on an interface or a subset of that traffic selected by access list criteria. It then compares the rate of the traffic to a configured token bucket and takes action based on the result. For example, CAR will drop the packet or rewrite the IP precedence, resetting the type of service (ToS) bits. You can configure CAR to transmit, drop, or set precedence.

This section explains these aspects of CAR rate limiting:

● Matching Criteria

● Rate Limits

- Conform and Exceed Actions

- Multiple Rate Policies

CAR utilizes a token bucket measurement. Tokens are inserted into the bucket at the committed rate. The depth of the bucket is the burst size. Traffic arriving at the bucket when sufficient tokens are available is said to conform and the corresponding number of tokens are removed from the bucket. If sufficient tokens are not available, then the traffic is said to exceed.

Matching Criteria

Traffic matching entails identification of traffic of interest for rate limiting, precedence setting, or both. Rate policies can be associated with one of the following:

- Incoming interface

- All IP traffic

- IP precedence (defined by a rate-limit access list)

- MAC address (defined by a rate-limit access list)

- IP access list (standard and extended)

CAR provides configurable actions, such as transmit, drop, or set precedence when traffic conforms to or exceeds the rate limit.

NOTE   Matching to IP access lists is more processor-intensive than matching based on other criteria.

Rate Limits

CAR propagates bursts. It does no smoothing or shaping of traffic, and therefore does no buffering and adds no delay. CAR is highly optimized to run on high-speed links—DS3, for example—in distributed mode on VIPs on the Cisco 7500 series.

CAR rate limits may be implemented either on input or output interfaces or subinterfaces including Frame Relay and ATM subinterfaces.

Rate limits define which packets conform to or exceed the defined rate based on the following three parameters:

- Average rate—The average rate determines the long-term average transmission rate. Traffic that falls under this rate will always conform.

- Normal burst size—The normal burst size determines how large traffic bursts can be before some traffic exceeds the rate limit.

- Excess Burst size—The Excess Burst (Be) size determines how large traffic bursts can be before all traffic exceeds the rate limit. CAR provides managed discard between the Be and extended Be parameters. Traffic that falls between the normal burst size and the Be size exceeds the rate limit with a probability that increases as the burst size increases.

A token bucket's tokens are replenished at regular intervals depending on the configured committed rate. The maximum number of tokens a bucket can ever contain is determined by the normal burst size configured for the token bucket.

When the CAR rate limit is applied to a packet, CAR removes from the bucket tokens that are equivalent in number to the byte size of the packet. If a packet arrives and there are fewer tokens available in the standard token bucket than are equal to the packet's byte size, extended burst capability is engaged if it is configured.

Extended burst is configured by setting the extended burst to a value that is greater than the normal burst value. Setting the extended burst value equal to the normal burst value excludes the extended burst capability. If extended burst is not configured, given the example scenario, CAR's exceed action takes effect because sufficient tokens are not available.

When extended burst is configured and this scenario occurs, the flow is allowed to borrow the needed tokens to allow the packet to be transmitted. This capability exists so as to avoid tail-drop behavior, and, instead, engage behavior like that of Random Early Detection (RED).

Here is how the extended burst capability works. If a packet arrives and needs to borrow n number of tokens because the token bucket contains fewer tokens than its packet size requires, then CAR compares the following two values:

- Extended burst parameter value.

- Compounded debt. Compounded debt is computed as the sum over all a_i.

  — a indicates the actual debt value of the flow after packet i is sent. Actual debt is simply a count of how many tokens the flow has currently borrowed.

  — i indicates the ith packet that attempts to borrow tokens since the last time a packet was dropped.

If the compounded debt is greater than the extended burst value, CAR's exceed action takes effect. After a packet is dropped, the compounded debt is effectively set to 0. CAR will compute a new compounded debt value equal to the actual debt for the next packet that needs to borrow tokens.

If the actual debt is greater than the extended limit, all packets will be dropped until the actual debt is reduced through accumulation of tokens in the token bucket.

Dropped packets do not count against any rate or burst limit. That is, when a packet is dropped, no tokens are removed from the token bucket.

Testing of Transmission Control Protocol (TCP) traffic suggests that the chosen normal and extended burst values should be on the order of several seconds worth of traffic at the configured average rate.

That is, if the average rate is 10 Mbps, then a normal burst size of 10 to 20 Mbps and a Be size of 20 to 40 Mbps would be appropriate.

Conform and Exceed Actions

CAR utilizes a token bucket, thus CAR can pass temporary bursts that exceed the rate limit as long as tokens are available.

Once a packet has been classified as conforming to or exceeding a particular rate limit, the router performs one of the following actions on the packet:

● Transmit—The packet is transmitted.

● Drop—The packet is discarded.

● Set precedence and transmit—The IP precedence (ToS) bits in the packet header are rewritten. The packet is then transmitted. You can use this action to either color (set precedence) or recolor (modify existing packet precedence) the packet.

● Continue—The packet is evaluated using the next rate policy in a chain of rate limits. If there is not another rate policy, the packet is transmitted.

Multiple Rate Policies

A single CAR rate policy includes information about the rate limit, conform actions, and exceed actions. Each interface can have multiple CAR rate policies corresponding to different types of traffic. For example, low priority traffic may be limited to a lower rate than high priority traffic. When there are multiple rate policies, the router examines each policy in the order entered until the packet matches. If no match is found, the default action is to transmit.

Rate policies can be independent: each rate policy deals with a different type of traffic. Alternatively, rate policies can be cascading: a packet may be compared to multiple different rate policies in succession.

Cascading of rate policies allows a series of rate limits to be applied to packets to specify more granular policies. For example, you could rate limit total traffic on an access link to a specified subrate bandwidth and then rate limit World Wide Web traffic on the same link to a given proportion of the subrate limit. You could configure CAR to match packets against an ordered sequence of policies until an applicable rate limit is encountered—that is, rate limiting several MAC addresses with different bandwidth allocations at an exchange point. You can configure up to 100 rate policies on a subinterface.

Restrictions

CAR and VIP-Distributed CAR can only be used with IP traffic. Non-IP traffic is not rate limited.

CAR or VIP-Distributed CAR can be configured on an interface or subinterface. However, CAR and VIP-Distributed CAR are not supported on the following interfaces:

- Fast EtherChannel

- Tunnel

- PRI

- Any interface that does not support CEF

Traffic Shaping

Cisco IOS QoS software includes two types of traffic shaping: GTS and FRTS. Both traffic shaping methods are similar in implementation, although their command-line interfaces differ somewhat and they use different types of queues to contain and shape traffic that is deferred. In particular, the underlying code that determines whether there is enough credit in the token bucket for a packet to be sent or whether that packet must be delayed is common to both features. If a packet is deferred, GTS uses a weighted fair queue to hold the delayed traffic. FRTS uses either a custom queue or a priority queue for the same, depending on what you have configured.

This section explains how traffic shaping works, then it describes the two Cisco IOS QoS traffic shaping mechanisms. It includes these subsections:

- About Traffic Shaping

- GTS

- FRTS

For description of a token bucket and explanation of how it works, see the section "What Is a Token Bucket?" earlier in this chapter.

About Traffic Shaping

Traffic shaping allows you to control the traffic going out an interface in order to match its flow to the speed of the remote, target interface and to ensure that the traffic conforms to policies contracted for it. Thus, traffic adhering to a particular profile can be shaped to meet downstream requirements, thereby eliminating bottlenecks in topologies with data-rate mismatches.

Why Use Traffic Shaping?

The primary reasons you would use traffic shaping are to control access to available bandwidth, to ensure that traffic conforms to the policies established for it, and to regulate the flow of traffic in order to avoid congestion that can occur when the transmitted traffic exceeds the access speed of its remote, target interface. Here are some examples:

● Control access to bandwidth when, for example, policy dictates that the rate of a given interface should not on the average exceed a certain rate even though the access rate exceeds the speed.

● Configure traffic shaping on an interface if you have a network with differing access rates. Suppose that one end of the link in a Frame Relay network runs at 256 kbps and the other end of the link runs at 128 kbps. Sending packets at 256 kbps could cause failure of the applications using the link.

A similar, more complicated case would be a link-layer network giving indications of congestion that has differing access rates on different attached date terminal equipment (DTE); the network may be able to deliver more transit speed to a given DTE at one time than another. (This scenario warrants that the token bucket be derived, and then its rate maintained.)

● Configure traffic shaping if you offer a subrate service. In this case, traffic shaping enables you to use the router to partition your T1 or T3 links into smaller channels.

Traffic shaping prevents packet loss. Use of it is especially important in Frame Relay networks because the switch cannot determine which packets take precedence, and therefore which packets should be dropped when congestion occurs. Moreover, it is of critical importance for real-time traffic such as Voice over Frame Relay that latency be bounded, thereby bounding the amount of traffic and traffic loss in the data link network at any given time by keeping the data in the router that is making the guarantees. Retaining the data in the router allows the router to prioritize traffic according to the guarantees it is making. (Packet loss can result in detrimental consequences for real-time and interactive applications.)

Traffic Shaping and Rate of Transfer

Traffic shaping limits the rate of transmission of data. You can limit the data transfer to one of the following:

● A specific configured rate

● A derived rate based on the level of congestion

As mentioned, the rate of transfer depends on these three components that constitute the token bucket: burst size, mean rate, measurement (time) interval. The mean rate is equal to the burst size divided by the interval.

When traffic shaping is enabled, the bit rate of the interface will not exceed the mean rate over any integral multiple of the interval. In other words, during every interval, a maximum of burst size can be transmitted. Within the interval, however, the bit rate may be faster than the mean rate at any given time.

One additional variable applies to traffic shaping: Be size. The Be size corresponds to the number of noncommitted bits—those outside the CIR—that are still accepted by the Frame Relay switch but marked as discard eligible.

In other words, the Be size allows more than the burst size to be sent during a time interval in certain situations. The switch will allow the packets belonging to the Be to go through but it will mark them by setting the discard eligible (DE) bit. Whether the packets are sent depends on how the switch is configured.

When the Be size equals 0, the interface sends no more than the burst size every interval, achieving an average rate no higher than the mean rate. However, when the Be size is greater than 0, the interface can send as many as Bc+Be bits in a burst, if in a previous time period the maximum amount was not transmitted. Whenever less than the burst size is transmitted during an interval, the remaining number of bits, up to the Be size, can be used to transmit more than the burst size in a later interval.

DE Bit

You can specify which Frame Relay packets have low priority or low time sensitivity and will be the first to be dropped when a Frame Relay switch is congested. The mechanism that allows a Frame Relay switch to identify such packets is the DE bit.

You can define DE lists that identify the characteristics of packets to be eligible for discarding, and you can also specify DE groups to identify the data-link connection identifier (DLCI) that is affected.

You can specify DE lists based on the protocol or the interface, and on characteristics such as fragmentation of the packet, a specific TCP or User Datagram Protocol (UDP) port, an access list number, or a packet size. For more information about the discard eligible bit, see Chapter 13, "Configuring Frame Relay and Frame Relay Traffic Shaping."

Differences Between GTS and FRTS

As mentioned, both GTS and FRTS are similar in implementation, sharing the same code and data structures, but they differ in regard to their command-line interfaces and the queue types they use.

Here are two ways in which GTS and FRTS differ:

- FRTS supports shaping on a per-DLCI basis, while GTS is configurable per interface or subinterface.

- For GTS, the shaping queue is a weighted fair queue (WFQ). For FRTS, WFQ is not supported; instead, the queue can be a CQ, PQ, or FIFO.

Table 11-1 summarizes these differences.

Table 11-1 *Differences Between FRTS and GTS*

	FRTS	GTS
Command-Line Interface	Classes of parameters	Applies parameters per subinterface
	Applies parameters to all VCs[1] on an interface through inheritance mechanism	**traffic group** command supported
	No traffic group command	
Queues Supported	CQ, PQ, FCFS per VC	WFQ per subinterface

1. VC = virtual channel

You can configure GTS to behave the same as FRTS by allocating one DLCI per subinterface and using GTS plus backward explicit congestion notification (BECN) support. The behavior of the two is then the same except for the different shaping queues used.

Traffic Shaping and Queuing

Traffic shaping smooths traffic by storing traffic above the configured rate in a queue.

When a packet arrives at the interface for transmission, the following happens:

- If the queue is empty, the arriving packet is processed by the traffic shaper.

  — If possible, the traffic shaper sends the packet.

  — Otherwise, the packet is placed in the queue.

- If the queue is not empty, the packet is placed in the queue.

When there are packets in the queue, the traffic shaper removes the number of packets it can transmit from the queue every time interval.

GTS

GTS shapes traffic by reducing outbound traffic flow to avoid congestion by constraining traffic to a particular bit rate using the token bucket mechanism. (See the section "What Is a Token Bucket?" earlier in this chapter.)

GTS applies on a per-interface basis and can use access lists to select the traffic to shape. It works with a variety of Layer 2 technologies, including Frame Relay, ATM, Switched Multimegabit Data Service (SMDS), and Ethernet.

On a Frame Relay subinterface, GTS can be set up to adapt dynamically to available bandwidth by integrating BECN signals, or set up simply to shape to a prespecified rate. GTS can also be configured on an ATM/AIP interface to respond to Resource Reservation Protocol (RSVP) signaled over statically configured ATM permanent virtual circuits (PVCs).

GTS is supported on most media and encapsulation types on the router. GTS can also be applied to a specific access list on an interface. Figure 11-1 shows how GTS works.

Figure 11-1 *GTS*

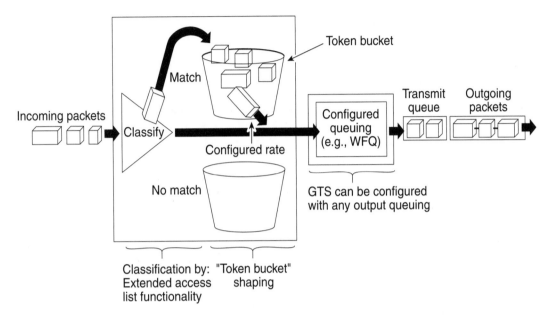

FRTS

Cisco has long provided support for forward explicit congestion notification (FECN) for DECnet and OSI, and BECN for Systems Network Architecture (SNA) traffic using LLC2 encapsulation via RFC 1490 and DE bit support. FRTS builds upon this existing Frame Relay support with additional capabilities that improve the scalability and performance of a Frame Relay network, increasing the density of virtual circuits and improving response time.

As is also true of GTS, FRTS can eliminate bottlenecks in Frame Relay networks that have high-speed connections at the central site and low-speed connections at branch sites. You can configure rate enforcement—a peak rate configured to limit outbound traffic—to limit the rate at which data is sent on the VC at the central site.

Using FRTS, you can configure rate enforcement to either the CIR or some other defined value such as the excess information rate, on a per-virtual-circuit VC basis. The ability to allow the transmission speed used by the router to be controlled by criteria other than line speed (that is, by the CIR or the excess information rate) provides a mechanism for sharing media by multiple VCs. You can preallocate bandwidth to each VC, creating a virtual time-division multiplexing network.

You can also define PQ, CQ, and WFQ at the VC or subinterface level. Using these queuing methods allows for finer granularity in the prioritization and queuing of traffic, providing more control over the traffic flow on an individual VC. If you combine CQ with the per-VC queuing and rate enforcement capabilities, you enable Frame Relay VCs to carry multiple traffic types such as IP, SNA, and Internetwork Packet Exchange (IPX) with bandwidth guaranteed for each traffic type.

Using information contained in the BECN-tagged packets received from the network, FRTS can also dynamically throttle traffic. With BECN-based throttling, packets are held in the router's buffers to reduce the data flow from the router into the Frame Relay network. The throttling is done on a per-VC basis and the transmission rate is adjusted based on the number of BECN-tagged packets received.

With Cisco's FRTS feature, you can integrate ATM ForeSight closed loop congestion control to actively adapt to downstream congestion conditions.

Derived Rates

In Frame Relay networks, BECNs and FECNs indicate congestion. BECN and FECN are specified by bits within a Frame Relay frame.

FECNs are generated when data is sent out a congested interface; they indicate to a DTE that congestion was encountered. Traffic is marked with BECN if the queue for the opposite direction is deep enough to trigger FECNs at the current time.

BECNs notify the sender to decrease the transmission rate. If the traffic is one-way only (such as multicast traffic), there is no reverse traffic with BECNs to notify the sender to slow down. Thus, when a DTE receives an FECN, it first determines if it is sending any data in return. If it is sending return data, this data will get marked with a BECN on its way to the other DTE. However, if the DTE is not sending any data, the DTE can send a Q.922 TEST RESPONSE message with the BECN bit set.

When an interface configured with traffic shaping receives a BECN, it immediately decreases its maximum rate by a large amount. If, after several intervals, the interface has not received another BECN and traffic is waiting in the queue, the maximum rate increases slightly. The dynamically adjusted maximum rate is called the derived rate.

The derived rate will always be between the upper bound and the lower bound configured on the interface.

Restrictions

Because of the method in which FRTS is implemented, Cisco recommends that you do not use it for real-time traffic. If FRTS is used and the traffic bursts to the Be rate, the router must wait for a period of time before transmitting again. Under certain conditions, this time can be up to 900 milliseconds, an unacceptable amount of time for real-time traffic.

FRTS applies only to Frame Relay PVCs and SVCs.

CHAPTER 12

Configuring Generic Traffic Shaping

This chapter describes the tasks for configuring QoS Generic Traffic Shaping (GTS) on a router. To locate documentation of related commands, you can search online at www.cisco.com.

NOTE GTS is not supported on ISDN, tunnel, and dialup interfaces. Traffic shaping is not supported with optimum, distributed, or flow switching. If you enable traffic shaping, all interfaces will revert to fast switching.

GTS Configuration Task List

To configure GTS, perform the tasks described in the following sections:

- Configure GTS
- Configure GTS for an Access List
- Configure Adaptive GTS for Frame Relay Networks
- Monitor the GTS Configuration

The section "GTS Configuration Examples" later in this chapter contains examples of these configuration tasks.

Configure GTS

To configure GTS for outbound traffic on an interface or subinterface, use the following command in interface configuration mode:

Command	Purpose
traffic-shape rate *bit-rate* [*burst-size* [*excess-burst-size*]]	Configures traffic shaping for outbound traffic on an interface.

Configure GTS for an Access List

To configure GTS for outbound traffic on an access list, use the following commands beginning in global configuration mode:

Step	Command	Purpose
1	**access-list** *access-list-number*	Assigns traffic to an access list.
2	**interface** *interface-type interface-number*	Enters interface configuration mode.
3	**traffic-shape group** *access-list bit-rate* [*burst-size* [*excess-burst-size*]]	Configures traffic shaping for outbound traffic on an interface for the specified access list.

Repeat steps 1 through 3 for each type of traffic you want to rate limit.

Configure Adaptive GTS for Frame Relay Networks

If traffic shaping is performed on a Frame Relay network with the **traffic-shape rate** command, you can also use the **traffic-shape adaptive** command to specify the minimum bit rate to which the traffic is shaped.

To configure adaptive GTS for outbound traffic on an interface or subinterface, use the following commands in interface configuration mode:

Step	Command	Purpose
1	**traffic-shape rate** *bit-rate* [*burst-size* [*excess-burst-size*]]	Enables traffic shaping for outbound traffic on an interface.
2	**traffic-shape adaptive** [*bit-rate*]	Configures minimum bit rate that traffic is shaped to when BECNs[1] are received on an interface.
3	**traffic-shape fecn-adapt**	Configures reflection of BECN signals as FECNs.[2]

1. BECN = backward explicit congestion notification
2. FECN = forward explicit congestion notification

With adaptive GTS, the router uses BECNs to estimate the available bandwidth and adjust the transmission rate accordingly. The actual maximum transmission rate will be between the rate specified in the **traffic-shape adaptive** command and the rate specified in the **traffic-shape rate** command.

Configure these commands on both ends of the link, enabling the router at the high-speed end to detect and adapt to congestion even when traffic is flowing primarily in one direction.

Monitor the GTS Configuration

To monitor the current traffic shaping configuration and statistics, use either of the following commands in EXEC mode:

Command	Purpose
show traffic-shape [*interface-name*]	Shows the current traffic-shaping configuration.
show traffic-shape statistics [*interface-name*]	Shows the current traffic-shaping statistics.

GTS Configuration Examples

This section provides the following examples of GTS configurations:

- Enable GTS on the Interface Example

- Constrained Access Rate Example

- Differing Controlled Rates through an IP Internet Example

- Frame Relay Adaptability to Congestion Example

- Accommodating Differing Access Speeds Example

Enable GTS on the Interface Example

This example shows the configuration of two traffic-shaped interfaces on a router. Ethernet 0 is configured to limit User Datagram Protocol (UDP) traffic to 1 Mbps. Ethernet 1 is configured to limit all output to 5 Mbps.

```
access-list 101 permit udp any any
interface Ethernet0
 traffic-shape group 101 1000000 125000 125000
!
interface Ethernet1
 traffic-shape rate 5000000 625000 625000
```

The following is a sample display for the **show traffic-shape** command for the example shown:

```
Router# show traffic-shape
```

I/F	access list	Target Rate	Byte Limit	Sustain bits/int	Excess bits/int	Interval (ms)	Increment (bytes)	Adapt Active
Et0	101	1000000	23437	125000	125000	63	7813	-
Et1		5000000	87889	625000	625000	16	9766	-

The following is a sample display for the **show traffic-shape statistics** command for the example shown:

```
Router# show traffic-shape statistics

        Access Queue    Packets   Bytes    Packets   Bytes    Shaping
I/F     List   Depth                       Delayed   Delayed  Active
Et0     101    0         2         180      0         0        no
Et1            0         0         0        0         0        no
```

Constrained Access Rate Example

In this example, a customer may use all of a T1 line for 30 seconds in a burst, but the long-term average is limited to 64 kbps. This configuration restricts the amount of load the system can induce on the outbound network interface.

```
interface <his interface or sub-interface>
 traffic-shape rate 64000 8000 46080000
```

If you need to restrict the amount of load the system can induce both outbound and inbound, and therefore the total load it can induce on the Internet service provider (ISP), configure traffic shaping on both the inbound and outbound interfaces, as in the following example:

```
interface <serial interface or sub-interface>
 traffic-shape rate 64000 8000 46320000
interface <LAN interface>
 traffic-shape rate 64000 8000 46320000
```

Differing Controlled Rates through an IP Internet Example

Perhaps you need to restrict the flow of NNTP to each of some set of sites across an intervening backbone out an interface to 64 kbps. This example illustrates how to configure that control and provide one site with 256 kbps:

```
access-list 101 permit <nntp to hither>
access-list 102 permit <nntp to thither>
access-list 103 permit <nntp to yon>
!
interface <the (sub-)interface leading to the above places>
 traffic-shape group 101 64000
 traffic-shape group 102 64000
 traffic-shape group 103 256000
```

Separate token buckets are maintained for each access list, and traffic not matching any access list is not shaped at all.

Frame Relay Adaptability to Congestion Example

This example does not restrict flow across a Frame Relay subinterface that has been layered onto a single DLC. However, in the presence of BECN bits from the network, the flow is throttled back to the committed information rate (CIR). The access rate of the interface is assumed to be 1544 kbps, and the CIR is 64 kbps.

```
interface <relevant sub-interface>
 traffic-shape rate 1544000
 traffic-shape adaptive 64000
 traffic-shape fecn-adapt
```

If the **traffic-shape fecn-adapt** command is configured at both ends of the link, the far end will reflect received FECNs as BECNs in a Q.922 TEST RESPONSE message.

Accommodating Differing Access Speeds Example

Frame Relay networks are often asymmetrical, that is, the access rate at one site may differ from the access rate at another. In such cases, it may be worthwhile to configure the faster rate to shape to the access rate of the slower, as well as to respond to BECNs. Using the previous example as a starting point, in which the access rate is 1544 kbps and the CIR is 64 kbps, and the access rate at the far end is 128 kbps, the configuration of the subinterfaces would be as follows:

```
interface <relevant sub-interface>
traffic-shape rate 128000
traffic-shape adaptive 64000
```

CHAPTER 13

Configuring Frame Relay and Frame Relay Traffic Shaping

This chapter describes the tasks for configuring Frame Relay and Frame Relay Traffic Shaping (FRTS) on a router. To locate documentation of related commands, you can search online at www.cisco.com.

FRTS Configuration Task List

To configure FRTS and verify that the information is correct, perform the tasks in the following sections:

- Configure a Map Class
- Configure FRTS
- Monitor the Frame Relay Connections

See the section "FRTS Configuration Examples" later in this chapter for ideas of how to configure FRTS on your network.

Configure a Map Class

To configure a map class, perform the following tasks. Only the first task is required.

- Specify the map class name.
- Specify a custom queue list for the map class.
- Specify a priority queue list for the map class.
- Enable backward explicit congestion notification (BECN) feedback to throttle the output rate on the switched virtual circuit (SVC) for the map class.
- Set the nondefault QoS values for the map class. You are not required to set the QoS values; default values are provided.

To configure a map class, use the following commands beginning in global configuration mode. Only the first command is required.

Step	Command	Purpose
1	**map-class frame-relay** *map-class-name*	Specifies the Frame Relay map class name and enter map-class configuration mode.
2	**frame-relay custom-queue-list** *list-number*	(Optional) Specifies a custom queue list to be used for the map class.
3	**frame-relay priority-group** *list-number*	(Optional) Assigns a priority list to virtual circuits (VCs) associated with the map class.
4	**frame-relay adaptive-shaping [becn	foresight]**[1]	(Optional) Selects either BECN or ForeSight as the congestion backward-notification mechanism to which traffic shaping will adapt.
5	**frame-relay cir out** *bps*[2]	(Optional) Specifies the outbound committed information rate (CIR).
6	**frame-relay mincir in** *bps*[2]	(Optional) Sets the minimum acceptable incoming CIR.
7	**frame-relay mincir out** *bps*[2]	(Optional) Sets the minimum acceptable outgoing CIR.
8	**frame-relay bc out** *bits*[2]	(Optional) Sets the outgoing Committed Burst (Bc) size.
9	**frame-relay be out** *bits*[2]	(Optional) Sets the outgoing Excess Burst (Be) size.
10	**frame-relay idle-timer** *duration*	(Optional) Sets the idle timeout interval.

1. This command replaces the **frame-relay becn-response-enable** command, which will be removed in a future Cisco IOS release. If you use the **frame-relay becn-response-enable** command in scripts, you should replace it with the **frame-relay adaptive-shaping becn** command.
2. The **in** and **out** keywords are optional. Configuring the command without the **in** and **out** keywords will apply that value to both the incoming and outgoing traffic values for the SVC setup. For example, **frame-relay cir 56000** applies 56000 to both incoming and outgoing traffic values for setting up the SVC.

For SVCs, you can define multiple map classes. A map class is associated with a static map, not with the interface or subinterface itself. Because of the flexibility this association allows, you can define different map classes for different destinations.

Configure FRTS

FRTS provides these capabilities:

- Rate enforcement on a per-VC basis—The peak rate for outbound traffic. The value can be set to match CIR or another value.

- Dynamic traffic throttling on a per-VC basis—When BECN packets indicate congestion on the network, the outbound traffic rate is automatically stepped down; when congestion eases, the outbound traffic rate is increased. This feature is enabled by default.

- Enhanced queuing support on a per-VC basis—Either custom queuing or priority queuing can be configured for individual VCs.

NOTE   FRTS is not effective for Layer 2 PVC switching using the **frame-relay route** command.

Virtual Circuits for Different Types of Traffic

By defining separate VCs for different types of traffic and specifying queuing and an outbound traffic rate for each VC, you can provide guaranteed bandwidth for each type of traffic. By specifying different traffic rates for different VCs over the same line, you can perform virtual time-division multiplexing. By throttling outbound traffic from high-speed lines in central offices to lower-speed lines in remote locations, you can ease congestion and data loss in the network; enhanced queuing also prevents congestion-caused data loss.

Traffic Shaping Tasks

Traffic shaping applies to both permanent virtual circuits (PVCs) and SVCs. To configure FRTS, perform the tasks in the following sections:

- Enable FRTS on the Interface
- Enable Enhanced Local Management Interface
- Specify a Traffic Shaping Map Class for the Interface
- Define a Map Class with Queuing and Traffic Shaping Parameters
- Define Access Lists
- Define Priority Queue Lists for the Map Class
- Define Custom Queue Lists for the Map Class
- Create a Broadcast Queue for an Interface
- Configure Discard Eligibility
- Configure DLCI Priority Levels

Enable FRTS on the Interface

Enabling FRTS on an interface enables both traffic shaping and per-VC queuing on all the interface's PVCs and SVCs. Traffic shaping enables the router to control the circuit's output rate and react to congestion notification information if also configured.

To enable FRTS on the specified interface, use the following command in interface configuration mode:

Command	Purpose
frame-relay traffic-shaping	Enables Frame Relay traffic shaping and per-VC queuing.

Understand the Frame Relay ForeSight Feature

The router ForeSight feature is the network traffic control software used in Cisco switches. The Cisco Frame Relay switch can extend ForeSight messages over a User-to-Network Interface (UNI), passing the backward explicit congestion notification (BECN) bit for VCs.

The ForeSight feature allows Cisco Frame Relay routers to process and react to ForeSight messages and adjust VC-level traffic shaping in a timely manner.

The ForeSight feature must be configured explicitly on both the Cisco router and the Cisco switch. It is enabled on the Cisco router when FRTS is configured. However, the router's response to the ForeSight feature is not applied to any VC until the **frame-relay adaptive-shaping foresight** command is added to the VC's map class. When the ForeSight feature is enabled on the switch, the switch will periodically send out a ForeSight message based on the time value configured. The time interval can range from 40 to 5000 milliseconds.

When a Cisco router receives a ForeSight message indicating that certain data-link connection identifiers (DLCIs) are experiencing congestion, the Cisco router reacts by activating its traffic shaping function to slow down the output rate. The router reacts as it would if it were to detect the congestion by receiving a packet with the BECN bit set.

Congestion Notification Methods

The difference between the BECN and ForeSight congestion notification methods is that BECN requires a user packet to be sent in the direction of the congested DLCI to convey the signal. The sending of user packets is not predictable and therefore is not reliable as a notification mechanism. Rather than wait for user packets to provide the congestion notification, timed ForeSight messages guarantee that the router receives notification before congestion becomes a problem. Traffic can be slowed down in the direction of the congested DLCI.

ForeSight Prerequisites

For the ForeSight feature to work, the following conditions must exist on the Cisco router:

● FRTS is enabled on the interface.

● The traffic shaping for a circuit is adapted to the ForeSight feature.

The following additional condition must exist on the Cisco switch: The UNI connecting to the router is Consolidated Link Layer Management (CLLM) enabled, with the proper time interval specified.

The ForeSight feature is enabled automatically when you use the **frame-relay traffic-shaping** command. However, you must issue the **map-class frame-relay** command and the **frame-relay adaptive-shaping foresight** command before the router will respond to the ForeSight feature and apply the traffic shaping effect on a specific interface, subinterface, or VC.

Enable Enhanced Local Management Interface

When used in conjunction with traffic shaping, the router can respond to changes in the network dynamically. This optional feature allows the router to learn QoS parameters from the Cisco switch and use them for traffic shaping, configuration, or management purposes.

Enhanced Local Management Interface (ELMI) also simplifies traffic shaping configuration on the router. Previously, users needed to configure traffic shaping rate enforcement values, possibly for every VC. Enabling ELMI reduces the chance of specifying inconsistent or incorrect values when configuring the router.

To enable ELMI, you must configure it on the main interface. Use the following optional commands in interface configuration mode:

Step	Command	Purpose
1	**interface** *interface-type interface-number*	Specifies the physical interface.
2	**encapsulation frame-relay** [**cisco** | **ietf**]	Enables Frame Relay encapsulation on the interface.
3	**frame-relay qos-autosense**	Enables the ELMI feature.

NOTE	ELMI enables automated exchange of Frame Relay QoS parameter information between the Cisco router and the Cisco switch. Routers can base congestion management and prioritization decisions on known QoS values, such as the CIR, Bc, and Be. The router senses QoS values from the switch and can be configured to use those values in traffic shaping. This enhancement works between Cisco routers and Cisco switches (BPX/MGX and IGX platforms).

It is not necessary to configure traffic shaping on the interface to enable ELMI. You might want to enable it to know the values being used by the switch. If you want the router to respond to the QoS information received from the switch by adjusting the output rate, you must configure traffic shaping on the interface using the **frame-relay traffic-shaping** command in interface configuration mode.

For an example of how to configure a Frame Relay interface with QoS autosense enabled, see the section "ELMI Example" later in this chapter.

Specify a Traffic Shaping Map Class for the Interface

When you specify a Frame Relay map class for a main interface, all the VCs on its subinterfaces inherit all the traffic shaping parameters defined for the class.

To specify a map class for a particular ELMI interface, use the following command in interface configuration mode:

Command	Purpose
frame-relay class *map-class-name*	Specifies a Frame Relay map class for the interface.

You can override the default for a specific DLCI on a specific subinterface by using the **frame-relay class** VC configuration command to assign the DLCI explicitly to a different class. For an example of assigning subinterface DLCIs to the default class and assigning others explicitly to a different class, see the section "FRTS Configuration Examples" later in this chapter.

Define a Map Class with Queuing and Traffic Shaping Parameters

When you define a map class for Frame Relay, you can define the average and peak rates (in bits per second) allowed on VCs associated with the map class. You can also specify either a custom queue list or a priority queue group to use on VCs associated with the map class.

To define a map class, use the following commands in global configuration mode:

Step	Command	Purpose
1	**map-class frame-relay** *map-class-name*	Specifies a map class to define.
2	**frame-relay traffic-rate** *average* [*peak*]	Defines the traffic rate for the map class.
3	**frame-relay custom-queue-list** *list-number*	Specifies a custom queue list.
4	**frame-relay priority-group** *list-number*	Specifies a priority queue list.
5	**frame-relay adaptive-shaping** {**becn** | **foresight**}[1]	Selects either BECN or ForeSight as the congestion backward notification mechanism to which traffic shaping will adapt.

1. This command replaces the **frame-relay becn-response-enable** command, which will be removed in a future Cisco IOS release. If you use the **frame-relay becn-response-enable** command in scripts, you should replace it with the **frame-relay adaptive-shaping becn** command.

Define Access Lists

You can specify access lists and associate them with the custom queue list defined for any map class. The list number specified in the access list and the custom queue list tie them together.

See the appropriate protocol chapters for information about defining access lists for the protocols you want to transmit on the Frame Relay network.

Define Priority Queue Lists for the Map Class

You can define a priority list for a protocol and you can also define a default priority list. The number used for a specific priority list ties the list to the Frame Relay priority group defined for a specified map class.

For example, if you enter the **frame relay priority-group 2** command for the map class *fast_vcs* and then you enter the **priority-list 2 protocol decnet high** command, that priority list is used for the map class *fast_vcs*. The average and peak traffic rates defined for the map class *fast_vcs* are used for DECnet traffic.

Define Custom Queue Lists for the Map Class

You can define a queue list for a protocol and a default queue list. You can also specify the maximum number of bytes to be transmitted in any cycle. The number used for a specific queue list ties the list to the Frame Relay custom queue list defined for a specified map class.

For example, if you enter the **frame relay custom-queue-list 1** command for the map class *slow_vcs* and then you enter the **queue-list 1 protocol ip list 100** command, that queue list is used for the map class *slow_vcs*; **access-list 100** definition is also used for that map class and queue. The average and peak traffic rates defined for the map class *slow_vcs* are used for IP traffic that meets the **access-list 100** criteria.

Create a Broadcast Queue for an Interface

Very large Frame Relay networks might have performance problems when many DLCIs terminate in a single router or access server that must replicate routing updates and service advertising updates on each DLCI. The updates can consume access-link bandwidth and cause significant latency variations in user traffic; the updates can also consume interface buffers and lead to higher packet rate loss for both user data and routing updates.

To avoid such problems, you can create a special broadcast queue for an interface. The broadcast queue is managed independently of the normal interface queue, has its own buffers, and has a configurable size and service rate.

A broadcast queue is given a maximum transmission rate (throughput) limit measured in both bytes per second and packets per second. The queue is serviced to ensure that no more than this maximum is provided. The broadcast queue has priority when transmitting at a rate below the configured maximum, and hence has a guaranteed minimum bandwidth allocation. The two transmission rate limits are intended to avoid flooding the interface with broadcasts. The actual transmission rate limit in any second is the first of the two rate limits that is reached.

To create a broadcast queue, use the following command in interface configuration mode:

Command	Purpose
frame-relay broadcast-queue *size byte-rate packet-rate*	Creates a broadcast queue for an interface.

Configure Discard Eligibility

You can specify which Frame Relay packets have low priority or low time sensitivity and will be the first to be dropped when a Frame Relay switch is congested. The mechanism that allows a Frame Relay switch to identify such packets is the discard eligible (DE) bit.

This feature requires that the Frame Relay network be able to interpret the DE bit. Some networks take no action when the DE bit is set. Other networks use the DE bit to determine which packets to discard. The most desirable interpretation is to use the DE bit to determine which packets should be dropped first and also which packets have lower time sensitivity.

You can define DE lists that identify the characteristics of packets to be eligible for discarding, and you can also specify DE groups to identify the DLCI that is affected.

To define a DE list specifying the packets that can be dropped when the Frame Relay switch is congested, use the following command in global configuration mode:

Command	Purpose
frame-relay de-list *list-number* {**protocol** *protocol* | **interface** *interface-type interface-number*} *characteristic*	Defines a DE list.

You can specify DE lists based on the protocol or the interface, and on characteristics such as fragmentation of the packet, a specific Transmission Control Protocol (TCP) or User Datagram Protocol (UDP) port, an access list number, or a packet size.

To define a DE group specifying the DE list and DLCI affected, use the following command in interface configuration mode:

Command	Purpose
frame-relay de-group *group-number dlci*	Defines a DE group.

Configure DLCI Priority Levels

DLCI priority levels allow you to separate different types of traffic and can provide a traffic management tool for congestion problems caused by the following situations:

● Mixing batch and interactive traffic over the same DLCI.

● Traffic from sites with high-speed access being queued at destination sites with lower speed access.

Before you configure the DLCI priority levels, complete the following tasks:

● Define a global priority list.

● Enable Frame Relay encapsulation, as described earlier in this chapter.

● Define static or dynamic address mapping, as described earlier in this chapter.

  Make sure that you define each of the DLCIs to which you intend to apply levels. You can associate priority-level DLCIs with subinterfaces.

● Configure ELMI, as described earlier in this chapter.

NOTE   DLCI priority levels provide a way to define multiple parallel DLCIs for different types of traffic. DLCI priority levels do not assign priority queues within the router or access server; in fact, they are independent of the device's priority queues. However, if you enable queuing and use the same DLCIs for queuing, then high-priority DLCIs can be put into high-priority queues.

To configure DLCI priority levels, use the following command in interface configuration mode:

Command	Purpose
frame-relay priority-dlci-group *group-number high-dlci medium-dlci normal-dlci low-dlci*	Enables multiple parallel DLCIs for different types of Frame Relay traffic, associate specified DLCIs with the same group, and define their levels.

NOTE   If you do not explicitly specify a DLCI for each of the priority levels, the last DLCI specified in the command line is used as the value of the remaining arguments. At a minimum, you must configure the high-priority and the medium-priority DLCIs.

Monitor the Frame Relay Connections

To monitor Frame Relay connections, use any of the following commands in EXEC mode:

Command	Purpose
clear frame-relay-inarp	Clears dynamically created Frame Relay maps, which are created by the use of Inverse ARP.
show interfaces type *interface-number*	Shows information about Frame Relay DLCIs and the LMI.
show frame-relay lmi [*interface-type interface-number*]	Shows LMI statistics.
show frame-relay map	Shows the current Frame Relay map entries.
show frame-relay pvc [*interface-type interface-number* [*dlci*]]	Shows PVC statistics.
show frame-relay route	Shows configured static routes.
show frame-relay traffic	Shows Frame Relay traffic statistics.
show frame-relay lapf	Shows information about the status of LAPF.
s**how frame-relay svc maplist**	Shows all the SVCs under a specified map list.

FRTS Configuration Examples

The following examples provide FRTS configuration examples for interfaces and subinterfaces:

- SVC Interface Example

- SVC Subinterface Example

- Traffic Shaping with Three Point-to-Point Subinterfaces Example

- Traffic Shaping with Router ForeSight Example

- ELMI Example

SVC Interface Example

The following example configures a physical interface, applies a map group to the physical interface, and then defines the map group:

```
interface serial 0
 ip address 172.10.8.6
 encapsulation frame-relay
 map-group bermuda
 frame-relay lmi-type q933a
 frame-relay svc
!
```

```
map-list bermuda source-addr E164 123456 dest-addr E164 654321
 ip 131.108.177.100 class hawaii
 appletalk 1000.2 class rainbow
!
map-class frame-relay rainbow
 frame-relay idle-timer 60
!
map-class frame-relay hawaii
 frame-relay cir in 64000
 frame-relay cir out 64000
```

SVC Subinterface Example

The following example configures a point-to-point interface for SVC operation. This example assumes that the main interface (serial 0) has been configured for signaling, and that SVC operation has been enabled on the main interface.

```
int s 0.1 point-point
! Define the map-group; details are specified under the map-list holiday command.
map-group holiday
!
! Associate the map-group with a specific source and destination.
map-list holiday local-addr X121 <X121-addr> dest-addr E164 <E164-addr>
! Specify destination protocol addresses for a map-class.
 ip 131.108.177.100 class hawaii IETF
 appletalk 1000.2 class rainbow IETF broadcast
!
! Define a map class and its QoS settings.
map-class hawaii
 frame-relay cir in 2000000
 frame-relay cir out 56000
 frame-relay be 9000
!
! Define another map class and its QOS settings.
map-class rainbow
 frame-relay cir in 64000
 frame-relay idle-timer 2000
```

Traffic Shaping with Three Point-to-Point Subinterfaces Example

In this example, the VCs on subinterfaces Serial0.1 and Serial0.2 inherit class parameters from the main interface, namely those defined in *slow_vcs*, but the VC defined on subinterface Serial0.2 (DLCI 102) is specifically configured to use map class *fast_vcs*.

Map class *slow_vcs* uses a peak rate of 9600 and average rate of 4800 bps. Because BECN feedback is enabled by default, the output rate will be cut back as low as 4800 bps in response to received BECNs. This map class is configured to use custom queuing using queue-list 1. In this example, queue-list 1 has three queues, with the first two being controlled by access lists 100 and 115.

Map class *fast_vcs* uses a peak rate of 64,000 and average rate of 16,000 bps. Because BECN feedback is enabled by default, the output rate will be cut back to as low as 4800 bps in response to received BECNs. This map class is configured for priority queuing using priority-group 2.

```
interface Serial0
 no ip address
 encapsulation frame-relay
 frame-relay lmi-type ansi
 frame-relay traffic-shaping
 frame-relay class slow_vcs
!
interface Serial0.1 point-to-point
 ip address 10.128.30.1 255.255.255.248
 ip ospf cost 200
 bandwidth 10
 frame-relay interface-dlci 101
!
interface Serial0.2 point-to-point
 ip address 10.128.30.9 255.255.255.248
 ip ospf cost 400
 bandwidth 10
 frame-relay interface-dlci 102
   class fast_vcs
!
interface Serial0.3 point-to-point
 ip address 10.128.30.17 255.255.255.248
 ip ospf cost 200
 bandwidth 10
 frame-relay interface-dlci 103
!
map-class frame-relay slow_vcs
 frame-relay traffic-rate 4800 9600
 frame-relay custom-queue-list 1
!
map-class frame-relay fast_vcs
 frame-relay traffic-rate 16000 64000
 frame-relay priority-group 2
!
access-list 100 permit tcp any any eq 2065
access-list 115 permit tcp any any eq 256
!
priority-list 2 protocol decnet high
priority-list 2 ip normal
priority-list 2 default medium
!
queue-list 1 protocol ip 1 list 100
queue-list 1 protocol ip 2 list 115
queue-list 1 default 3
queue-list 1 queue 1 byte-count 1600 limit 200
queue-list 1 queue 2 byte-count 600 limit 200
queue-list 1 queue 3 byte-count 500 limit 200
```

Traffic Shaping with Router ForeSight Example

The following example illustrates a router configuration with traffic shaping enabled. DLCIs 100 and 101 on subinterfaces Serial3.2 and Serial3.3 inherit class parameters from the main interface. The traffic shaping for these two VCs will be adaptive to the ForeSight notification.

For serial interface 0, the output rate for DLCI 103 will not be affected by the ForeSight function.

```
interface Serial0
 no ip address
 encapsulation frame-relay
 frame-relay lmi-type ansi
 frame-relay traffic-shaping
!
interface Serial0.2 point-to-point
 ip address 10.128.30.17 255.255.255.248
 frame-relay interface-dlci 102
 class fast_vcs
!
interface Serial0.3 point-to-point
 ip address 10.128.30.5 255.255.255.248
 ip ospf cost 200
 frame-relay interface-dlci 103
 class slow_vcs
!
interface serial 3
 no ip address
 encapsulation frame-relay
 frame-relay traffic-shaping
 frame-relay class fast_vcs
!
interface Serial3.2 multipoint
 ip address 100.120.20.13 255.255.255.248
 frame-relay map ip 100.120.20.6 16 ietf broadcast
!
interface Serial3.3 point-to-point
 ip address 100.120.10.13 255.255.255.248
 frame-relay interface-dlci 101
!
map-class frame-relay slow_vcs
 frame-relay adaptive-shaping becn
 frame-relay traffic-rate 4800 9600
!
map-class frame-relay fast_vcs
 frame-relay adaptive-shaping foresight
 frame-relay traffic-rate 16000 64000
 frame-relay cir 56000
 frame-relay bc 64000
```

ELMI Example

Figure 13-1 illustrates a Cisco switch and a Cisco router, both configured with ELMI enabled. The switch sends QoS information to the router, which uses it for traffic rate enforcement.

Figure 13-1 *ELMI—Sent Between the Cisco Switch and the Cisco Router*

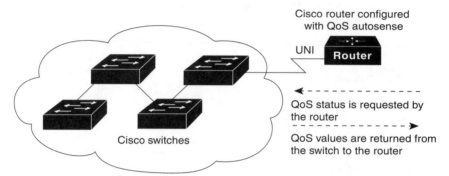

The following configuration example shows a Frame Relay interface enabled with QoS autosense. The router receives messages from the Cisco switch, which is also configured with QoS autosense enabled. When ELMI is configured in conjunction with traffic shaping, the router receives congestion information through BECN or ForeSight congestion signaling and reduces its output rate to the value specified in the traffic shaping configuration.

```
interface serial0
  no ip address
  encapsulation frame-relay
  frame-relay lmi-type ansi
  frame-relay traffic-shaping
  frame-relay qos-autosense
!
interface serial0.1 point-to-point
  no ip address
  frame-relay interface-dlci 101
```

Signaling

CHAPTER 14

Signaling Overview

In the most general sense, QoS signaling is a form of network communication that provides a way for an end station or network node to communicate with, or signal, its neighbors to request special handling of certain traffic. QoS signaling is useful for coordinating the traffic handling techniques provided by other QoS features. It plays a key role in configuring successful overall end-to-end QoS service across your network.

True end-to-end QoS requires that every element in the network path—switch, router, firewall, host, client, and so forth—deliver its part of QoS, and all of these entities must be coordinated with QoS signaling.

Many viable QoS signaling solutions provide QoS at some places in the infrastructure; however, they often have limited scope across the network. To achieve end-to-end QoS, signaling must span the entire network.

Cisco IOS QoS software takes advantage of the Internet Protocol (IP) to meet the challenge of finding a robust QoS signaling solution that can operate over heterogeneous network infrastructures. It overlays Layer 2 technology-specific QoS signaling solutions with Layer 3 IP QoS signaling methods of Resource Reservation Protocol (RSVP) and IP precedence.

An IP network can achieve end-to-end QoS, for example, by using part of the IP packet header to request special handling of priority or time-sensitive traffic. Given the ubiquity of IP, QoS signaling that takes advantage of IP provides powerful end-to-end signaling. Both IP precedence and RSVP fit this category.

Either in-band (IP precedence, 802.1p) or out-of-band (RSVP) signaling is used to indicate that a particular QoS service is desired for a particular traffic classification. IP precedence signals for differentiated QoS and RSVP for guaranteed QoS.

IP Precedence

As shown in Figure 14-1, IP precedence utilizes the three precedence bits in the IPv4 header's type of service (ToS) field to specify class of service for each packet. You can partition traffic in up to six classes of service using IP precedence. The queuing technologies throughout the network can then use this signal to provide the appropriate expedited handling.

Figure 14-1 *IP Precedence ToS Field*

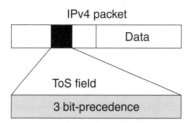

You can use features such as policy-based routing (PBR) and committed access rate (CAR) to set precedence based on extended access list classification. Use of these features allows considerable flexibility of precedence assignment, including assignment by application or user, or by destination or source subnet. Typically, you deploy these features as close to the edge of the network or the administrative domain as possible, so that each subsequent network element can provide service based on the determined policy. IP precedence can also be set in the host or the network client; however, IP precedence can be overridden by policy within the network.

IP precedence enables service classes to be established using existing network queuing mechanisms, such as WFQ and WRED, with no changes to existing applications and with no complicated network requirements.

RSVP

RSVP is the first significant industry-standard protocol for dynamically setting up end-to-end QoS across a heterogeneous network. RSVP, which runs over IP, allows an application to dynamically reserve network bandwidth. Using RSVP, applications can request a certain level of QoS for a data flow across a network.

The Cisco IOS QoS implementation allows RSVP to be initiated within the network using configured proxy RSVP. Using this capability, network managers can take advantage of the benefits of RSVP in the network even for non-RSVP enabled applications and hosts. RSVP is the only standard signaling protocol designed to guarantee network bandwidth from end-to-end for IP networks.

RSVP does not perform its own routing; instead it uses underlying routing protocols to determine where it should carry reservation requests. As routing changes paths to adapt to topology changes, RSVP adapts its reservation to the new paths wherever reservations are in place. This modularity does not prevent RSVP from using other routing services. RSVP provides transparent operation through router nodes that do not support RSVP.

RSVP works in conjunction with, not in place of, current queuing mechanisms. RSVP requests the particular QoS, but it is up to the particular interface queuing mechanism, such as WFQ or WRED to implement the reservation.

You can use RSVP to make two types of dynamic reservations: controlled load and guaranteed rate services, both of which are briefly described in the Introduction, "Quality of Service Overview."

A primary feature of RSVP is its scalability. RSVP scales well using multicast's inherent scalability. RSVP scales to very large multicast groups because it uses receiver-oriented reservation requests that merge as they progress up the multicast tree. Although RSVP is designed specifically for multicast applications, it may also make unicast reservations though it does not scale as well with a large number of unicast reservations.

RSVP is an important QoS feature, but it does not solve all problems addressed by QoS, and it imposes a few hindrances such as the time required to set up end-to-end reservation.

How It Works

Hosts and routers use RSVP to deliver QoS requests to the routers along the paths of the data stream and to maintain router and host state to provide the requested service, usually bandwidth and latency. RSVP uses a mean data rate, the largest amount of data the router will keep in the queue, and minimum QoS to determine bandwidth reservation.

A host uses RSVP to request a specific QoS service from the network on behalf of an application data stream. RSVP requests the particular QoS, but it is up to the interface queuing mechanism to implement the reservation. RSVP carries the request through the network, visiting each node the network uses to carry the stream. At each node, RSVP attempts to make a resource reservation for the stream using its own admission control module, exclusive to RSVP, which determines whether the node has sufficient available resources to supply the requested QoS.

If either resource is unavailable or the user is denied administrative permission, the RSVP program returns an error notification to the application process that originated the request. If both attempts succeed, the RSVP daemon sets parameters in a packet classifier and packet scheduler to obtain the desired QoS. The packet classifier determines the QoS class for each packet and the scheduler orders packet transmission to achieve the promised QoS for each stream.

WFQ or WRED sets up the packet classification and the scheduling required for the reserved flows. Using WFQ, RSVP can deliver an integrated services Guaranteed Rate Service. Using WRED, it can deliver a Controlled Load Service.

CHAPTER 15

Configuring RSVP

This chapter describes how to configure Resource Reservation Protocol (RSVP), which is an IP service that allows end systems or hosts on either side of a router network to establish a reserved-bandwidth path between them to predetermine and ensure QoS for their data transmission.

To locate documentation of related commands, you can search online at www.cisco.com.

RSVP allows end systems to request QoS guarantees from the network. The need for network resource reservations differs for data traffic versus for real-time traffic, as follows:

- Data traffic seldom needs reserved bandwidth because internetworks provide datagram services for data traffic. This asynchronous packet switching may not need guarantees of service quality. End-to-end controls between data traffic senders and receivers help ensure adequate transmission of bursts of information.

- Real-time traffic (that is, voice or video information) experiences problems when operating over datagram services. Because real-time traffic sends an almost constant flow of information, the network "pipes" must be consistent. Some guarantee must be provided that service between real-time hosts will not vary. Routers operating on a first-in, first-out (FIFO) basis risk unrecoverable disruption of the real-time information that is being transmitted.

Data applications, with little need for resource guarantees, frequently demand relatively lower bandwidth than real-time traffic. The almost constant high bit-rate demands of a video conference application and the bursty low bit-rate demands of an interactive data application share available network resources.

RSVP prevents the demands of traffic such as large file transfers from impairing the bandwidth resources necessary for bursty data traffic. When RSVP is used, the routers sort and prioritize packets much like a statistical time-division multiplexer would sort and prioritize several signal sources that share a single channel.

RSVP mechanisms enable real-time traffic to reserve resources necessary for consistent latency. A video conferencing application can use settings in the router to propagate a request for a path with the required bandwidth and delay for video conferencing destinations. RSVP will check and repeat reservations at regular intervals. By this process, RSVP can adjust and alter the path between RSVP end systems to recover from route changes.

Real-time traffic (unlike data traffic) requires a guaranteed network consistency. Without consistent QoS, real-time traffic faces the following problems:

- Jitter—A slight time or phase movement in a transmission signal can introduce loss of synchronization or other errors.

- Insufficient bandwidth—Voice calls use a digital signal level 0 (DS0 at 64 kbps); video conferencing uses T1/E1 (1.544 Mbps or 2.048 Mbps); and higher-fidelity video uses much more.

- Delay variations—If the wait time between when signal elements are sent and when they arrive varies, the real-time traffic will no longer be synchronized and may fail.

- Information loss—When signal elements drop or arrive too late, lost audio causes distortions with noise or crackle sounds. The lost video causes image blurring, distortions, or blackouts.

RSVP works in conjunction with WFQ or RED. This conjunction of reservation setting with packet queuing uses two key concepts: end-to-end flows with RSVP and router-to-router conversations with WFQ:

- RSVP flow—This is a stream that operates "multidestination simplex," because data travels across it in only one direction: from the origin to the targets. Flows travel from a set of senders to a set of receivers. The flows can be merged or left unmerged, and the method of merging them varies according to the attributes of the application using the flow.

- WFQ Conversation—This is the traffic for a single transport layer session or network layer flow that crosses a given interface. This conversation is identified from the source and destination address, protocol type, port number, or other attributes in the relevant communications layer.

RSVP allows for hosts to send packets to a subset of all hosts (multicasting). RSVP assumes that resource reservation applies primarily to multicast applications (such as video conferencing). Although the primary target for RSVP is multimedia traffic, a clear interest exists for the reservation of bandwidth for unicast traffic (such as Network File System [NFS] and virtual private network management). A unicast transmission involves a host sending packets to a single host.

RSVP Reservation Types

These are the two types of multicast flows:

- Distinct Reservation. This constitutes a flow that originates from exactly one sender.

- Shared Reservation. This constitutes a flow that originates from one or more senders.

RSVP describes these reservations as having certain algorithmic attributes.

Distinct Reservation

An example of a distinct reservation is a video application in which each sender emits a distinct data stream that requires admission and management in a queue. Such a flow, therefore, requires a separate reservation per sender on each transmission facility it crosses (such as Ethernet, an HDLC line, a Frame Relay data-link connection identifier, or an ATM virtual channel). RSVP refers to this distinct reservation as explicit and installs it using a Fixed Filter style of reservation.

Use of RSVP for unicast applications is generally a degenerate case of a distinct flow.

Shared Reservation

An example of a shared reservation is an audio application in which each sender also emits a distinct data stream that requires admission and management in a queue. However, because of the nature of the application, a limited number of senders are transmitting data at any given time. Such a flow, therefore, does not require a separate reservation per sender. Instead, it uses a single reservation that can be applied to any sender within a set as needed.

RSVP installs a shared reservation using a Wild Card or Shared Explicit style of reservation, with the difference between the two determined by the scope of application (which is either wild or explicit):

● The Wild Card Filter reserves bandwidth and delay characteristics for any sender and is limited by the list of source addresses carried in the reservation message.

● The Shared Explicit reservation style identifies the flows for specific network resources.

Planning for RSVP Configuration

You must plan carefully to successfully configure and use RSVP on your network. At a minimum, RSVP must reflect your assessment of bandwidth needs on router interfaces. Consider the following questions as you plan for RSVP configuration:

● How much bandwidth should RSVP allow per end-user application flow? You must understand the "feeds and speeds" of your applications. By default, the amount reservable by a single flow can be the entire reservable bandwidth. You can, however, limit individual reservations to smaller amounts using the single flow bandwidth parameter. The reserved bandwidth value may not exceed the interface reservable amount, and no one flow may reserve more than the amount specified.

● How much bandwidth is available for RSVP? By default, 75 percent of the bandwidth available on an interface is reservable. If you are using a tunnel interface, RSVP can make a reservation for the tunnel whose bandwidth is the sum of the bandwidths reserved within the tunnel.

● How much bandwidth must be excluded from RSVP so that it can fairly provide the timely service required by low-volume data conversations? End-to-end controls for data traffic assume that all sessions will behave so as to avoid congestion dynamically. Real-time demands do not follow this behavior. Determine the bandwidth to set aside so bursty data traffic will not be deprived as a side effect of the RSVP QoS configuration.

Plan for RSVP before entering the details needed as RSVP configuration parameters.

RSVP Implementation Considerations

You should be aware of RSVP implementation considerations as you design your reservation system. RSVP does not model all data links likely to be present on the internetwork. RSVP models an interface as having a queuing system that completely determines the mix of traffic on the interface; bandwidth or delay characteristics are only deterministic to the extent that this model holds. Unfortunately, data links are often imperfectly modeled this way. Use the following guidelines:

● Serial line interfaces—Point-to-Point Protocol, High-Level Data Link Control, Link Access Procedure, Balanced, High-Speed Serial Interface, and similar serial line interfaces are well modeled by RSVP. The device can, therefore, make guarantees on these interfaces. Nonbroadcast multiaccess (NBMA) interfaces are also most in need of reservations.

● Multiaccess LANs—These data links are not modeled well by RSVP interfaces because the LAN itself represents a queuing system that is not under the control of the device making the guarantees. The device guarantees what load it will offer, but cannot guarantee the competing loads or timings of loads that neighboring LAN systems will offer. The network administrator can use admission controls to control how much traffic is placed on the LAN. The network administrator, however, should focus on the use of admission in network design in order to use RSVP effectively.

● Public X.25 networks—It is not clear that rate or delay reservations can be usefully made on public X.25 networks.

You must use a specialized configuration on Frame Relay and ATM networks, as discussed in the next sections.

Frame Relay Internetwork Considerations

The following RSVP implementation considerations apply as you design your reservation system for a Frame Relay internetwork:

● Reservations are made for an interface or subinterface. If subinterfaces contain more than one data-link control (DLC), the bandwidth required and the bandwidth reserved may differ. Therefore, RSVP subinterfaces of Frame Relay interfaces must contain exactly one DLC to operate correctly.

● In addition, Frame Relay DLCs have committed information rates (CIR) and burst controls (Bc and Be) that may not be reflected in the configuration and may differ markedly from the interface speed (either adding up to exceed it or being significantly smaller). Therefore, the **ip rsvp bandwidth** interface configuration command must be entered for both the interface and the subinterface. Both bandwidths are used as admission criteria.

For example, suppose that a Frame Relay interface runs at a T1 rate (1.544 Mbps) and supports several DLCs to remote offices served by 128-kbps and 56-kbps lines. You must configure the amount of the total interface (75 percent of which being 1.158 Mbps) and the amount of each receiving interface (75 percent of which would be 96 and 42 kbps, respectively) that may be reserved. Admission succeeds if, and only if, enough bandwidth is available on the DLC (the subinterface) and on the aggregate interface.

ATM Internetwork Considerations

The following RSVP implementation considerations apply as you design your reservation system for an ATM internetwork:

- When ATM is configured, it most likely uses a usable bit rate (UBR) or an available bit rate (ABR) virtual channel (VC) connecting individual routers. With these classes of service, the ATM network makes a "best effort" to meet the traffic's bit-rate requirements and assumes that the end stations are responsible for information that does not get through the network.

- This ATM service can open separate channels for reserved traffic having the necessary characteristics. RSVP should open these VCs and adjust the cache to make effective use of the VC for this purpose.

Resource Reservation Protocol Configuration Task List

After you have planned your RSVP configuration, enter the Cisco IOS commands that implement your configuration plan. To configure RSVP, perform the tasks in the following sections. You must enable RSVP on an interface in order to use it; the other tasks are optional.

- Enable RSVP

- Enter Senders in the RSVP Database

- Enter Receivers in the RSVP Database

- Enter Multicast Addresses

- Control Which RSVP Neighbor Can Offer a Reservation

- Monitor RSVP

Enable RSVP

By default, RSPV is disabled so that it is backward compatible with systems that do not implement RSVP. To enable RSVP on an interface, use the following command in interface configuration mode:

Command	Purpose
ip rsvp bandwidth [*interface-kbps*] [*single-flow-kbps*]	Enables RSVP for IP on an interface.

This command starts RSVP and sets the bandwidth and single-flow limits. The default maximum bandwidth is up to 75 percent of the bandwidth available on the interface. By default, the amount reservable by a flow can be up to the entire reservable bandwidth.

On subinterfaces, this command applies the more restrictive of the available bandwidths of the physical interface and the subinterface. For example, a Frame Relay interface might have a T1 connector nominally capable of 1.536 Mbps, and 64-kbps subinterfaces on 128-kbps circuits (64-KB CIR), with 1200 and 100 kbps, respectively.

Reservations on individual circuits that do not exceed 100 kbps normally succeed. If, however, reservations have been made on other circuits adding up to 1.2 Mbps, and a reservation is made on a subinterface that itself has enough remaining bandwidth, the reservation will still be refused because the physical interface lacks supporting bandwidth.

Enter Senders in the RSVP Database

You can configure the router to behave as though it is periodically receiving an RSVP PATH message from the sender or previous hop routes containing the indicated attributes. To enter senders in the RSVP database, use the following command in interface configuration mode:

Command	Purpose
ip rsvp sender *session-ip-address sender-ip-address* [**tcp** | **udp** | *ip-protocol*] *session-dport sender-sport previous-hop-ip-address previous-hop-interface bandwidth burst-size*	Enters the senders in the RSVP database.

Enter Receivers in the RSVP Database

You can configure the router to behave as though it is continuously receiving an RSVP RESV message from the originator containing the indicated attributes. To enter receivers in the RSVP database, use the following command in global configuration mode:

Command	Purpose
ip rsvp reservation *session-ip-address sender-ip-address* [**tcp** | **udp** | *ip-protocol*] *session-dport sender-sport next-hop-ip-address next-hop-interface* {**ff** | **se** | **wf**} {**rate** | **load**} *bandwidth burst-size*	Enters the receivers in the RSVP database.

Enter Multicast Addresses

If RSVP neighbors are discovered to be using UDP encapsulation, the router will automatically generate UDP-encapsulated messages for consumption by the neighbors.

To enter multicast addresses, use the following command in global configuration mode:

Command	Purpose
ip rsvp udp-multicast [**multicast-address**]	Enters any multicast addresses necessary if you use UDP.

However, in some cases, a host will not originate such a message until it has first heard from the router, which it can only do via UDP. You must instruct the router to generate UDP-encapsulated RSVP multicasts whenever it generates an IP-encapsulated multicast.

Control Which RSVP Neighbor Can Offer a Reservation

By default, any RSVP neighbor may offer a reservation. To control which RSVP neighbors can offer a reservation, use the following command in global configuration mode:

Command	Purpose
ip rsvp neighbors **access-list-number**	Limits which routers may offer reservations.

When this command is configured, only neighbors conforming to the access list are accepted. The access list is applied to the IP header.

Monitor RSVP

After you configure the RSVP reservations that reflect your network resource policy, you can verify the resulting RSVP operations. To do so, use the following commands in EXEC mode:

Command	Purpose
show ip rsvp interface [*type number*]	Displays RSVP-related interface information.
show ip rsvp installed [*type number*]	Displays RSVP-related filters and bandwidth information.
show ip rsvp neighbor [*type number*]	Displays current RSVP neighbors.
show ip rsvp sender [*type number*]	Displays RSVP sender information.
show ip rsvp request [*type number*]	Displays RSVP request information.
show ip rsvp reservation [*type number*]	Displays RSVP receiver information.

RSVP Configuration for a Multicast Session Example

This section describes configuration of RSVP on three Cisco 4500 routers for a multicast session. The three routers form the router network between an RSVP sender application running on an upstream (end-system) host and an RSVP receiver application running on a downstream (end-system) host—neither host is shown in this example.

The router network includes three routers: Router A, Router B, and Router C. The example presumes that Router A's upstream interface Hssi0 links to the upstream host. Router A and Router B are connected by Router A's downstream interface Ethernet1, which links to Router B's upstream interface Ethernet 1. Router B and Router C are connected by Router B's downstream interface Hssi0, which links to Router C's upstream interface Hssi0. The example presumes that Router C's downstream interface Ethernet2 links to the downstream host.

Typically, an RSVP-capable application running on an end system host on one side of a router network sends out either unicast or multicast RSVP PATH (Set Up) messages to the destination end system or host on the other side of the router network with which it wishes to communicate. The initiating application is referred to as the sender; the target or destination application is called the receiver. In this example, the sender runs on the host upstream from Router A and the receiver runs on the host downstream from Router C. The router network delivers the RSVP PATH messages from the sender to the receiver. The receiver replies with RSVP RESV messages in an attempt to reserve across the network the requested resources that are required between itself and the sender. The RSVP RESV messages specify the parameters for the requisite QoS that the router network connecting the systems should attempt to offer.

This example does not show the host that would run the sender application and the host that would run the receiver application. Normally, the first router downstream from the sender in the router network—in this case, Router A—would receive the RSVP PATH message from the sender. Normally, the last router in the router network—that is, the next hop upstream from the host running the receiver application, in this case, Router C—would receive an RSVP RESV message from the receiver.

Because this example does not explicitly include the hosts on which the sender and receiver applications run, the routers have been configured to act as if they were receiving PATH messages from a sender and RESV messages from a receiver. The commands used for this purpose, allowing RSVP to be more fully illustrated in the example, are the **ip rsvp sender** command and the **ip rsvp reservation** command. On Router A, the following command has been issued:

```
ip rsvp sender 225.1.1.1 12.1.2.1 UDP 7001 7000 12.1.2.1 Hs0 20 1
```

This command causes the router to act as if it were receiving PATH messages destined to multicast address 225.1.1.1 from a source 12.1.2.1. The previous hop of the PATH message is 12.1.2.1, and the message was received on interface Hssi0.

On Router B, the following command has been issued:

```
ip rsvp reservation 225.1.1.1 12.1.2.1 UDP 7001 7000 9.1.2.1 Et2 FF LOAD 8 1
```

This command causes the router to act as if it were receiving RESV messages for the session with multicast destination 225.1.1.1. The messages request a Fixed Filter reservation to source 12.1.1.1, and act as if they had arrived from a receiver on interface Ethernet2 with address 9.1.2.1.

In the example, the RSVP PATH messages flow in one direction: downstream from the sender, which in this example is Router A. (If the host were to initiate the RSVP PATH message, the message would flow from the host to Router A.) Router A sends the message downstream to Router B, and Router B sends it downstream to Router C. (If the downstream host were the actual receiver, Router C would send the RSVP PATH message downstream to the receiver host.) Each router in the router network must process the RSVP PATH message and route it to the next downstream hop.

The RSVP RESV messages flow in one direction: upstream from the receiver—in this example, Router C—upstream from Router C to Router B, and upstream from Router B to Router A. If the downstream host were the receiver, the message would originate with the host, which would send it to Router C. If the upstream host were the sender, the final destination of the RSVP RESV message would be the upstream host. At each hop, the router receiving the RSVP RESV message must determine whether it can honor the reservation request.

The **ip rsvp bandwidth** command both enables RSVP on an interface and specifies the amount of bandwidth on the interface that can be reserved (as well as the amount of bandwidth that can be allocated to a single flow). To ensure QoS for the RSVP reservation, WFQ is configured on the interfaces enabled for the reservation.

If the router network is capable of offering the specified (QoS) level of service, then an end-to-end reserved path is established. If not, the reservation attempt is rejected and a reservation error message is sent to the receiver. The ability of each router in the network to honor the requested level of service is verified, link by link, as the RSVP RESV messages are sent across the router network to the sender. However, the data itself for which the bandwidth is reserved travels one way only: from the sender to receiver across an established PATH. Therefore, the QoS is effective in only one direction. This is the common case for one-to-many multicast data flows.

After the three routers in the example are configured, the **show ip rsvp sender** and **show ip rsvp reservation** commands will make visible the PATH and RESV state.

On Router A, RSVP is enabled on Ethernet1 with 10 kbps to be reserved for the data transmission. A weighted fair queue is reserved on this interface to ensure RSVP QoS. (On Router A, RSVP is also enabled on interface Hssi0 with 1 kbps reserved, but this bandwidth is used simply for passing messages.)

Router A

```
!
version 12.0
service config
service timestamps debug uptime
service timestamps log uptime
no service password-encryption
```

```
service udp-small-servers
service tcp-small-servers
!
hostname routerA
!
ip subnet-zero
no ip domain-lookup
ip multicast-routing
ip dvmrp route-limit 20000
!
!
interface Ethernet0
 ip address 2.0.0.193 255.0.0.0
 no ip directed-broadcast
 no ip route-cache
 no ip mroute-cache
 media-type 10BaseT
!
interface Ethernet1
 ip address 11.1.1.2 255.0.0.0
 no ip directed-broadcast
 ip pim dense-mode
 ip rsvp bandwidth 10 10
 fair-queue 64 256 1000
 media-type 10BaseT
!
interface Hssi0
 ip address 12.1.1.1 255.0.0.0
 no ip directed-broadcast
 ip pim dense-mode
 ip rsvp bandwidth 1 1
!
interface ATM0
 no ip address
 no ip directed-broadcast
 shutdown
!
router ospf 100
 network 11.0.0.0 0.255.255.255 area 10
 network 12.0.0.0 0.255.255.255 area 10
!
ip classless
ip rsvp sender 225.1.1.1 12.1.2.1 UDP 7001 7000 12.1.2.1 Hs0 20 1
!
!
!
line con 0
 exec-timeout 0 0
 length 0
 transport input none
line aux 0
line vty 0 4
 login
!
end
```

On Router B, RSVP is enabled on interface Hssi0 with 20 kbps to be reserved for the data transmission. A weighted fair queue is reserved on this interface to ensure RSVP QoS. (On Router B, RSVP is also enabled on interface Ethernet1 with 1 kbps reserved, but this bandwidth is used simply for passing messages.)

Router B

```
!
!
version 12.0
service config
service timestamps debug uptime
service timestamps log uptime
no service password-encryption
service udp-small-servers
service tcp-small-servers
!
hostname routerB
!
ip subnet-zero
no ip domain-lookup
ip multicast-routing
ip dvmrp route-limit 20000
clock calendar-valid
!
!
interface Ethernet0
 ip address 2.0.0.194 255.0.0.0
 no ip directed-broadcast
 no ip route-cache
 no ip mroute-cache
 media-type 10BaseT
!
interface Ethernet1
 ip address 11.1.1.1 255.0.0.0
 no ip directed-broadcast
 ip pim dense-mode
 ip rsvp bandwidth 1 1
 media-type 10BaseT
!
interface Hssi0
 ip address 10.1.1.2 255.0.0.0
 no ip directed-broadcast
 ip pim dense-mode
 ip rsvp bandwidth 20 20
 fair-queue 64 256 1000
 hssi internal-clock
!
interface ATM0
 no ip address
```

```
 no ip directed-broadcast
 shutdown
!
router ospf 100
 network 10.0.0.0 0.255.255.255 area 10
 network 11.0.0.0 0.255.255.255 area 10
!
ip classless
!
!
!
line con 0
 exec-timeout 0 0
 length 0
 transport input none
line aux 0
line vty 0 4
 login
!
end
```

On Router C, RSVP is enabled on interface Ethernet2 with 20 kbps to be reserved for the data transmission. A weighted fair queue is reserved on this interface to ensure RSVP QoS. (On Router C, RSVP is also enabled on interface Hssi0 with 1 kbps reserved, but this bandwidth is used simply for passing messages.)

Router C

```
!
version 12.0
service config
service timestamps debug uptime
service timestamps log uptime
no service password-encryption
service udp-small-servers
service tcp-small-servers
!
hostname routerC
!
ip subnet-zero
no ip domain-lookup
ip multicast-routing
ip dvmrp route-limit 20000
!
!
interface Ethernet0
 ip address 2.0.0.195 255.0.0.0
 no ip directed-broadcast
 no ip route-cache
 no ip mroute-cache
 media-type 10BaseT
!
```

```
interface Ethernet1
 no ip address
 no ip directed-broadcast
 shutdown
 media-type 10BaseT
!
interface Ethernet2
 ip address 9.1.1.2 255.0.0.0
 no ip directed-broadcast
 ip pim dense-mode
 ip rsvp bandwidth 20 20
 fair-queue 64 256 1000
 media-type 10BaseT
!
interface Ethernet3
 no ip address
 no ip directed-broadcast
 shutdown
 media-type 10BaseT
!
interface Ethernet4
 no ip address
 no ip directed-broadcast
 shutdown
 media-type 10BaseT
!
interface Ethernet5
 no ip address
 no ip directed-broadcast
 shutdown
 media-type 10BaseT
!
interface Hssi0
 ip address 10.1.1.1 255.0.0.0
 no ip directed-broadcast
 ip pim dense-mode
 ip rsvp bandwidth 1 1
 hssi internal-clock
!
interface ATM0
 no ip address
 no ip directed-broadcast
 shutdown
!
router ospf 100
 network 9.0.0.0 0.255.255.255 area 10
 network 10.0.0.0 0.255.255.255 area 10
 network 11.0.0.0 0.255.255.255 area 10
!
ip classless
ip rsvp reservation 225.1.1.1 12.1.2.1 UDP 7001 7000 9.1.2.1 Et2 FF LOAD 8 1
!
!
!
line con 0
```

```
 exec-timeout 0 0
 length 0
 transport input none
line aux 0
line vty 0 4
 login
!
end
```

PART VI

Link Efficiency Mechanisms

CHAPTER 16

Link Efficiency Mechanisms Overview

Cisco IOS offers two link-layer efficiency mechanisms—Link Fragmentation and Interleaving (LFI) for Multilink Point-to-Point Protocol (MLP) and Compressed Real-Time Protocol (CRTP) header—that work with queuing and traffic shaping to improve the efficiency and predictability of the application service levels.

This chapter gives a brief introduction to these link-layer efficiency mechanisms described in the following sections:

- Link Fragmentation and Interleaving
- CRTP Header

Link Fragmentation and Interleaving

Interactive traffic such as Telnet and Voice over IP is susceptible to increased latency when the network processes large packets such as LAN-to-LAN File Transfer Protocol (FTP) transfers traversing a WAN. Packet delay is especially significant when the FTP packets are queued on slower links within the WAN. To solve delay problems on slow bandwidth links, a method for fragmenting larger packets and then queuing the smaller packets between fragments of the large packets is required.

The Cisco IOS LFI feature reduces delay on slower-speed links by breaking up large datagrams and interleaving low-delay traffic packets with the smaller packets resulting from the fragmented datagram. The Cisco IOS LFI feature uses Cisco's implementation of MLP, which supports the fragmentation and packet sequencing specifications in RFC 1717.

LFI allows reserve queues to be set up so that Real-Time Protocol (RTP) streams can be mapped into a higher priority queue in the configured weighted fair queue set.

NOTE A related IETF Draft called "Multiclass Extensions to Multilink PPP (MCML)" describes the MCML feature, which implements nearly the same function as LFI.

How It Works

To understand how LFI using MLP works, it helps to understand the problem it addresses. The complete end-to-end delay target for real-time packets, especially voice packets, is 150 to 200 milliseconds (ms). The IP-based datagram transmission techniques for audio transmission do not adequately address the problems posed by limited bandwidth and the very stringent telephony delay bound of 150 ms.

Unacceptable queuing delays for small real-time packets exist regardless of use of QoS features such as RSVP and WFQ, and use of voice compression algorithms such as Compressed Encoding for Linear Prediction (CELP), which reduces the inherent bit rate from 64 kbps to as low as 8 kbps. Despite these measures, real-time delay continues to exist because per-packet header overhead is too large, and large maximum transmission units (MTUs) are needed to produce acceptable bulk transmission efficiency.

A large MTU of 1500 bytes takes 215 ms to traverse a 56-kbps line, which exceeds the delay target. Therefore, to limit the delay of real-time packets on relatively slow bandwidth links—links such as 56-kpbs Frame Relay or 64-kbps ISDN B channels—a method for fragmenting larger packets and queuing smaller packets between fragments of the large packet is needed. MLP helps to solve this problem through LFI.

MLP provides a method of splitting, recombining, and sequencing datagrams across multiple logical data links. The LFI scheme is relatively simple: Large datagrams are multilink encapsulated and fragmented to packets of a size small enough to satisfy the delay requirements of the delay-sensitive traffic; small delay-sensitive packets are not multilink encapsulated but are interleaved between fragments of the large datagram.

MLP allows the fragmented packets to be sent at the same time over multiple point-to-point links to the same remote address. The multiple links come up in response to a dialer load threshold that you define. The load can be calculated on inbound traffic, outbound traffic, or on either, as needed for the traffic between the specific sites. MLP provides bandwidth on demand and reduces transmission latency across WAN links.

Figure 16-1 shows the mix of traffic destined for an interface as including both jumbograms and smaller, time-sensitive IP voice packets. Based on their classifications, these arriving packets are sorted into queues. After the packets are queued, the jumbogram is fragmented into smaller packets in preparation for interleaving with the time-sensitive IP voice packets. Because WFQ is configured for the interface, packets from each queue—that is, the jumbogram packet fragments and the IP voice packets—are interleaved and scheduled (fairly and based on their weight) for transmission in the output interface queue.

To ensure correct order of transmission and reassembly, LFI adds multilink headers to the datagram fragments after the packets are dequeued and ready to transmit.

Figure 16-1 *Link Fragmentation and Interleaving*

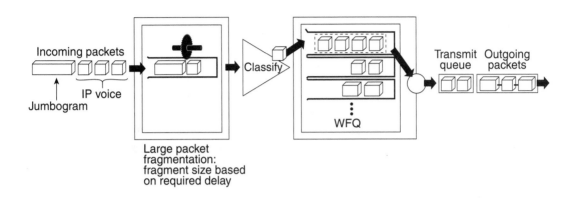

Interleaving can occur at process-fast paths. However, because it relies on MLP, its performance is closely tied with multilink behavior.

CRTP Header

RTP header is the Internet-standard protocol for the transport of real-time data. It is intended to provide end-to-end network transport functions for applications that support audio, video, or simulation data over multicast or unicast network services. RTP is not intended for data traffic that uses Transmission Control Protocol (TCP) or User Datagram Protocol (UDP) as its transport protocol.

RTP provides support for real-time conferencing of groups of any size within the Internet. This support includes source identification and support for gateways such as audio and video bridges as well as multicast-to-unicast translators. RTP offers QoS feedback from receivers to the multicast group, as well as support for the synchronization of different media streams.

RTP includes a data portion and a header portion. The data portion of RTP is a thin protocol that provides support for the real-time properties of applications, such as continuous media, including timing reconstruction, loss detection, and content identification.

The header portion of RTP is considerably large. As shown in Figure 16-2, the minimal 12 bytes of the RTP header, combined with 20 bytes of IP header (IPH) and 8 bytes of UDP header, create a 40-byte IP/UDP/RTP header. For compressed-payload audio applications, the RTP packet typically has a 20-byte to 160-byte payload. Given the size of the IP/UDP/RTP header combinations, it is inefficient to transmit the IP/UDP/RTP header without compressing it.

To avoid the unnecessary consumption of available bandwidth, the RTP header compression feature—referred to as CRTP—is used on a link-by-link basis.

How It Works

CRTP compresses the IP/UDP/RTP header in an RTP data packet from 40 bytes to approximately 2 to 5 bytes. Figure 16-2 illustrates this process.

Figure 16-2 *RTP Header Compression*

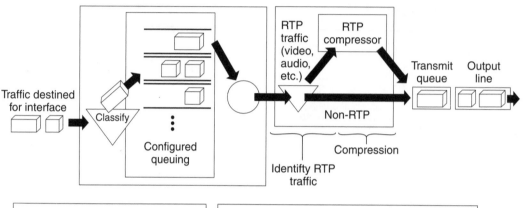

CRTP accrues major gain in terms of packet compression because although several fields in the header change in every packet, the difference from packet to packet is often constant, and therefore the second-order difference is zero. The decompressor can reconstruct the original header without any loss of information.

CRTP is a hop-by-hop compression scheme similar to RFC 1144 for TCP header compression.

Why Use Compressed Real-Time Protocol Header?

CRTP's reduction in line overhead for multimedia RTP traffic results in a corresponding reduction in delay; CRTP is especially beneficial when the RTP payload size is small, for example, for compressed audio payloads of 20 to 50 bytes.

You should use CRTP on any WAN interface where bandwidth is a concern and there is a high portion of RTP traffic. CRTP can be used for media-on-demand and interactive services such as Internet telephony. As with RTP, CRTP provides support for real-time conferencing of groups of any size within the Internet. This support includes source identification and support for gateways such as audio and video bridges as well as multicast-to-unicast translators. CRTP can benefit both telephony voice and multicast backbone (MBONE) applications running over slow links.

You should not use CRTP on any high-speed interfaces—that is, anything over T1 speed—because the trade-offs are not desired.

CRTP is supported on serial lines using Frame Relay, High-Level Data Link Control (HDLC), or Point-to-Point Protocol (PPP) encapsulation. It is also supported over Integrated Services Digital Network (ISDN) interfaces.

CHAPTER 17

Configuring Link Fragmentation and Interleaving for Multilink PPP

The Cisco IOS Link Fragmentation and Interleaving (LFI) feature uses Multilink Point-to-Point Protocol (MLP). MLP provides a method of splitting, recombining, and sequencing datagrams across multiple logical data links. MLP allows packets to be fragmented and the fragments to be sent at the same time over multiple point-to-point links to the same remote address.

This chapter describes the tasks required to configure MLP, and it includes example configurations. To locate documentation of related commands, you can search online at www.cisco.com.

Interleaving for Multilink PPP Configuration Task List

To configure MLP, perform the tasks in the following sections.

- Configure MLP Interleaving and Queuing for Real-Time Traffic
- Monitor PPP and MLP Interfaces

Configure MLP Interleaving and Queuing for Real-Time Traffic

Interleaving on MLP allows large packets to be multilink encapsulated and fragmented into a small enough size to satisfy the delay requirements of real-time traffic; small real-time packets are not multilink encapsulated and are transmitted between fragments of the large packets.

The interleaving feature also provides a special transmit queue for the smaller, delay-sensitive packets, enabling them to be transmitted earlier than other flows.

WFQ on MLP works at the packet level, not at the level of multilink fragments. Thus, if a small real-time packet gets queued behind a larger best-effort packet and no special queue has been reserved for real-time packets, the small packet will be scheduled for transmission only after all the fragments of the larger packet are scheduled for transmission.

WFQ is supported on all interfaces that support MLP, including MLP virtual access interfaces and virtual interface templates.

Fair queuing on MLP overcomes a prior restriction. Previously, fair queuing was not allowed on virtual access interfaces and virtual interface templates. Interleaving provides the delay bounds for delay-sensitive voice packets on a slow link that is used for other best-effort traffic.

Restrictions

Interleaving applies only to interfaces that can configure a multilink bundle interface. These interfaces include virtual templates, dialer interfaces, and ISDN BRI or PRI interfaces.

Multilink and fair queuing are not supported when a multilink bundle is off-loaded to a different system using Multichassis Multilink PPP (MMP). Thus, interleaving is not supported in MMP networking designs.

MLP Interleaving Configuration Tasks

MLP support for interleaving can be configured on virtual templates, dialer interfaces, and ISDN BRI or PRI interfaces. To configure interleaving, perform the following tasks:

> **Step 1**   Configure the dialer interface, BRI interface, PRI interface, or virtual interface template, as defined in the relevant Cisco IOS documents.
>
> **Step 2**   Configure MLP and interleaving on the interface or template.

NOTE   Fair queuing, which is enabled by default, must remain enabled on the interface.

To configure MLP and interleaving on a configured and operational interface or virtual interface template, use the following commands in interface configuration mode:

Step	Command	Purpose
1	**ppp multilink**	Enables MLP.
2	**ppp multilink interleave**	Enables real-time packet interleaving.
3	**ppp multilink fragment-delay** *milliseconds*	Optionally, configures a maximum fragment delay. If, for example, you want a voice stream to have a maximum bound on delay of 20 ms and you specify 20 ms using this command, MLP will choose a fragment size based on the configured value.

Step	Command	Purpose
4	**ip rtp reserve** *lowest-UDP-port range-of-ports* [*maximum-bandwidth*]	Reserves a special queue for real-time packet flows to specified destination User Datagram Protocol (UDP) ports, allowing real-time traffic to have higher priority than other flows. If the bandwidth exceeds the limit specified, the reserved queue is degraded to a best-effort queue. (Use of this command is helpful in improving delay bounds of real-time traffic, such as voice streams, by giving them a higher priority.)
5	multilink virtual-template [1]	For virtual interface templates only, applies the virtual interface template to the multilink bundle.[1]

1. This step is not used for ISDN or dialer interfaces.

Interleaving statistics can be displayed by using the **show interfaces** command, specifying the particular interface on which interleaving is enabled. Interleaving data is displayed only if there are interleaves. For example, the following line shows interleaves:

```
Output queue: 315/64/164974/31191 (size/threshold/drops/interleaves)
```

Monitor PPP and MLP Interfaces

To monitor virtual interfaces, use the following command in EXEC mode:

Command	Purpose
show ppp multilink	Displays MLP and MMP.

MLP Interleaving and Link Fragmentation Examples

The following example defines a virtual interface template that configures MLP interleaving and a maximum real-time traffic delay of 20 ms, and then applies that virtual template to the MLP bundle:

```
interface virtual-template 1
 ip unnumbered ethernet 0
 ppp multilink
 ppp multilink interleave
 ppp multilink fragment-delay 20
 ip rtp interleave 32768 20 1000
multilink virtual-template 1
```

The following example configures MLP interleaving on a dialer interface that controls a rotary group of BRI interfaces. This configuration permits IP packets to trigger calls.

```
interface BRI0
 description connected into a rotary group
 encapsulation ppp
 dialer rotary-group 1
!
interface BRI1
 no ip address
 encapsulation ppp
 dialer rotary-group 1

interface BRI2
 encapsulation ppp
 dialer rotary-group 1
!
interface BRI3
 no ip address
 encapsulation ppp
 dialer rotary-group 1
!
interface BRI4
 encapsulation ppp
 dialer rotary-group 1
!
interface Dialer0
 description Dialer group controlling the BRIs
 ip address 8.1.1.1 255.255.255.0
 encapsulation ppp
 dialer map ip 8.1.1.2 name angus 14802616900
 dialer-group 1
 ppp authentication chap
! Enables Multilink PPP interleaving on the dialer interface and reserves
! a special queue.
 ppp multilink
 ppp multilink interleave
 ip rtp reserve 32768 20 1000
! Keeps fragments of large packets small enough to ensure delay of 20 ms or less.
 ppp multilink fragment-delay 20
dialer-list 1 protocol ip permit
```

Configuring Compressed Real-Time Protocol

This chapter describes how to configure Compressed Real-Time Protocol (CRTP) header on serial lines using Frame Relay, High-Level Data Link Control (HDLC), or Point-to-Point Protocol (PPP) encapsulation. You can also use CRTP over Integrated Services Digital Network (ISDN) interfaces.

To locate documentation of related commands, you can search online at www.cisco.com.

CRTP Configuration Task List

To configure CRTP header, perform the tasks in the following sections. Either one of the first two tasks is required.

- Enable CRTP on a Serial Interface
- Enable CRTP with Frame Relay Encapsulation
- Change the Number of Header Compression Connections
- Display System and Network Statistics

NOTE   You must enable compression on both ends of a serial connection.

Before You Configure CRTP

CRTP is supported on serial lines using Frame Relay, HDLC, or PPP encapsulation. It is also supported over ISDN interfaces.

You should configure CRTP if the following conditions exist in your network:

- Slow links
- The need to save bandwidth

NOTE   CRTP should not be used on links greater than 2 Mbps.

Enabling compression on both ends of a low-bandwidth serial link can greatly reduce the network overhead if it carries a lot of Real-Time Protocol (RTP) traffic. Although the MBONE-style RTP traffic has higher payload sizes, compact encodings such as Compressed Encoding for Linear Prediction (CELP) can also help considerably.

Before you can enable RTP header compression, you must have configured a serial line that uses either Frame Relay, HDLC, or PPP encapsulation, or an ISDN interface. To configure RTP header compression, perform the tasks in the following sections.

Enable CRTP on a Serial Interface

To enable CRTP header for serial encapsulations HDLC or PPP, use the following command in interface configuration mode: (You must enable compression on both ends of a serial connection.)

Command	Purpose
ip rtp header-compression [**passive**]	Enables RTP header compression.

If you include the **passive** keyword, the software compresses outgoing RTP packets only if incoming RTP packets on the same interface are compressed. If you use the command without the **passive** keyword, the software compresses all RTP traffic.

Enable CRTP with Frame Relay Encapsulation

To enable CRTP header with Frame Relay encapsulation, use one of the following commands in interface configuration mode:

Command	Purpose
frame-relay ip rtp header-compression [**passive**]	Enables RTP header compression on the physical interface and all the interface maps will inherit it. Subsequently, all maps will perform RTP/IP header compression.
frame-relay map ip *ip-address dlci* [**broadcast**] **rtp header-compression** [**active** | **passive**]	Enables RTP header compression only on the particular map specified.
frame-relay map ip *ip-address dlci* [**broadcast**] **compress**	Enables both RTP and TCP header compression on this link.

Change the Number of Header Compression Connections

By default, the software supports a total of 16 RTP header compression connections on an interface. To change that number, use the following command in interface configuration mode:

Command	Purpose
ip rtp compression connections *number*	Specifies the total number of RTP header compression connections supported on an interface.

Display System and Network Statistics

You can display specific statistics such as the contents of IP routing tables, caches, and databases. Information provided can be used to determine resource utilization and solve network problems. You can also display information about node reachability and discover the routing path your device's packets are taking through the network.

To display various routing statistics, use the following commands in EXEC mode:

Command	Purpose
show frame-relay ip rtp header-compression [**interface** *type number*]	Displays Frame Relay RTP header compression statistics.
show ip rtp header-compression [*type number*] [**detail**]	Displays RTP header compression statistics.

CRTP Configuration Examples

The following example enables RTP header compression for a serial, ISDN, or asynchronous interface. For ISDN, you also need a broadcast dialer map.

```
interface serial 0 :or interface bri 0
 ip rtp header-compression
 encapsulation ppp
 ip rtp compression-connections 25
```

The following example for Frame Relay encapsulation enables RTP header compression on the specified map:

```
interface serial 0
 ip address 1.0.0.2 255.0.0.0
 encapsulation frame-relay
 no keepalive
 clockrate 64000
 frame-relay map ip 1.0.0.1 17 broadcast rtp header-compression
```

CHAPTER 19

Quality of Service Commands

Use the commands in this chapter to configure quality of service (QoS), a measure of performance for a transmission system that reflects its transmission quality and service availability. The commands are arranged alphabetically.

access-list rate-limit

To configure an access list for use with committed access rate (CAR) policies, use the **access-list rate-limit** global configuration command. To remove the access list from the configuration, use the **no** form of this command.

> **access-list rate-limit** *acl-index* {*precedence* | *mac-address* | **mask** *prec-mask*}
> **no access-list rate-limit** *acl-index* {*precedence* | *mac-address* | **mask** *prec-mask*}

Syntax	Description
acl-index	Access list number. Use any number from 1 to 99 to classify packets by precedence or precedence mask, and use any number from 100 to 199 to classify by MAC address.
precedence	IP precedence.
mac-address	Address of the MAC.
mask *prec-mask*	IP precedence mask; a two-digit hexadecimal number. Use this option when you want to assign multiple precedences to the same rate-limit access list.

Default
No CAR access lists are configured.

Command Mode
Global configuration

Usage Guidelines
This command first appeared in Cisco IOS Release 11.1 CC.

This command classifies packets by the specified IP precedence or MAC address for a particular CAR access list. You can then apply CAR policies, using the **rate-limit** command, to individual rate limit access lists. Thus, packets with different IP precedences or MAC addresses are treated differently by the CAR process.

You can specify only one command for each rate limit access list. If you enter this command multiple times with the same access list number, the new command will overwrite the previous command.

Use the **mask** keyword to assign multiple IP precedences to the same rate-limit list. To determine the mask value, perform the following steps:

Step 1   Decide which precedences you want to assign to this rate-limit access list.

Step 2   Convert the precedences into an 8-bit number with each bit corresponding to one precedence. For example, an IP precedence of 0 corresponds to 00000001, 1 corresponds to 00000010, 6 corresponds to 01000000, and 7 corresponds to 10000000.

Step 3   Add the 8-bit numbers for the selected precedences. For example, the mask for precedences 1 and 6 is 01000010.

Step 4   The command expects hexadecimal format. Convert the binary mask into the corresponding hexadecimal number. For example, 01000010 becomes 42. This value is used in the **access-list rate-limit** command. Any packets that have an IP precedence of 1 or 6 will match this access list.

A mask of FF matches any precedence, and 00 does not match any precedence.

Examples

The following example assigns any packets with a MAC address of 00e0.34b0.7777 to rate-limit access list 100:

```
router(config)# access-list rate-limit 100 00e0.34b0.7777
```

The following example assigns packets with an IP precedence of 0, 1, or 2 to the rate-limit access list 25:

```
router(config)# access-list rate-limit 25 mask 42
```

Related Commands

To locate documentation of related commands, you can search online at www.cisco.com.

show access-lists rate-limit
show ip cef

bgp-policy

To enable QoS policy propagation via Border Gateway Protocol (BGP) on the interface, use the **bgp-policy** interface configuration command. To disable QoS policy propagation via BGP, use the **no** form of this command.

> **bgp-policy ip-prec-map**
> **no bgp-policy ip-prec-map**

Syntax   Description

ip-prec-map   QoS policy based on the IP precedence.

Default

QoS policy propagation via BGP is disabled.

Command Mode

Interface configuration

Usage Guidelines

This command first appeared in Cisco IOS Release 11.1 CC.

For the QoS policy propagation via BGP feature to work, you must enable BGP and CEF/DCEF. In addition, the proper route-map configuration must be in place to specify the IP precedence (for example, **set ip precedence** route-map configuration command).

| NOTE | If you specify both **source** and **destination** on the interface, the software looks up the source address in the routing table and classifies the packet based on the source address first; then the software looks up the destination address in the routing table and reclassifies the packet based on the destination address. |

To display QoS policy information for the interface, use the **show ip interface** command.

Example

The following example enables QoS policy propagation via BGP on an interface based on the source address and the IP precedence setting:

```
router# configure terminal
router(config)# interface ethernet 4/0/0
router(config-if)# bgp-policy ip-prec-map
router(config-if)# end
router#
```

custom-queue-list

To assign a custom queue list to an interface, use the **custom-queue-list** interface configuration command. To remove a specific list or all list assignments, use the **no** form of the command.

> **custom-queue-list** *list*
> **no custom-queue-list** [*list*]

Syntax   Description

list   Any number from 1 to 16 for the custom queue list.

Default

No custom queue list is assigned.

Command Mode

Interface configuration

Usage Guidelines

This command first appeared in Cisco IOS Release 10.0.

Only one queue list can be assigned per interface. Use this command in place of the **priority-list** command (not in addition to it). Custom queuing allows a fairness not provided with priority queuing. With custom queuing, you can control the interface's available bandwidth when it is unable to accommodate the aggregate traffic enqueued. Associated with each output queue is a configurable byte count, which specifies how many bytes of data should be delivered from the current queue by the system before the system moves on to the next queue. When a particular queue is being processed, packets are sent until the number of bytes sent exceeds the queue byte count or until the queue is empty.

Use the **show queuing custom** and **show interface** commands to display the current status of the custom output queues.

Example

In the following example, custom queue list number 3 is assigned to serial interface 0:

```
router(config)# interface serial 0
router(config-if)# custom-queue-list 3
```

Related Commands

To locate documentation of related commands, you can search online at www.cisco.com.

queue-list default
queue-list interface
queue-list queue byte-count
queue-list queue limit
show interfaces
show queue
show queuing

fair-queue

To enable weighted fair queuing (WFQ) for an interface, use the **fair-queue** interface configuration command. To disable WFQ for an interface, use the **no** form of this command.

> **fair-queue** [*congestive-discard-threshold* [*dynamic-queues* [*reservable-queues*]]]
> **no fair-queue**

Syntax	Description
congestive-discard-threshold	(Optional) Number of messages allowed in each queue. The default is 64 messages, and a new threshold must be a power of 2 in the range 16 to 4096. When a conversation reaches this threshold, new message packets are discarded.
dynamic-queues	(Optional) Number of dynamic queues used for best-effort conversations (that is, a normal conversation not requiring any special network services). Values are 16, 32, 64, 128, 256, 512, 1024, 2048, and 4096. The default is 256.
reservable-queues	(Optional) Number of reservable queues used for reserved conversations in the range 0 to 1000. The default is 0. Reservable queues are used for interfaces configured for features such as Resource Reservation Protocol (RSVP).

Part
VI

Command Reference

Default

Fair queuing is enabled by default for physical interfaces whose bandwidth is less than or equal to 2.048 Mbps and that do not use the following: X.25 and Synchronous Data Link Control (SDLC) encapsulations; Link Access Procedure, Balanced (LAPB); tunnels; loopbacks; dialer; bridges; or virtual interfaces. Fair queuing is not an option for these protocols. However, if custom queuing or priority queuing is enabled for a qualifying link, it overrides fair queuing, effectively disabling it. Additionally, fair queuing is automatically disabled if you enable the autonomous or silicon switching engine mechanisms. Fair queuing is also enabled automatically on interfaces configured for Multilink PPP.

Command Mode

Interface configuration

Usage Guidelines

This command first appeared in Cisco IOS Release 11.0.

The command enables WFQ. With WFQ, packets are classified by flow. For example, packets with the same source IP address, destination IP address, source TCP or UDP port, destination TCP or UDP port, protocol, and type of service (ToS) field belong to the same flow; see Table 19-1 for a full list of protocols and traffic stream discrimination fields.

When enabled for an interface, WFQ provides traffic priority management that automatically sorts among individual traffic streams without requiring that you first define access lists. Enabling WFQ requires use of this command only.

When WFQ is enabled for an interface, new messages for high-bandwidth traffic streams are discarded after the configured or default congestive discard threshold has been met. However, low-bandwidth conversations, which include control message conversations, continue to enqueue data. As a result, the fair queue may occasionally contain more messages than its configured threshold number specifies.

WFQ uses a traffic data stream discrimination registry service to determine which traffic stream a message belongs to. For each forwarding protocol, Table 19-1 shows the attributes of a message that are used to classify traffic into data streams.

Table 19-1 *WFQ Traffic Stream Discrimination Fields*

Forwarder	Fields Used
AppleTalk	• Source net, node, socket
	• Destination net, node, socket
	• Type

Table 19-1 *WFQ Traffic Stream Discrimination Fields (Continued)*

Forwarder	Fields Used
CLNS	• Source NSAP • Destination NSAP
DECnet	• Source address • Destination address
Frame Relay switching	• DLCI value
IP	• ToS • IP protocol • Source IP address (if message is not fragmented) • Destination IP address (if message is not fragmented) • Source TCP/UDP port • Destination TCP/UDP port
Transparent bridging	• Unicast: source MAC, destination MAC • Ethertype SAP/SNAP multicast: destination MAC address
Source-route bridging	• Unicast: source MAC, destination MAC • SAP/SNAP multicast: destination MAC address
VINES	• Source network/host • Destination network/host • Level 2 protocol
Apollo	• Source network/host/socket • Destination network/host/socket • Level 2 protocol
XNS	• Source/destination network/host/socket • Level 2 protocol
Novell NetWare	• Source/destination network/host/socket • Level 2 protocol
All others (default)	• Control protocols (one queue per protocol)

It is important to note that IP precedence, congestion in Frame Relay switching, and discard eligibility flags affect the weights used for queuing.

IP precedence, which is set by the host or by policy maps, is a number in the range of 0 to 7. Data streams of precedence *number* are weighted so that they are given an effective bit rate of *number*+1 times as fast as a data stream of precedence 0, which is normal.

In Frame Relay switching, message flags for forward explicit congestion notification (FECN), backward explicit congestion notification (BECN), and discard eligibility (DE) message flags cause the algorithm to select weights that effectively impose reduced queue priority, which provides the application with "slow down" feedback and sorting traffic and gives the best service to applications within their committed information rate (CIR).

Fair queuing is supported for all LAN and line (WAN) protocols except X.25, including LAPB and SDLC; see the notes in the section "Default." Because tunnels are software interfaces that are themselves routed over physical interfaces, fair queuing is not supported for tunnels. Fair queuing is on by default for interfaces with bandwidth less than or equal to 2 Mbps.

NOTE   For Release 10.3 and earlier for the Cisco 7000 and 7500 routers with an RSP card, if you used the **tx-queue-limit** command to set the transmit limit available to an interface on an MCI or SCI card and you configured custom queuing or priority queuing for that interface, the configured transmit limit was automatically overridden and set to 1. With Cisco IOS Release 12.0, for WFQ, custom queuing, and priority queuing, the configured transmit limit is derived from the bandwidth value set for the interface using the **bandwidth** command. Bandwidth value divided by 512 rounded up yields the effective transmit limit. However, the derived value only applies in the absence of a **tx-queue-limit** command; that is, a configured transmit limit overrides this derivation.

When Resource Reservation Protocol (RSVP) is configured on an interface that supports fair queuing or on an interface that is configured for fair queuing with the reservable queues set to 0 (the default), the reservable queue size is automatically configured using the following method: interface bandwidth divided by 32 kbps. You can override this default by specifying a reservable queue other than 0.

Examples

The following example enables use of WFQ on serial interface 0, with a congestive threshold of 300. This threshold means that messages will be discarded from the queuing system only when 300 or more messages have been queued and the message is in a data stream that has more than one message in the queue. The transmit queue limit is set to 2, based on the 384-kilobit (Kb) line set by the **bandwidth** command:

```
router(config)# interface serial 0
router(config-if)# bandwidth 384
router(config-if)# fair-queue 300
```

Unspecified parameters take the default values.

The following example requests a fair queue with a congestive discard threshold of 64 messages, 512 dynamic queues, and 18 RSVP queues:

```
router(config)# interface Serial 3/0
router(config-if)# ip unnumbered Ethernet 0/0
router(config-if)# fair-queue 64 512 18
```

Related Commands

To locate documentation of related commands, you can search online at www.cisco.com.

custom-queue-list
priority-group
priority-list default
show interfaces
show queue
show queuing

fair-queue (DWFQ)

To enable distributed weighted fair queuing (DWFQ), use the **fair-queue** interface configuration command. The command enables DWFQ on an interface using a VIP2-40 or greater interface processor. To disable DWFQ, use the **no** form of this command.

> **fair-queue**
> **no fair-queue**

Syntax Description

This command has no arguments or keywords.

Default

DWFQ is enabled by default for physical interfaces whose bandwidth is less than or equal to 2.048 Mbps.

DWFQ can be configured on interfaces but not subinterfaces. It is not supported on Fast EtherChannel, tunnel, or other logical or virtual interfaces such as Multilink Point-to-Point Protocol.

Table 19-2 lists the default queue lengths and thresholds.

Table 19-2 *Default Fair Queues and Thresholds*

Queue or Threshold	Default
Congestive discard threshold	64 messages
Dynamic queues	256

Table 19-2 *Default Fair Queues and Thresholds*

Queue or Threshold	Default
Reservable queues	0

Command Mode

Interface configuration

Usage Guidelines

This command first appeared in Cisco IOS Release 11.1.

With DWFQ, packets are classified by flow. Packets with the same source IP address, destination IP address, source TCP or UDP port, destination TCP or UDP port, protocol, and type of service (ToS) field belong to the same flow.

DWFQ allocates an equal share of the bandwidth to each flow.

Example

The following example enables DWFQ on the HSSI 0/0/0 interface:

```
router(config)# interface Hssi0/0/0
router(config-if)# description 45Mbps to R2
router(config-if)# ip address 200.200.14.250 255.255.255.252
router(config-if)# fair-queue
```

Related Commands

show interfaces
show interfaces fair-queue

ip rsvp bandwidth

To enable RSVP for IP on an interface, use the **ip rsvp bandwidth** interface configuration command. To disable RSVP, use the **no** form of the command.

> **ip rsvp bandwidth** [*interface-kbps* [*single-flow-kbps*]]
> **no ip rsvp bandwidth** [*interface-kbps* [*single-flow-kbps*]]

Syntax	Description
interface-kbps	(Optional) Amount of bandwidth (in kbps) on interface to be reserved. The range is 1 to 10,000,000.
single-flow-kbps	(Optional) Amount of bandwidth (in kbps) allocated to a single flow. The range is 1 to 10,000,000.

Default

RSVP is disabled if this command is not entered. When enabled without the optional arguments, RSVP is enabled on 75 percent of the link bandwidth.

Command Mode

Interface configuration

Usage Guidelines

This command first appeared in Cisco IOS Release 11.2.

This command is not supported on VIP-based routers. RSVP is disabled by default to allow backward compatibility with systems that do not implement RSVP. Weighted Random Early Detection (WRED) or fair queuing must be enabled first.

Example

The following example shows a T1 (1536 kbps) link configured to permit RSVP reservation of up to 1158 kbps, but no more than 100 kbps for any given flow on serial interface 0. Fair queuing is configured with 15 reservable queues to support those reserved flows, should they be required.

```
router(config)# interface serial 0
router(config-if)# fair-queue 64 256 15
router(config-if)# ip rsvp bandwidth 1158 100
```

Related Commands

To locate documentation of related commands, you can search online at www.cisco.com.

fair-queue
ip rsvp neighbors
ip rsvp reservation
ip rsvp sender
ip rsvp udp-multicast
random-detect

Part
VI

Command Reference

show ip rsvp installed
show ip rsvp interface
show ip rsvp neighbor
show ip rsvp reservation
show ip rsvp sender

ip rsvp neighbors

To enable neighbors to request a reservation, use the **ip rsvp neighbors** interface configuration command. To disable this feature, use the **no** form of the command.

> **ip rsvp neighbors** *access-list-number*
> **no ip rsvp neighbors** *access-list-number*

Syntax

Description

Syntax	Description
access-list-number	Number of a standard or extended access list. It can be any number from 1 to 199.

Default

The router accepts messages from any neighbor.

Command Mode

Interface configuration

Usage Guidelines

This command first appeared in Cisco IOS Release 11.2.

This command is not supported on VIP-based routers. Use this command to allow only specific RSVP neighbors to make a reservation. If no limits are specified, any neighbor can request a reservation. If an access list is specified, only neighbors meeting the specified access list requirements can make a reservation.

Example

The following example allows neighbors meeting access list 1 requirements to request a reservation:

```
router(config)# interface ethernet 0
router(config-if)# ip rsvp neighbors 1
```

Related Commands

To locate documentation of related commands, you can search online at www.cisco.com.

fair-queue
ip rsvp bandwidth
ip rsvp reservation
ip rsvp sender
ip rsvp udp-multicast
random-detect
show ip rsvp installed
show ip rsvp interface
show ip rsvp neighbor
show ip rsvp reservation
show ip rsvp sender

ip rsvp reservation

To enable a router to generate an RSVP RESV message, use the **ip rsvp reservation** interface configuration command. To disable this feature, use the **no** form of the command.

> **ip rsvp reservation** *session-ip-address sender-ip-address* {**tcp** | **udp** | *ip-protocol*}
> *session-dport sender-sport next-hop-ip-address next-hop-interface* {**ff** | **se** | **wf**} {**rate** |
> **load**} [*bandwidth* [*burst-size*]]

> **no ip rsvp reservation** *session-ip-address sender-ip-address* {**tcp** | **udp** | *ip-protocol*}
> *session-dport sender-sport next-hop-ip-address next-hop-interface* {**ff** | **se** | **wf**}
> {**rate** | **load**} [*bandwidth* [*burst-size*]]

Syntax	Description
session-ip-address	For unicast sessions, this is the address of the intended receiver; for multicast sessions, it is the IP multicast address of the session.
sender-ip-address	The IP address of the sender.
tcp | **udp** | *ip-protocol*	TCP, UDP, or IP protocol in the range 0 to 255.
session-dport *sender-sport*	*Session-dport* is the destination port. *Sender-sport* is the source port. Port numbers are specified in all cases, because the use of 16-bit ports following the IP header is not limited to UDP or TCP. If destination is zero, source must be zero, and the implication is that ports are not checked. If destination is nonzero, source must be nonzero.
next-hop-ip-address	Host name or address of the receiver or the router closest to the receiver.

Part
VI

Command Reference

Syntax	Description
next-hop-interface	Next hop interface or subinterface type and number. Interface type can be **ethernet**, **loopback**, **null**, or **serial**.
ff | **se** | **wf**	Reservation style:
	Fixed Filter (**ff**) is single reservation.
	Shared Explicit (**se**) is shared reservation, limited scope.
	Wild Card Filter (**wf**) is shared reservation, unlimited scope.
rate | **load**	QoS guaranteed bit rate service or controlled load service.
bandwidth	(Optional) Average bit rate (kbps) to reserve up to 75 percent of total on interface. The range is 1 to 10,000,000.
burst-size	(Optional) Maximum burst size (kilobytes of data in queue). The range is 1 to 65,535.

Default

The router does not simulate receiving an RSVP RESV message by default.

Command Mode

Interface configuration

Usage Guidelines

This command first appeared in Cisco IOS Release 11.2.

Use this command to force the router to act like it is generating RSVP RESV messages from the receiver.

This command is not supported on VIP-based routers.

Examples

The following example specifies the use of a Shared Explicit Filter style of reservation and the Controlled Load Service, with token buckets of 100 or 150 kbps and 60 or 65 kbps maximum queue depth:

```
router(config)# interface ethernet 0
router(config-if)# ip rsvp reservation 224.250.0.2 132.240.1.1 UDP 20 30 132.240.4.1 Et1 se
load 100 60
router(config-if)# ip rsvp reservation 224.250.0.2 132.240.2.1 TCP 20 30 132.240.4.1 Et1 se
load 150 65
```

The following example specifies the use of a Wild Card Filter style of reservation and the Guaranteed Bit Rate Service with token buckets of 300 or 350 kbps and 60 or 65 kbps maximum queue depth:

```
router(config)# interface ethernet 0
router(config-if)# ip rsvp reservation 224.250.0.3 0.0.0.0 UDP 20 0 132.240.4.1  Et1 wf rate
300 60
router(config-if)# ip rsvp reservation 224.250.0.3 0.0.0.0 UDP 20 0 132.240.4.1  Et1 wf rate
350 65
```

Note that the Wild Card Filter does not admit the specification of the sender; it accepts all senders. This action is denoted by setting the source address and port to zero. If, in any filter style, the destination port is specified to be zero, RSVP does not permit the source port to be anything else; it understands that such protocols do not use ports or that the specification applies to all ports.

Related Commands

To locate documentation of related commands, you can search online at www.cisco.com.

fair-queue
ip rsvp bandwidth
ip rsvp neighbors
ip rsvp sender
ip rsvp udp-multicast
random-detect
show ip rsvp installed
show ip rsvp interface
show ip rsvp neighbor
show ip rsvp reservation
show ip rsvp sender

ip rsvp sender

To enable a router to generate an RSVP PATH message, use the **ip rsvp sender** interface configuration command. To disable this feature, use the **no** form of the command.

ip rsvp sender *session-ip-address sender-ip-address* {**tcp** | **udp** | *ip-protocol*} *session-dport sender-sport previous-hop-ip-address previous-hop-interface* [*bandwidth*] [*burst-size*]

no ip rsvp sender *session-ip-address sender-ip-address* {**tcp** | **udp** | *ip-protocol*} *session-dport sender-sport previous-hop-ip-address previous-hop-interface* [*bandwidth*] [*burst-size*]

Syntax	Description
session-ip-address	For unicast sessions, this is the address of the intended receiver; for multicast sessions, it is the IP multicast address of the session.
sender-ip-address	The IP address of the sender.
tcp | **udp** | *ip-protocol*	TCP, UDP, or IP protocol in the range 0 to 255.
session-dport *sender-sport*	*Session-dport* is the destination port. *Sender-sport* is the source port. Port numbers are specified in all cases, because the use of 16-bit ports following the IP header is not limited to UDP or TCP. If destination is zero, source must be zero, and the implication is that ports are not checked. If destination is nonzero, source must be nonzero.
previous-hop-ip-address	Address of the sender or the router closest to the sender.
previous-hop-interface	Address of the previous hop interface or subinterface. Interface type can be **ethernet**, **loopback**, **null**, or **serial**.
bandwidth	(Optional) Average bit rate (kbps) to reserve up to 75 percent of total on interface. The range is 1 to 10,000,000.
burst-size	(Optional) Maximum burst size (kilobytes of data in queue). The range is 1 to 65,535.

Default
The router does not simulate RSVP PATH message generation by default.

Command Mode
Interface configuration

Usage Guidelines
This command first appeared in Cisco IOS Release 11.2.

Use this command to force the router to act like it is receiving RSVP PATH messages from the sender.

This command is not supported on VIP-based routers.

Example
The following example sets up the router to act like it is receiving RSVP PATH messages using UDP over the loopback 1 interface:

```
router(config)# interface ethernet 0
router(config-if)# ip rsvp sender 224.250.0.1 132.240.2.1 udp 20 30 132.240.2.1 loopback 1
50 5
router(config-if)# ip rsvp sender 224.250.0.2 132.240.2.1 udp 20 30 132.240.2.1 loopback 1
50 5
router(config-if)# ip rsvp sender 224.250.0.2 132.240.2.28 udp 20 30 132.240.2.28 loopback
1 50 5
```

Related Commands

To locate documentation of related commands, you can search online at www.cisco.com.

fair-queue
ip rsvp bandwidth
ip rsvp neighbors
ip rsvp reservation
ip rsvp udp-multicast
random-detect
show ip rsvp installed
show ip rsvp interface
show ip rsvp neighbor
show ip rsvp reservation
show ip rsvp sender

ip rsvp udp-multicast

To instruct the router to generate UDP-encapsulated RSVP multicasts whenever it generates an IP-encapsulated multicast packet, use the **ip rsvp udp-multicast** interface configuration command. To disable this feature, use the **no** form of the command.

> **ip rsvp udp-multicast** [*multicast-address*]
> **no ip rsvp udp-multicast** [*multicast-address*]

Syntax	Description
multicast-address	(Optional) Host name or UDP multicast address of router.

Default

The generation of UDP multicasts is disabled. If a system sends a UDP-encapsulated RSVP message to the router, the router starts using UDP for contact with the neighboring system. The router uses multicast address 224.0.0.14 and starts sending to UDP port 1699. If the command is entered without specifying a multicast address, the router uses the same multicast address.

Command Mode

Interface configuration

Usage Guidelines

This command first appeared in Cisco IOS Release 11.2.

Use this command to instruct a router to generate UDP-encapsulated RSVP multicasts whenever it generates an IP-encapsulated multicast packet. Some hosts require this trigger from the router.

Example

The following example reserves up to 7500 kbps on Ethernet interface 2, with up to 1 Mbps per flow. The router is configured to use UDP encapsulation with the multicast address 224.0.0.14.

```
router(config)# interface ethernet 2
router(config-if)# ip rsvp bandwidth 7500 1000
router(config-if)# ip rsvp udp-multicast 224.0.0.14
```

Related Commands

To locate documentation of related commands, you can search online at www.cisco.com.

ip rsvp bandwidth
ip rsvp neighbors
ip rsvp reservation
ip rsvp sender

priority-group

To assign the specified priority list to an interface, use the **priority-group** interface configuration command. To remove the specified priority group assignment, use the **no** form of this command.

> **priority-group** *list-number*
> **no priority-group**

Syntax	Description
list-number	Priority list number assigned to the interface. Any number from 1 to 16.

Default
This command is not enabled by default.

Command Mode
Interface configuration

Usage Guidelines
This command first appeared in Cisco IOS Release 10.0.

Only one list can be assigned per interface. Priority output queuing provides a mechanism to prioritize packets transmitted on an interface.

Use the **show queuing priority** and **show interface** commands to display the current status of the output queues.

Example
The following example causes packets for transmission on serial interface 0 to be classified by priority list 1:

```
router(config)# interface serial 0
router(config-if)# priority-group 1
```

Related Commands
To locate documentation of related commands, you can search online at www.cisco.com.

priority-list default
priority-list interface
priority-list protocol
priority-list queue-limit
show interfaces
show queue
show queuing

priority-list default

To assign a priority queue for those packets that do not match any other rule in the priority list, use the **priority-list default** global configuration command. To return to the default or assign **normal** as the default, use the **no** form of this command.

> **priority-list** *list-number* **default** {**high** | **medium** | **normal** | **low**}
> **no priority-list** *list-number*

Syntax

Syntax	Description
list-number	Any number from 1 to 16 that identifies the priority list.
high	**medium**	**normal**	**low**	Priority queue level.

Default

The **normal** queue, if you use the **no** form of the command.

Command Mode

Global configuration

Usage Guidelines

This command first appeared in Cisco IOS Release 10.0.

When you use multiple rules, remember that the system reads the priority settings in order of appearance. When classifying a packet, the system searches the list of rules specified by **priority-list** commands for a matching protocol or interface type. When a match is found, the system assigns the packet to the appropriate queue. The system searches the list in the order it is specified, and the first matching rule terminates the search.

Example

The following example sets the priority queue for those packets that do not match any other rule in the priority list to a low priority:

```
router(config)# priority-list 1 default low
```

Related Commands

To locate documentation of related commands, you can search online at www.cisco.com.

priority-group
priority-list interface
priority-list protocol
priority-list queue-limit
show queue
show queuing

priority-list interface

To establish queuing priorities on packets entering from a given interface, use the **priority-list interface** global configuration command. To remove an entry from the list, use the **no** form of this command with the appropriate arguments.

> **priority-list** *list-number* **interface** *interface-type interface-number* {**high** | **medium** |
> **normal** | **low**}
> **no priority-list** *list-number*

Syntax

Syntax	Description
list-number	Arbitrary integer from 1 to 16 that identifies the priority list selected by the user.
interface-type	The name of the interface.
interface-number	The number of the interface.
high | **medium** | **normal** | **low**	Priority queue level.

Default

No queuing priorities are established.

Command Mode

Interface configuration

Usage Guidelines

This command first appeared in Cisco IOS Release 10.0.

When you use multiple rules, remember that the system reads the priority settings in order of appearance. When classifying a packet, the system searches the list of rules specified by **priority-list** commands for a matching protocol or interface type. When a match is found, the system assigns the packet to the appropriate queue. The system searches the list in the order it is specified, and the first matching rule terminates the search.

Example

The following example assigns a list entering on serial interface 0 to a medium priority queue level:

```
router(config)# interface serial 0
router(config-if)# priority-list 3 interface serial 0 medium
```

NOTE	These commands define a rule that determines how packets are attached to an interface. Once the rule is defined, the packet is actually attached to the interface using the **priority-group** command.

Related Commands

To locate documentation of related commands, you can search online at www.cisco.com.

priority-group
priority-list default
priority-list protocol
priority-list queue-limit
show queue
show queuing

priority-list protocol

To establish queuing priorities based upon the protocol type, use the **priority-list protocol** global configuration command. To remove a priority list entry assigned by protocol type, use the **no** form of the command followed by the appropriate *list-number* argument and the **protocol** keyword.

> **priority-list** *list-number* **protocol** [*protocol-name* {**high** | **medium** | **normal** | **low**}
> *queue-keyword keyword-value*]
> **no priority-list** *list-number* **protocol** [*protocol-name* {**high** | **medium** | **normal** | **low**}
> *queue-keyword keyword-value*]

Syntax	Description
list-number	Any number from 1 to 16 that identifies the priority list selected by the user.
protocol-name	Protocol type: **aarp**, **apollo**, **appletalk**, **arp**, **bridge** (transparent), **clns**, **clns_es**, **clns_is**, **compressedtcp**, **cmns**, **decnet**, **decnet_node**, **decnet_router-l1**, **decnet_router-l2**, **dlsw**, **ip**, **ipx**, **pad**, **rsrb**, **stun**, **vines**, **xns**, and **x25**.
high | **medium** | **normal** | **low**	Priority queue level.
queue-keyword keyword-value	Possible keywords are **fragments**, **gt**, **list**, **lt**, **tcp**, and **udp**. See Table 19-3.

Default

No queuing priorities are established.

Command Mode

Global configuration

Usage Guidelines

This command first appeared in Cisco IOS Release 10.0.

When you use multiple rules for a single protocol, remember that the system reads the priority settings in order of appearance. When classifying a packet, the system searches the list of rules specified by **priority-list** commands for a matching protocol type. When a match is found, the system assigns the packet to the appropriate queue. The system searches the list in the order it is specified, and the first matching rule terminates the search.

The **decnet_router-l1** keyword refers to the multicast address for all level 1 routers, which are intra-area routers, and the **decnet_router-l2** keyword refers to all level 2 routers, which are interarea routers.

The **dlsw**, **rsrb**, and **stun** keywords refer only to direct encapsulation.

Use Table 19-3, Table 19-4, and Table 19-5 to configure the queuing priorities for your system.

Part
VI

Command Reference

Table 19-3 *Protocol Priority Queue Keywords and Values*

Option	Description
fragments	Assigns the priority level defined to fragmented IP packets (for use with the IP protocol only). More specifically, this command matches IP packets whose fragment offset field is nonzero. The initial fragment of a fragmented IP packet has a fragment offset of zero, so such packets are not matched by this command.
	Note that packets with a nonzero fragment offset do not contain TCP or UDP headers, so other instances of this command that use the **tcp** or **udp** keyword will always fail to match such packets.
gt *byte-count*	Specifies a greater-than count. The priority level assigned goes into effect when a packet size exceeds the value entered for the argument *byte-count.*
	Note that the size of the packet must also include additional bytes because of MAC encapsulation on the outgoing interface.
list *list-number*	Assigns traffic priorities according to a specified list when used with AppleTalk, bridging, IP, IPX, VINES, or XNS. The argument *list-number* is the access list number as specified by the **access-list** global configuration command for the specified *protocol-name*. For example, if the protocol is AppleTalk, *list-number* should be a valid AppleTalk access list number.
lt *byte-count*	Specifies a less-than count. The priority level assigned goes into effect when a packet size is less than the value entered for the argument *byte-count.*
	Note that the size of the packet must also include additional bytes because of MAC encapsulation on the outgoing interface.
tcp *port*	Assigns the priority level defined to TCP segments originating from or destined to a specified port (for use with the IP protocol only). Table 19-4 lists common TCP services and their port numbers.
udp *port*	Assigns the priority level defined to UDP packets originating from or destined to a specified port (for use with the IP protocol only). Table 19-5 lists common UDP services and their port numbers.

Table 19-4 *Common TCP Services and Their Port Numbers*

Service	Port
FTP data	20
FTP	21
SMTP	25
Telnet	23

Table 19-5 *Common UDP Services and Their Port Numbers*

Service	Port
DNS	53
NFS	2049
RPC	111
SNMP	161
TFTP	69

NOTE   Table 19-4 and Table 19-5 include some of the more common TCP and UDP port numbers. However, you can specify any port number to be prioritized; you are not limited to those listed. For some protocols, such as TFTP and FTP, only the initial request uses port 69. Subsequent packets use a randomly chosen port number. For these types of protocols, the use of port numbers fails to be an effective method to manage queued traffic.

Examples

The following example assigns 1 as the arbitrary priority list number, specifies DECnet as the protocol type, and assigns a high-priority level to the DECnet packets transmitted on this interface:

```
router(config)# priority-list 1 protocol decnet high
```

The following example assigns a medium-priority level to every DECnet packet with a size greater than 200 bytes:

```
router(config)# priority-list 2 protocol decnet medium gt 200
```

The following example assigns a medium-priority level to every DECnet packet with a size less than 200 bytes:

```
router(config)# priority-list 4 protocol decnet medium lt 200
```

The following example assigns a high-priority level to traffic that matches IP access list 10:

```
router(config)# priority-list 1 protocol ip high list 10
```

The following example assigns a medium-priority level to Telnet packets:

```
router(config)# priority-list 4 protocol ip medium tcp 23
```

The following example assigns a medium-priority level to UDP Domain Name Service packets:

```
router(config)# priority-list 4 protocol ip medium udp 53
```

Part VI

Command Reference

The following example assigns a high-priority level to traffic that matches Ethernet type code access list 201:

```
router(config)# priority-list 1 protocol bridge high list 201
```

The following example assigns a high-priority level to DLSw+ traffic with TCP encapsulation:

```
router(config)# priority-list 1 protocol ip high tcp 2065
```

The following example assigns a high-priority level to DLSw+ traffic with direct encapsulation:

```
router(config)# priority-list 1 protocol dlsw high
```

NOTE   These commands define a rule that determines how packets are attached to an interface. Once the rule is defined, the packet is actually attached to the interface using the **priority-group** command.

Related Commands

To locate documentation of related commands, you can search online at www.cisco.com.

priority-group
priority-list default
priority-list interface
priority-list queue-limit
show queue
show queuing

priority-list queue-limit

To specify the maximum number of packets that can be waiting in each of the priority queues, use the **priority-list queue-limit** global configuration command. To select the normal queue, use the **no** form of this command.

> **priority-list** *list-number* **queue-limit** [*high-limit* [*medium-limit* [*normal-limit* [*low-limit*]]]]
> **no priority-list** *list-number* **queue-limit**

Syntax	Description
list-number	Any number from 1 to 16 that identifies the priority list.
high-limit *medium-limit* *normal-limit* *low-limit*	(Optional) Priority queue maximum length. A value of 0 for any of the four arguments means that the queue can be of unlimited size for that particular queue.

Default

The default queue limit arguments are listed in Table 19-6.

Table 19-6 *Default Priority Queue Packet Limits*

Priority Queue Argument	Packet Limits
high-limit	20
medium-limit	40
normal-limit	60
low-limit	80

Command Mode

Global configuration

Usage Guidelines

This command first appeared in Cisco IOS Release 10.0.

If a priority queue overflows, excess packets are discarded and quench messages can be sent, if appropriate, for the protocol.

Example

The following example sets the maximum packets in the priority queue to 10:

```
router(config)# priority-list 2 queue-limit 10 40 60 80
```

Part VI

Command Reference

Related Commands

To locate documentation of related commands, you can search online at www.cisco.com.

priority-group
priority-list default
priority-list interface
priority-list protocol
show queue
show queuing

queue-list default

To assign a priority queue for those packets that do not match any other rule in the queue list, use the **queue-list default** global configuration command. To restore the default value, use the **no** form of this command.

> **queue-list** *list-number* **default** *queue-number*
> **no queue-list** *list-number* **default** *queue-number*

Syntax   Description

list-number   Number of the queue list. Any number from 1 to 16.

queue-number   Number of the queue. Any number from 1 to 16.

Default

The default number of the queue list is queue number 1.

Command Mode

Global configuration

Usage Guidelines

This command first appeared in Cisco IOS Release 10.0.

When you use multiple rules, remember that the system reads the **queue-list** commands in order of appearance. When classifying a packet, the system searches the list of rules specified by **queue-list** commands for a matching protocol or interface type. When a match is found, the system assigns the packet to the appropriate queue. The system searches the list in the order it is specified, and the first matching rule terminates the search.

Queue number 0 is a system queue. It is emptied before any of the other queues are processed. The system enqueues high-priority packets, such as keepalives, to this queue.

Use the **show interfaces** command to display the current status of the output queues.

Example

In the following example, the default queue for list 10 is set to queue number 2:

```
router(config)# queue-list 10 default 2
```

Related Commands

To locate documentation of related commands, you can search online at www.cisco.com.

custom-queue-list
queue-list interface
queue-list protocol
queue-list queue byte-count
queue-list queue limit
show queue
show queuing

queue-list interface

To establish queuing priorities on packets entering on an interface, use the **queue-list interface** global configuration command. To remove an entry from the list, use the **no** form of the command.

> **queue-list** *list-number* **interface** *interface-type interface-number queue-number*
> **no queue-list** *list-number* **interface** *interface-type interface-number queue-number*

Syntax	Description
list-number	Number of the queue list. Any number from 1 to 16.
interface-type	Name of the interface.
interface-number	Number of the interface.
queue-number	Number of the queue. Any number from 1 to 16.

Default

No queuing priorities are established.

Command Mode

Global configuration

Usage Guidelines

This command first appeared in Cisco IOS Release 10.0.

When you use multiple rules, remember that the system reads the **queue-list** commands in order of appearance. When classifying a packet, the system searches the list of rules specified by **queue-list** commands for a matching protocol or interface type. When a match is found, the system assigns the packet to the appropriate queue. The list is searched in the order it is specified, and the first matching rule terminates the search.

Example

In the following example, queue list 4 establishes queuing priorities for packets entering on interface tunnel 3. The queue number assigned is 10.

```
router(config)# queue-list 4 interface tunnel 3 10
```

Related Commands

To locate documentation of related commands, you can search online at www.cisco.com.

custom-queue-list
queue-list default
queue-list protocol
queue-list queue byte-count
queue-list queue limit
show queue
show queuing

queue-list protocol

To establish queuing priority based upon the protocol type, use the **queue-list protocol** global configuration command. To remove an entry from the list, use the **no** form of this command with the appropriate list number.

> **queue-list** *list-number* **protocol** *protocol-name queue-number queue-keyword keyword-value*
> **no queue-list** *list-number* **protocol** *protocol-name queue-number queue-keyword keyword-value*

Syntax	Description
list-number	Number of the queue list. Any number from 1 to 16.
protocol-name	Required argument that specifies the protocol type: **aarp**, **apollo**, **appletalk**, **arp**, **bridge** (transparent), **clns**, **clns_es**, **clns_is**, **cmns**, **compressedtcp**, **decnet**, **decnet_node**, **decnet_routerl1**, **decnet_routerl2**, **dlsw**, **ip**, **ipx**, **pad**, **rsrb**, **stun**, **vines**, **xns**, and **x25**.
queue-number	Number of the queue. Any number from 1 to 16.
queue-keyword keyword-value	Possible keywords are **gt**, **list**, **lt**, **tcp**, and **udp**. See Table 19-3.

Default

No queuing priorities are established.

Command Mode

Global configuration

Usage Guidelines

This command first appeared in Cisco IOS Release 10.0.

When you use multiple rules, remember that the system reads the **queue-list** commands in order of appearance. When classifying a packet, the system searches the list of rules specified by **queue-list** commands for a matching protocol or interface type. When a match is found, the packet is assigned to the appropriate queue. The list is searched in the order it is specified, and the first matching rule terminates the search.

The **decnet_router-l1** keyword refers to the multicast address for all level 1 routers, which are intra-area routers, and the **decnet_router-l2** keyword refers to all level 2 routers, which are interarea routers.

The **dlsw**, **rsrb**, and **stun** keywords refer only to direct encapsulation.

Use Table 19-3, Table 19-4, and Table 19-5 from the **priority-list protocol** command to configure the queuing priorities for your system.

Examples

The following example assigns 1 as the custom queue list, specifies DECnet as the protocol type, and assigns 3 as a queue number to the packets transmitted on this interface:

```
router(config)# queue-list 1 protocol decnet 3
```

The following example assigns DECnet packets with a size greater than 200 bytes to queue number 2:

```
router(config)# queue-list 2 protocol decnet 2 gt 200
```

The following example assigns DECnet packets with a size less than 200 bytes to queue number 2:

```
router(config)# queue-list 4 protocol decnet 2 lt 200
```

The following example assigns traffic that matches IP access list 10 to queue number 1:

```
router(config)# queue-list 1 protocol ip 1 list 10
```

The following example assigns Telnet packets to queue number 2:

```
router(config)# queue-list 4 protocol ip 2 tcp 23
```

The following example assigns UDP Domain Name Service packets to queue number 2:

```
router(config)# queue-list 4 protocol ip 2 udp 53
```

The following example assigns traffic that matches Ethernet type code access list 201 to queue number 1:

```
router(config)# queue-list 1 protocol bridge 1 list 201
```

Related Commands

To locate documentation of related commands, you can search online at www.cisco.com.

custom-queue-list
queue-list default
queue-list queue byte-count
queue-list queue limit
show queue
show queuing

queue-list queue byte-count

To specify how many bytes the system allows to be delivered from a given queue during a particular cycle, use the **queue-list queue byte-count** global configuration command. To return the byte count to the default value, use the **no** form of the command.

> **queue-list** *list-number* **queue** *queue-number* **byte-count** *byte-count-number*
> **no queue-list** *list-number* **queue** *queue-number* **byte-count** *byte-count-number*

Syntax	Description
list-number	Number of the queue list. Any number from 1 to 16.
queue-number	Number of the queue. Any number from 1 to 16.
byte-count-number	The lower boundary on how many bytes the system allows to be delivered from a given queue during a particular cycle.

Default
The default byte count is 1500 bytes.

Command Mode
Global configuration

Usage Guidelines
This command first appeared in Cisco IOS Release 10.0.

Example
In the following example, queue list 9 establishes the byte count as 1400 for queue number 10:

```
router(config)# queue-list 9 queue 10 byte-count 1400
```

Related Commands
To locate documentation of related commands, you can search online at www.cisco.com.

custom-queue-list
queue-list default
queue-list interface
queue-list protocol
queue-list queue limit
show queue
show queuing

queue-list queue limit

To designate the queue length limit for a queue, use the **queue-list queue limit** global configuration command. To return the queue length to the default value, use the **no** form of the command.

> **queue-list** *list-number* **queue** *queue-number* **limit** *limit-number*
> **no queue-list** *list-number* **queue** *queue-number* **limit** *limit-number*

Syntax | Description

Syntax	Description
list-number	Number of the queue list. Any number from 1 to 16.
queue-number	Number of the queue. Any number from 1 to 16.
limit-number	Maximum number of packets that can be enqueued at any time. The range is 0 to 32,767 queue entries. A value of 0 means that the queue can be of unlimited size.

Default

The default queue is 20 entries.

Command Mode

Global configuration

Usage Guidelines

This command first appeared in Cisco IOS Release 10.0.

Example

In the following example, the queue length of queue 10 is increased to 40:

```
router(config)# queue-list 5 queue 10 limit 40
```

Related Commands

To locate documentation of related commands, you can search online at www.cisco.com.

custom-queue-list
queue-list default
queue-list interface
queue-list protocol
queue-list queue byte-count
show queue
show queuing

random-detect

To enable Weighted Random Early Detection (WRED) or Distributed WRED (DWRED), use the **random-detect** interface configuration command. To disable WRED and DWRED, use the **no** form of this command.

> **random-detect**
> **no random-detect**

Syntax Description

This command has no arguments or keywords.

Default

WRED and DWRED are disabled by default.

Command Mode

Interface configuration

Usage Guidelines

This command first appeared in Cisco IOS Releases 11.2 and 11.1 CC.

WRED is a congestion avoidance mechanism that slows traffic by randomly dropping packets when there is congestion. WRED is only useful with protocols like TCP that respond to dropped packets by decreasing the transmission rate.

The router automatically determines parameters to use in the WRED calculations. To change these parameters, use the **random-detect precedence** command.

The WRED feature is supported on these Cisco router platforms:

- Cisco 1600 series
- Cisco 2500 series
- Cisco 3600 series
- Cisco 4000 series (including 4500 and 4700 series)
- Cisco 7200 series
- Cisco 7500 series with RSP interface card

The DWRED feature is only supported on Cisco 7000 series routers with an RSP7000 card and Cisco 7500 series routers with a VIP2-40 or greater interface processor. A VIP2-50 interface processor is strongly recommended when the aggregate line rate of the port adapters on the VIP is greater than DS3. A VIP2-50 interface processor is required for OC-3 rates. To use DWRED, distributed Cisco Express Forwarding (DCEF) switching must first be enabled on the interface.

Example

The following example configures WRED on the HSSI 0/0/0 interface:

```
router(config)# interface Hssi0/0/0
router(config-if)# random-detect
```

Related Commands

To locate documentation of related commands, you can search online at www.cisco.com.

random-detect exponential-weighting-constant
random-detect precedence
show interfaces
show queue
show queuing

random-detect exponential-weighting-constant

To configure the Weighted Random Early Detection (WRED) and Distributed WRED (DWRED) exponential weight factor for the average queue size calculation, use the **random-detect exponential-weighting-constant** interface configuration command. To return the value to the default, use the **no** form of this command.

> **random-detect exponential-weighting-constant** *exponent*
> **no random-detect exponential-weighting-constant**

Syntax   Description

exponent   Exponent from 1 to 16 used in the average queue size calculation.

Default

The default exponential weight factor is 9.

Command Mode

Interface configuration

Usage Guidelines

This command first appeared in Cisco IOS Release 11.1 CC.

WRED is a congestion avoidance mechanism that slows traffic by randomly dropping packets when there is congestion. WRED is only useful with protocols like TCP, which respond to dropped packets by decreasing the transmission rate.

Use this command to change the exponent used in the average queue size calculation for the WRED and DWRED services.

NOTE	The default WRED parameter values are based on the best available data. Cisco recommends that you do not change the parameters from their default values unless you have determined that your applications would benefit from the changed values.

The WRED feature is supported on these Cisco router platforms:

- Cisco 1600 series
- Cisco 2500 series
- Cisco 3600 series
- Cisco 4000 series (including 4500 and 4700 series)
- Cisco 7200 series
- Cisco 7500 series with RSP interface card

The DWRED feature is only supported on Cisco 7000 series routers with an RSP7000 card and Cisco 7500 series routers with a VIP2-40 or greater interface processor. A VIP2-50 interface processor is strongly recommended when the aggregate line rate of the port adapters on the VIP is greater than DS3. A VIP2-50 interface processor is required for OC-3 rates. To use DWRED, Distributed Cisco Express Forwarding (DCEF) switching must first be enabled on the interface.

Example

The following example configures WRED on an interface with a weight factor of 10:

```
router(config)# interface Hssi0/0/0
router(config-if)# description 45Mbps to R1
router(config-if)# ip address 200.200.14.250 255.255.255.252
router(config-if)# random-detect
router(config-if)# random-detect exponential-weighting-constant 10
```

Related Commands

To locate documentation of related commands, you can search online at www.cisco.com.

random-detect
random-detect precedence
show interfaces
show queue
show queuing

random-detect precedence

To configure Weighted Random Early Detection (WRED) and Distributed WRED (DWRED) parameters for a particular IP precedence, use the **random-detect precedence** interface configuration command. To return the values to the default for the precedence, use the **no** form of this command.

> **random-detect precedence** *precedence min-threshold max-threshold mark-prob-denominator*
> **no random-detect precedence** *precedence min-threshold max-threshold*
>   *mark-prob-denominator*

Syntax	Description
precedence	IP precedence number. The value range is 0 to 7 and RSVP. For Cisco 7000 series routers with an RSP7000 interface processor and Cisco 7500 series routers with a VIP2-40 interface processor (VIP2-50 interface processor strongly recommended), the precedence value ranges from 0 to 7 only; see Table 19-7.
min-threshold	Minimum threshold in number of packets. The value range of this argument is 1 to 4096. When the average queue length reaches the minimum threshold, WRED drops all packets with the specified IP precedence.
max-threshold	Maximum threshold in number of packets. The value range of this argument is the value of the *min-threshold* argument to 4096. When the average queue length exceeds the maximum threshold, WRED drops all packets with the specified IP precedence.
mark-prob-denominator	Denominator for the fraction of packets dropped when the average queue depth is at the maximum threshold. For example, if the denominator is 512, one out of every 512 packets is dropped when the average queue is at the maximum threshold. The value range is 1 to 65,536. The default is 10; one out of every ten packets is dropped at the maximum threshold.

Default

For all precedences, the *mark-prob-denominator* is 10, and the *max-threshold* is based on the output buffering capacity and the transmission speed for the interface.

The default *min-threshold* depends on the precedence. The *min-threshold* for IP precedence 0 corresponds to half of the *max-threshold*. The values for the remaining precedences fall between half the *max-threshold* and the *max-threshold* at evenly spaced intervals.

Table 19-7 lists the default minimum threshold valuefor each IP precedence.

Table 19-7 *Default WRED and DWRED Minimum Threshold Values*

| IP Precedence | Minimum Threshold Value (Fraction of Maximum Threshold Value) | |
	WRED	DWRED
0	9/18	8/16
1	10/18	9/16
2	11/18	10/16
3	12/18	11/16
4	13/18	12/16
5	14/18	13/16
6	15/18	14/16
7	16/18	15/16
RSVP	17/18	N/A

Command Mode

Interface configuration

Usage Guidelines

This command first appeared in Cisco IOS Release 11.1 CC.

When you configure the **random-detect** command on an interface, packets are given preferential treatment based on the IP precedence of the packet. Use the **random-detect precedence** command to adjust the treatment for different IP precedences.

If you want WRED to ignore the precedence when determining which packets to drop, enter this command with the same parameters for each precedence. Remember to use reasonable values for the minimum and maximum thresholds.

NOTE   The default WRED parameter values are based on the best available data. Cisco recommends that you do not change the parameters from their default values unless you have determined that your applications would benefit from the changed values.

The WRED feature is supported on these Cisco router platforms:

● Cisco 1600 series

● Cisco 2500 series

● Cisco 3600 series

● Cisco 4000 series (including 4500 and 4700 series)

● Cisco 7200 series

● Cisco 7500 series with RSP interface card

The DWRED feature is only supported on Cisco 7000 series routers with an RSP7000 card and Cisco 7500 series routers with a VIP2-40 or greater interface processor. A VIP2-50 interface processor is strongly recommended when the aggregate line rate of the port adapters on the VIP is greater than DS3. A VIP2-50 interface processor is required for OC-3 rates. To use DWRED, Distributed Cisco Express Forwarding (DCEF) switching must first be enabled on the interface.

Example

The following example enables WRED on the interface and specifies parameters for the different IP precedences:

```
router(config)# interface Hssi0/0/0
router(config-if)# description 45Mbps to R1
router(config-if)# ip address 200.200.14.250 255.255.255.252
router(config-if)# random-detect
router(config-if)# random-detect precedence 0 32 256 100
router(config-if)# random-detect precedence 1 64 256 100
router(config-if)# random-detect precedence 2 96 256 100
router(config-if)# random-detect precedence 3 120 256 100
router(config-if)# random-detect precedence 4 140 256 100
router(config-if)# random-detect precedence 5 170 256 100
router(config-if)# random-detect precedence 6 290 256 100
router(config-if)# random-detect precedence 7 210 256 100
router(config-if)# random-detect precedence rsvp 230 256 100
```

Related Commands

To locate documentation of related commands, you can search online at www.cisco.com.

random-detect
random-detect exponential-weighting-constant
show interfaces
show queue
show queuing

rate-limit

To configure committed access rate (CAR) and Distributed CAR (DCAR) policies, use the **rate-limit** interface configuration command. To remove the rate limit from the configuration, use the **no** form of this command.

> **rate-limit** {**input** | **output**} [**access-group** [**rate-limit**] *acl-index*] *bps*
>   *burst-normal burst-max* **conform-action** *action* **exceed-action** *action*
> **no rate-limit** {**input** | **output**} [**access-group** [**rate-limit**] *acl-index*] *bps*
>   *burst-normal burst-max* **conform-action** *action* **exceed-action** *action*

Syntax	Description
input	Applies this CAR traffic policy to packets received on this interface.
output	Applies this CAR traffic policy to packets sent on this interface.
access-group	(Optional) Applies this CAR traffic policy to the specified access list.
rate-limit	(Optional) The access list is a rate-limit access list.
acl-index	(Optional) Access list number.
bps	Average rate in bits per second. The value must be in increments of 8 kbps.
burst-normal	Normal burst size in bytes. The minimum value is bps divided by 2000.
burst-max	Excess burst size in bytes.
conform-action	Action to take on packets that conform to the rate limit.

Syntax	Description
action	Action to take on packets. Specify one of the following keywords:
	• **continue**—Evaluate the next **rate-limit** command.
	• **drop**—Drop the packet.
	• **set-prec-continue** *new-prec*—Set the IP precedence and evaluate the next **rate-limit** command.
	• **set-prec-transmit** *new-prec*—Set the IP precedence and transmit the packet.
	• **transmit**—Transmit the packet.
exceed-action	Action to take on packets that exceed the rate limit.

Default

CAR and DCAR are disabled on the interface.

Command Mode

Interface configuration

Usage Guidelines

This command first appeared in Cisco IOS Release 11.1 CC.

Use this command to configure your CAR policy on an interface. To specify multiple policies, enter this command once for each policy.

Distributed CAR is only supported on Cisco 7000 series routers with an RSP7000 or Cisco 7500 series routers with VIP2-40 or greater interface processor. A VIP2-50 interface processor is strongly recommended when the aggregate line rate of the port adapters on the VIP is greater than DS3. A VIP2-50 interface processor is required for OC-3 rates.

CAR and DCAR can only be used with IP traffic. Non-IP traffic is not rate limited.

CAR and DCAR can be configured on an interface or subinterface. However, CAR and DCAR are not supported on the Fast EtherChannel, tunnel, or PRI interfaces, nor on any interface that does not support Cisco Express Forwarding (CEF).

DCAR is not supported on ATM subinterfaces, nor with the ATM encapsulations AAL5-MUX and AAL5-NLPID.

CEF must be enabled on the interface before you configure CAR or DCAR.

Example

The example illustrated below limits the rate by application:

- All World Wide Web traffic is transmitted. However, the IP precedence for Web traffic that conforms to the first rate policy is set to 5. For nonconforming traffic, the IP precedence is set to 0 (best effort).

- FTP traffic is transmitted with an IP precedence of 5 if it conforms to the second rate policy. If the FTP traffic exceeds the rate policy, it is dropped.

- Any remaining traffic is limited to 8 Mbps, with a normal burst size of 16000 bytes and an excess burst size of 24000 bytes. Traffic that conforms is transmitted with an IP precedence of 5. Traffic that does not conform is dropped.

Notice that two access lists are created to classify the Web and FTP traffic so that they can be handled separately by the CAR feature.

```
router(config)# interface Hssi0/0/0
router(config-if)# description 45Mbps to R2
router(config-if)# rate-limit input access-group 101 20000000 24000 32000
  conform-action set-prec-transmit 5 exceed-action set-prec-transmit 0
router(config-if)# rate-limit input access-group 102 10000000 24000 32000
  conform-action set-prec-transmit 5 exceed-action drop
router(config-if)# rate-limit input 8000000 16000 24000 conform-action
  set-prec-transmit 5 exceed-action drop
router(config-if)# ip address 200.200.14.250 255.255.255.252
!
router(config-if)# access-list 101 permit tcp any any eq www
router(config-if)# access-list 102 permit tcp any any eq ftp
```

Related Commands

To locate documentation of related commands, you can search online at www.cisco.com.

access-list rate-limit
show access-lists rate-limit
show interfaces rate-limit
show ip cef

set ip precedence

To set the precedence value in the IP header, use the **set ip precedence** route-map configuration command. To leave the precedence value alone, use the **no** form of this command.

> **set ip precedence** [*number* | *name*]
> **no set ip precedence**

Syntax Description

(Optional) A number or name that sets the precedence bits in the IP header. The values for *number* and the corresponding *name* are as follows, listed from least to most important:

number	name
0	**routine**
1	**priority**
2	**immediate**
3	**flash**
4	**flash-override**
5	**critical**
6	**internet**
7	**network**

Default

The software leaves the existing value.

Command Mode

Route-map configuration

Usage Guidelines

This command first appeared in Cisco IOS Release 11.0.

You can set the precedence using either a number or the corresponding name. Once the IP precedence bits are set, other QoS services such as weighted fair queuing (WFQ) and Weighted Random Early Detection (WRED) then operate on the bit settings.

The network gives priority (or some type of expedited handling) to the marked traffic through the application of WFQ or WRED at points downstream in the network. Typically, you would set IP precedence at the edge of the network (or administrative domain) and have queuing act on it thereafter. WFQ can speed up handling for high precedence traffic at congestion points. WRED ensures high precedence traffic has lower loss rates than other traffic during times of congestion.

The mapping from keywords such as **routine** and **priority** to a precedence value is useful only in some instances. That is, the use of the precedence bit is evolving. You can define the meaning of a precedence value by enabling other features that use the value. In the case of Cisco's high-end Internet QoS, IP precedences can be used to establish classes of service that do not necessarily correspond numerically to better or worse handling in the network.

Use the **route-map** global configuration command with **match** and **set** route-map configuration commands to define the conditions for redistributing routes from one routing protocol into another, or for policy routing. Each **route-map** command has an associated list of **match** and **set** commands. The match commands specify the match criteria—the conditions under which redistribution or policy routing is allowed for the current **route-map** command. The **set** commands specify the set actions—the particular redistribution or policy routing actions to perform if the criteria enforced by the match commands are met. The **no route-map** command deletes the route map.

The **set route-map** configuration commands specify the redistribution set actions to be performed when all of a route map's match criteria are met.

Example

The following example sets the IP precedence to 5 (critical) for packets that pass the route-map match:

```
router(config)# interface serial 0
router(config-if)# ip policy route-map texas
!
router(config)# route-map texas
router(config)# match length 68 128
router(config)# set ip precedence 5
```

Related Commands

To locate documentation of related commands, you can search online at www.cisco.com.

fair-queue
ip policy route-map
random-detect
rate-limit
route-map
traffic-shape adaptive
traffic-shape fecn-adapt
traffic-shape group
traffic-shape rate

set ip qos-group

To set a group ID that can be used later to classify packets, use the **set ip qos-group** route-map configuration command. To remove the group ID, use the **no** form of this command.

>**set ip qos-group** *group-id*
>**no set ip qos-group** *group-id*

Syntax Description

group-id   Group ID number in the range 0 to 99.

Default

No group ID is specified.

Command Mode

Route-map configuration

Usage Guidelines

This command first appeared in Cisco IOS Release 11.1 CC.

This command allows you to set a group ID in the routing table that can be used later to classify packets into QoS groups based on prefix, autonomous system, and community string. These packets can then be rate limited or weighted fair queued based on the QoS group ID.

To display QoS group information, use the **show ip cef** command.

Example

The following example sets the QoS group to 1 for all packets that match community 1. These packets are then rate limited based on the QoS group ID.

```
router# configure terminal
router(config)# route-map precedence-map permit 10
router(config)# match community 1
router(config)# set ip qos-group 1
router(config)# interface hssi0/0/0
router(config-if)# bgp-policy source qos-group
router(config-if)# end
```

show access-lists

To display the contents of current IP and rate-limit access lists, use the **show access-lists** privileged EXEC command.

> **show access-lists** [*access-list-number*]

Syntax	Description
access-list-number	(Optional) Access list number to display. The range is 1 to 199.

Default

The system displays all access lists by default.

Command Mode

Privileged EXEC

Usage Guidelines

This command appeared before Cisco IOS Release 10.0.

Sample Displays

The following is sample output from the **show access-lists** command when rate-limit access lists are configured:

```
Router# show access-lists

Standard IP access list 1
    permit any
Standard IP access list 1300
    permit any
Rate-limit access list 1
    0
Rate-limit access list 2
    1
Rate-limit access list 3
    2
Rate-limit access list 4
    3
Rate-limit access list 5
    4
Rate-limit access list 6
    5
```

```
Rate-limit access list 9
    mask FF
Rate-limit access list 10
    mask 0F
Rate-limit access list 11
    mask F0
Rate-limit access list 100
    1001.0110.1111
Rate-limit access list 101
    00E0.34B8.D840
Rate-limit access list 199
    1111.1111.1111
```

The following is sample output from the **show access-lists** command when access lists numbered 1 are displayed:

```
Router# show access-lists 1

Standard IP access list 1
    permit any
Rate-limit access list 1
    0
```

The following is sample output from the **show access-lists** command when an extended access list is configured:

```
Router# show access-lists 101

Extended IP access list 101
    permit tcp host 198.92.32.130 any established (4304 matches)
    permit udp host 198.92.32.130 any eq domain (129 matches)
    permit icmp host 198.92.32.130 any
    permit tcp host 198.92.32.130 host 171.69.2.141 gt 1023
    permit tcp host 198.92.32.130 host 171.69.2.135 eq smtp (2 matches)
    permit tcp host 198.92.32.130 host 198.92.30.32 eq smtp
    permit tcp host 198.92.32.130 host 171.69.108.33 eq smtp
    permit udp host 198.92.32.130 host 171.68.225.190 eq syslog
    permit udp host 198.92.32.130 host 171.68.225.126 eq syslog
    deny   ip 150.136.0.0 0.0.255.255 224.0.0.0 15.255.255.255
    deny   ip 171.68.0.0 0.1.255.255 224.0.0.0 15.255.255.255 (2 matches)
    deny   ip 172.24.24.0 0.0.1.255 224.0.0.0 15.255.255.255
    deny   ip 192.82.152.0 0.0.0.255 224.0.0.0 15.255.255.255
    deny   ip 192.122.173.0 0.0.0.255 224.0.0.0 15.255.255.255
    deny   ip 192.122.174.0 0.0.0.255 224.0.0.0 15.255.255.255
    deny   ip 192.135.239.0 0.0.0.255 224.0.0.0 15.255.255.255
    deny   ip 192.135.240.0 0.0.7.255 224.0.0.0 15.255.255.255
    deny   ip 192.135.248.0 0.0.3.255 224.0.0.0 15.255.255.255
    deny   ip 192.150.42.0 0.0.0.255 224.0.0.0 15.255.255.255
```

An access list counter counts how many packets are allowed by each line of the access list. This number is displayed as the number of matches.

Related Commands

To locate documentation of related commands, you can search online at www.cisco.com.

access-list (extended)
access-list (standard)
access-list rate-limit
clear access-list counters
clear access-temp
ip access-list
show access-lists rate-limit
show ip access-list

show access-lists rate-limit

To display information about rate-limit access lists, use the **show access-lists rate-limit** EXEC command.

> **show access-lists rate-limit** [*acl-index*]

Syntax   Description

acl-index	(Optional) Rate-limit access list number from 1 to 199.

Command Mode

EXEC

Usage Guidelines

This command first appeared in Cisco IOS Release 11.1 CC.

Sample Displays

The following is sample output from the **show access-lists rate-limit** command:

```
Router# show access-lists rate-limit

Rate-limit access list 1
    0
Rate-limit access list 2
    1
Rate-limit access list 3
    2
Rate-limit access list 4
    3
```

```
Rate-limit access list 5
    4
Rate-limit access list 6
    5
Rate-limit access list 9
    mask FF
Rate-limit access list 10
    mask 0F
Rate-limit access list 11
    mask F0
Rate-limit access list 100
    1001.0110.1111
Rate-limit access list 101
    00E0.34B8.D840
Rate-limit access list 199
    1111.1111.1111
```

The following is sample output from the **show access-lists rate-limit** command when specific rate-limit access lists are specified:

```
Router# show access-lists rate-limit 1

Rate-limit access list 1
    0

Router# show access-lists rate-limit 9

Rate-limit access list 9
    mask FF

Router# show access-lists rate-limit 101

Rate-limit access list 101
    00E0.34B8.D840
```

Table 19-8 describes the fields shown in these displays.

Table 19-8 *show access-lists rate-limit Field Descriptions*

Field	Description
Rate-limit access list	Rate-limit access list number. A number from 1 to 99 represents a precedence-based access list. A number from 100 to 199 indicates a MAC address-based access list.
0	IP precedence for packets in this rate-limit access list.
mask FF	IP precedence mask for packets in this rate-limit access list.
1001.0110.1111	MAC address for packets in this rate-limit access list.

Related Commands

To locate documentation of related commands, you can search online at www.cisco.com.

access-list rate-limit

show interfaces

To display statistics for all interfaces, use the **show interfaces** EXEC command. The resulting output varies depending on the network for which an interface has been configured.

> **show interfaces** [*type slot / port-adapter / port*] (for ports on VIP interface processors in the Cisco 7500 series routers)

Syntax	Description
type	(Optional) Type of interface.
slot	(Optional) Refer to the appropriate hardware manual for slot information.
port-adapter	(Optional) Refer to the appropriate hardware manual for information about port adapter compatibility.
port	(Optional) Refer to the appropriate hardware manual for port information.

Command Mode

EXEC

Usage Guidelines

This command first appeared in Cisco IOS Release 10.0.

The **show interfaces** command displays statistics for the network interfaces.

The output of the **show interfaces** command varies based on the interface type and configuration.

This document describes the output related to these features and services:

● Distributed weighted fair queuing (DWFQ)

● Weighted Random Early Detection (WRED)

Refer to the Cisco IOS Release 11.1 command reference documents for a complete description of the entire output.

Sample Display for DWFQ

The following is sample output from the **show interfaces** command when DWFQ is enabled on an interface. Notice that the queuing strategy is listed as "VIP-based fair queuing."

```
Router# show interfaces FastEthernet1/1/0

FastEthernet1/1/0 is up, line protocol is up
  Hardware is cyBus FastEthernet Interface, address is 0007.f618.4448 (bia 00e0)
  Description: pkt input i/f for WRL tests (to pagent)
  Internet address is 80.0.2.70/24
  MTU 1500 bytes, BW 100000 Kbit, DLY 100 usec, rely 255/255, load 1/255
  Encapsulation ARPA, loopback not set, keepalive not set, fdx, 100BaseTX/FX
  ARP type: ARPA, ARP Timeout 04:00:00
  Last input never, output 01:11:01, output hang never
  Last clearing of "show interface" counters 01:12:31
  Queuing strategy: VIP-based fair queuing
  Output queue 0/40, 0 drops; input queue 0/75, 0 drops
  30 second input rate 0 bits/sec, 0 packets/sec
  30 second output rate 0 bits/sec, 0 packets/sec
     0 packets input, 0 bytes, 0 no buffer
     Received 0 broadcasts, 0 runts, 0 giants
     0 input errors, 0 CRC, 0 frame, 0 overrun, 0 ignored, 0 abort
     0 watchdog, 0 multicast
     0 input packets with dribble condition detected
     1 packets output, 60 bytes, 0 underruns
     0 output errors, 0 collisions, 0 interface resets
     0 babbles, 0 late collision, 0 deferred
     0 lost carrier, 0 no carrier
     0 output buffers copied, 0 interrupts, 0 failures
```

Sample Display for DWRED

The following is sample output from the **show interfaces** command when DWRED is enabled on an interface. Notice that the packet drop strategy is listed as "VIP-based weighted RED."

```
Router# show interfaces hssi0/0/0

Hssi0/0/0 is up, line protocol is up
  Hardware is cyBus HSSI
  Description: 45Mbps to R1
  Internet address is 200.200.14.250/30
  MTU 4470 bytes, BW 45045 Kbit, DLY 200 usec, rely 255/255, load 1/255
  Encapsulation HDLC, loopback not set, keepalive set (10 sec)
  Last input 00:00:02, output 00:00:03, output hang never
  Last clearing of "show interface" counters never
  Queuing strategy: fifo
  Packet Drop strategy: VIP-based weighted RED
  Output queue 0/40, 0 drops; input queue 0/75, 0 drops
  5 minute input rate 0 bits/sec, 0 packets/sec
  5 minute output rate 0 bits/sec, 0 packets/sec
  1976 packets input, 131263 bytes, 0 no buffer
  Received 1577 broadcasts, 0 runts, 0 giants
  0 parity
```

```
4 input errors, 4 CRC, 0 frame, 0 overrun, 0 ignored, 0 abort
1939 packets output, 130910 bytes, 0 underruns
0 output errors, 0 applique, 3 interface resets
0 output buffers copied, 0 interrupts, 0 failures
```

show interfaces fair-queue

To display information and statistics about weighted fair queuing (WFQ) for a VIP-based interface, use the **show interfaces fair-queue** EXEC command.

>**show interfaces** [*interface-type interface-number*] **fair-queue**

Syntax	Description
interface-type	(Optional) The name of the interface.
interface-number	(Optional) The number of the interface.

Command Mode

EXEC

Usage Guidelines

This command first appeared in Cisco IOS Release 11.1 CC.

Sample Display

The following is sample output from the **show interfaces fair-queue** command:

```
Router# show interfaces fair-queue

Hssi0/0/0 queue size 0
      packets output 1417079, drops 2
 WFQ: aggregate queue limit 54, individual queue limit 27
    max available buffers 54

    Class 0: weight 10 limit 27 qsize 0 packets output 1150 drops 0
    Class 1: weight 20 limit 27 qsize 0 packets output 0 drops 0
    Class 2: weight 30 limit 27 qsize 0 packets output 775482 drops 1
    Class 3: weight 40 limit 27 qsize 0 packets output 0 drops 0
```

Table 19-9 describes the fields and statistics shown in this display.

Table 19-9 *show interfaces fair-queue* Field Descriptions

Field	Description
queue size	Current output queue size for this interface.
packets output	Number of packets transmitted out this interface, or number of packets in this class transmitted out the interface.
drops	Number of packets dropped, or number of packets in this class dropped.
aggregate queue limit	Aggregate limit in number of packets.
individual queue limit	Individual limit in number of packets.
max available buffers	Available buffer space allocated to aggregate queue limit in number of packets.
Class	QoS group or ToS class.
weight	Percent of bandwidth allocated to this class during periods of congestion.
limit	Queue limit for this class in number of packets.
qsize	Current size of the queue for this class.

show interfaces random-detect

To display information about Weighted Random Early Detection (WRED) for a VIP-based interface, use the **show interfaces random-detect** EXEC command.

> **show interfaces** [*interface-type interface-number*] **random-detect**

Syntax   Description

interface-type   (Optional) The name of the interface.

interface-number   (Optional) The number of the interface.

Command Mode
EXEC

Usage Guidelines
This command first appeared in Cisco IOS Release 11.1 CC.

Sample Display

The following is sample output from the **show interfaces random-detect** command:

```
Router# show interfaces random-detect

FastEthernet1/0/0 queue size 0
      packets output 29692, drops 0
WRED: queue average 0
      weight 1/512
    Precedence 0: 109 min threshold, 218 max threshold, 1/10 mark weight
      1 packets output, drops: 0 random, 0 threshold
    Precedence 1: 122 min threshold, 218 max threshold, 1/10 mark weight
      (no traffic)
    Precedence 2: 135 min threshold, 218 max threshold, 1/10 mark weight
      14845 packets output, drops: 0 random, 0 threshold
    Precedence 3: 148 min threshold, 218 max threshold, 1/10 mark weight
      (no traffic)
    Precedence 4: 161 min threshold, 218 max threshold, 1/10 mark weight
      (no traffic)
    Precedence 5: 174 min threshold, 218 max threshold, 1/10 mark weight
      (no traffic)
    Precedence 6: 187 min threshold, 218 max threshold, 1/10 mark weight
      14846 packets output, drops: 0 random, 0 threshold
    Precedence 7: 200 min threshold, 218 max threshold, 1/10 mark weight
      (no traffic)
```

Table 19-10 describes the fields shown in this display.

Table 19-10 *show interfaces random-detect Field Descriptions*

Field	Description
queue size	Current output queue size for this interface.
packets output	Number of packets transmitted out this interface.
drops	Number of packets dropped.
queue average	Average queue length.
weight	Weighting factor used to determine the average queue size.
Precedence	WRED parameters for this precedence.
min threshold	Minimum threshold for this precedence.
max threshold	Maximum length of the queue. When the average queue is this long, any additional packets will be dropped.
mark weight	Probability of a packet being dropped if the average queue is at the maximum threshold.

Continues

Table 19-10 *show interfaces random-detect Field Descriptions (Continued)*

Field	Description
packets output	Number of packets with this precedence that have been transmitted.
random	Number of packets dropped randomly through the WRED process.
threshold	Number of packets dropped automatically because the average queue was at the maximum threshold length.
(no traffic)	No packets with this precedence.

Related Commands

To locate documentation of related commands, you can search online at www.cisco.com.

random-detect
random-detect exponential-weighting-constant
random-detect precedence

show interfaces rate-limit

To display information about committed access rate (CAR) for an interface, use the **show interfaces rate-limit** EXEC command.

> **show interfaces** [*interface-type interface-number*] **rate-limit**

Syntax   Description

interface-type   (Optional) The name of the interface.

interface-number   (Optional) The number of the interface.

Command Mode
EXEC

Usage Guidelines
This command first appeared in Cisco IOS Release 11.1 CC.

Sample Display

The following is sample output from the **show interfaces rate-limit** command:

```
Router# show interfaces fddi2/1/0 rate-limit

Fddi2/1/0
 Input
  matches: access-group rate-limit 100
   params: 800000000 bps, 64000 limit, 80000 extended limit
   conformed 0 packets, 0 bytes; action: set-prec-continue 1
   exceeded 0 packets, 0 bytes; action: set-prec-continue 0
   last packet: 4737508ms ago, current burst: 0 bytes
   last cleared 01:05:47 ago, conformed 0 bps, exceeded 0 bps
  matches: access-group 101
   params: 80000000 bps, 56000 limit, 72000 extended limit
   conformed 0 packets, 0 bytes; action: set-prec-transmit 5
   exceeded 0 packets, 0 bytes; action: set-prec-transmit 0
   last packet: 4738036ms ago, current burst: 0 bytes
   last cleared 01:02:05 ago, conformed 0 bps, exceeded 0 bps
  matches: all traffic
   params: 50000000 bps, 48000 limit, 64000 extended limit
   conformed 0 packets, 0 bytes; action: set-prec-transmit 5
   exceeded 0 packets, 0 bytes; action: set-prec-transmit 0
   last packet: 4738036ms ago, current burst: 0 bytes
   last cleared 01:00:22 ago, conformed 0 bps, exceeded 0 bps
 Output
  matches: all traffic
   params: 80000000 bps, 64000 limit, 80000 extended limit
   conformed 0 packets, 0 bytes; action: transmit
   exceeded 0 packets, 0 bytes; action: drop
   last packet: 4809528ms ago, current burst: 0 bytes
   last cleared 00:59:42 ago, conformed 0 bps, exceeded 0 bps
```

Table 19-11 describes the fields shown in this display.

Table 19-11 *show interfaces rate-limit Field Descriptions*

Field	Description
Input	These rate limits apply to packets received by the interface.
matches	Packets that match this rate limit.
params	Parameters for this rate limit as configured by the **rate-limit** command.
bps	Average rate in bits per second.
limit	Normal burst size in bytes.
extended limit	Excess burst size in bytes.

Continues

Table 19-11   *show interfaces rate-limit Field Descriptions (Continued)*

Field	Description
conformed action	Number of packets that have conformed with the rate limit. Conform action.
exceeded action	Number of packets that have exceeded the rate limit. Exceed action.
last packet	Time since the last packet in milliseconds.
current burst	Instantaneous burst size at the current time.

last cleared
  conformed
 	
  exceeded
	Time since the burst counter was set back to zero by the **clear counters** command.
	Number of packets conforming since the counter last cleared with the **clear counters** command.
	Number of packets exceeding since the counter last cleared with the **clear counters** command.

Output	These rate limits apply to packets sent by the interface.

Related Commands

To locate documentation of related commands, you can search online at www.cisco.com.

access-list rate-limit
clear counters
show access-lists rate-limit

show ip cef

To display entries in the FIB table based on the IP address, use the **show ip cef** EXEC command.

> **show ip cef** *network* [*mask* [**longer-prefix**]] [**detail**]

Syntax	Description
network	FIB entry for the specific destination network.
mask	(Optional) FIB entry for the specified destination network and mask.
longer-prefix	(Optional) FIB entries for all more specific destinations.
detail	(Optional) Detailed FIB information.

Command Mode
EXEC

Usage Guidelines

This command was updated in Cisco IOS Release 11.1 CC to add information on the QoS group ID.

Sample Display

The following is sample output from the **show ip cef** command for the network address 51.0.0.0:

```
Router# show ip cef 51.0.0.0

51.0.0.0/8, version 161, cached adjacency 200.31.51.2
0 packets, 0 bytes, precedence priority (1), qos-group 1
  via 50.50.50.1, 0 dependencies, recursive
    next hop 200.31.51.2, FastEthernet5/1/0 via 50.0.0.0/8
    valid cached adjacency
```

show ip interface

To display the usability status of interfaces configured for IP, use the **show ip interface** EXEC command.

> **show ip interface** [*interface-type interface-number*]

Syntax   Description

interface-type   (Optional) The name of the interface.

interface-number (Optional) The number of the interface.

Command Mode
EXEC

Usage Guidelines

This command first appeared in Cisco IOS Release 10.0. This command was updated in Cisco IOS Release 11.1 CC to add information on QoS policy propagation.

The Cisco IOS software automatically enters a directly connected route in the routing table if the interface is usable. A usable interface is one through which the software can send and receive packets. If the software determines that an interface is not usable, it removes the directly connected routing entry from the routing table. Removing the entry allows the software to use dynamic routing protocols to determine backup routes to the network (if any).

If the interface can provide two-way communication, the line protocol is marked "up." If the interface hardware is usable, the interface is marked "up."

If you specify an optional interface type, you will see only information on that specific interface.

If you specify no optional arguments, you will see information on all the interfaces.

When an asynchronous interface is encapsulated with the Point-to-Point Protocol (PPP) or the Serial Line Internet Protocol (SLIP), IP fast switching is enabled. A **show ip interface** command on an asynchronous interface encapsulated with PPP or SLIP displays a message indicating that IP fast switching is enabled.

Sample Display

The following is sample output from the **show ip interface** command:

```
Router# show ip interface hssi 5/0/0.1

Hssi5/0/0.1 is up, line protocol is up
 Internet address is 200.28.38.2/24
 Broadcast address is 255.255.255.255
 Address determined by non-volatile memory
 MTU is 4470 bytes
 Helper address is not set
 Directed broadcast forwarding is enabled
 Outgoing access list is not set
 Inbound access list is not set
 Proxy ARP is enabled
 Security level is default
 Split horizon is enabled
 ICMP redirects are always sent
 ICMP unreachables are always sent
 ICMP mask replies are never sent
 IP fast switching is enabled
 IP fast switching on the same interface is enabled
 IP Optimum switching is disabled
 IP Flow switching is enabled
 IP CEF switching is enabled
 IP Distributed switching is enabled
 IP LES Flow switching turbo vector
 IP Flow CEF switching turbo vector
 IP multicast fast switching is disabled
 IP multicast distributed fast switching is disabled
 Router Discovery is disabled
 IP output packet accounting is disabled
 IP access violation accounting is disabled
 TCP/IP header compression is disabled
 Probe proxy name replies are disabled
 Gateway Discovery is disabled
 Policy routing is disabled
 Web Cache Redirect is disabled
 BGP Policy Mapping is enabled (source ip-prec-map)
```

Table 19-12 describes the fields in this display.

Table 19-12 *show ip interface* Field Descriptions

Field	Description
Hssi5/0/0.1 is up	If the interface hardware is usable, the interface is marked "up." For an interface to be usable, both the interface hardware and line protocol must be up.
line protocol is up	If the interface can provide two-way communication, the line protocol is marked "up." For an interface to be usable, both the interface hardware and line protocol must be up.
Internet address and subnet mask	IP Internet address and subnet mask of the interface.
Broadcast address	The broadcast address.
Address determined by non-volatile memory	Indicates how the IP address of the interface was determined.
MTU	The MTU value set on the interface.
Helper address	A helper address if one has been set.
Secondary address	A secondary address if one has been set.
Directed broadcast forwarding	Indicates whether directed broadcast forwarding is enabled.
Multicast groups joined	Indicates the multicast groups to which this interface is a member.
Outgoing access list	Indicates whether the interface has an outgoing access list set.
Inbound access list	Indicates whether the interface has an incoming access list set.
Proxy ARP	Indicates whether Proxy ARP is enabled for the interface.
Security level	Specifies the IPSO security level set for this interface.
Split horizon	Indicates split horizon is enabled.
ICMP redirects	Specifies whether redirects will be sent on this interface.
ICMP unreachables	Specifies whether unreachable messages will be sent on this interface.
ICMP mask replies	Specifies whether mask replies will be sent on this interface.
IP fast switching	Specifies whether fast switching has been enabled for this interface. It is generally enabled on serial interfaces, such as this one.
IP fast switching on the same interface	Specifies whether fast switching has been enabled on the same interface.
IP Optimum switching	Specifies whether IP optimum switching is enabled.
IP Flow switching	Specifies whether IP flow switching is enabled.
IP CEF switching	Specifies whether IP CEF switching is enabled.

Continues

Table 19-12 *show ip interface Field Descriptions (Continued)*

Field	Description
IP Distributed switching	Specifies whether IP distributed switching is enabled.
IP LES Flow switching	Specifies whether the IP LES Flow switching is enabled.
IP Flow CEF switching	Specifies whether the IP flow CEF switching is enabled.
IP multicast fast switching	Specifies whether IP multicast fast switching is enabled.
IP multicast distributed fast switching	Specifies whether IP multicast distributed fast switching is enabled.
Router Discovery	Specifies whether the discovery process has been enabled for this interface. It is generally disabled on serial interfaces.
IP output packet accounting	Specifies whether IP accounting is enabled for this interface and the threshold (maximum number of entries).
IP access violation accounting	Indicates whether IP access violation accounting is enabled or disabled.
TCP/IP header compression	Indicates whether compression is enabled or disabled.
Probe proxy name	Indicates whether HP probe proxy name replies are generated.
Gateway Discovery	Specifies whether gateway discovery is enabled.
Policy routing	Specifies whether policy routing is enabled.
Web Cache Redirect	Specifies whether web cache redirect is enabled.
BGP Policy Mapping	Specifies whether BGP policy mapping is enabled and the current settings on the interface.

show ip rsvp installed

To display RSVP-related installed filters and corresponding bandwidth information, use the **show ip rsvp installed** EXEC command.

>   **show ip rsvp installed** [*interface-type interface-number*]

Syntax	Description
interface-type	(Optional) The name of the interface.
interface-number	(Optional) The number of the interface.

Command Mode
EXEC

Usage Guidelines

This command first appeared in Cisco IOS Release 11.2.

The command displays the current installed RSVP filters and the corresponding bandwidth information for a specified interface or all interfaces.

Sample Display

The following is sample output from the **show ip rsvp installed** command:

```
Router# show ip rsvp installed

RSVP:
RSVP: Ethernet1: has no installed reservations
RSVP: Serial0:
    kbps   To              From         Protocol DPort Sport Weight Conversation
    0      224.250.250.1   132.240.2.28    UDP 20    30    128    270
    150    224.250.250.1   132.240.2.1     UDP 20    30    128    268
    100    224.250.250.1   132.240.1.1     UDP 20    30    128    267
    200    224.250.250.1   132.240.1.25    UDP 20    30    256    265
    200    224.250.250.2   132.240.1.25    UDP 20    30    128    271
    0      224.250.250.2   132.240.2.28    UDP 20    30    128    269
    150    224.250.250.2   132.240.2.1     UDP 20    30    128    266
    350    224.250.250.3   0.0.0.0         UDP 20    0     128    26
```

Table 19-13 describes significant fields shown in this display.

Table 19-13 *show ip rsvp installed* Field Descriptions

Field	Description
kbps	Reserved rate.
To	IP address of the source device.
From	IP address of the destination device.
Protocol DPort	Protocol type of the destination UDP/TCP port (no longer the usual protocol).
Sport	Source UDP/TCP port.
Weight	Weight used in WFQ.
Conversation	WFQ conversation number. If the WFQ is not configured on the interface, weight and conversation will be zero.

show ip rsvp interface

To display RSVP-related interface information, use the **show ip rsvp interface** EXEC command.

show ip rsvp interface [*interface-type interface-number*]

Syntax   Description

interface-type   (Optional) The name of the interface.

interface-number   (Optional) The number of the interface.

Command Mode

EXEC

Usage Guidelines

This command first appeared in Cisco IOS Release 11.2.

Use this command to show the current allocation budget and maximum allocatable bandwidth.

Sample Display

The following is sample output from the **show ip rsvp interface** command:

```
Router# show ip rsvp interface

interfac allocate i/f max  flow max per/255 UDP  IP   UDP_IP   UDP M/C
Et1      0M       7500K    7500K    0  /255 0    0    0        0
Se0      0M       1158K    1158K    0  /255 0    0    0        0
Se1      30K      1158K    1158K    6  /255 0    1    0        0
```

Table 19-14 describes significant fields shown in this display.

Table 19-14 *show ip rsvp interface Field Descriptions*

Field	Description
interface	Interface name.
allocate	Current allocation budget.
i/f max	Maximum allocatable bandwidth.
flow max	Maximum flow possible on this interface.
per /255	Percent of bandwidth utilized.

Continues

Table 19-14 *show ip rsvp interface Field Descriptions (Continued)*

Field	Description
UDP	Number of neighbors sending UDP-encapsulated RSVP.
IP	Number of neighbors sending IP-encapsulated RSVP.
UDP_IP	Number of neighbors sending both UDP- and IP-encapsulated RSVP.
UDP M/C	Is router configured for UDP on this interface?

show ip rsvp neighbor

To display current RSVP neighbors, use the **show ip rsvp neighbor** EXEC command.

>   **show ip rsvp neighbor** [*interface-type interface-number*]

Syntax   Description

interface-type   (Optional) The name of the interface.

interface-number   (Optional) The number of the interface.

Command Mode
EXEC

Usage Guidelines
This command first appeared in Cisco IOS Release 11.2.

Use this command to show the current RSVP neighbors and identify if the neighbor is using IP, UDP, or RSVP encapsulation for a specified interface or all interfaces.

Sample Display
The following is sample output from the **show ip rsvp neighbor** command:

```
Router# show ip rsvp neighbor

Interfac Neighbor        Encapsulation
Se1      132.240.1.49    RSVP
```

show ip rsvp request

To display RSVP-related request information being requested upstream, use the **show ip rsvp request** EXEC command.

>   **show ip rsvp request** [*interface-type interface-number*]

Syntax   Description

interface-type   (Optional) The name of the interface.

interface-number   (Optional) The number of the interface.

Command Mode
EXEC

Usage Guidelines

This command first appeared in Cisco IOS Release 11.2.

Use this command to show the RSVP reservations currently being requested upstream for a specified interface or all interfaces. The received reservations may differ from requests because of aggregated or refused reservations.

Sample Display

The following is sample output from the **show ip rsvp request** command:

```
Router# show ip rsvp request

To            From        Pro DPort Sport Next Hop      I/F    Fi Serv BPS Bytes
132.240.1.49  132.240.4.53 1   0     0     132.240.3.53 Et1    FF LOAD 30K 3K
```

Table 19-15 describes significant fields shown in this display.

Table 19-15 *show ip rsvp request Field Descriptions*

Field	Description
To	IP address of the receiver.
From	IP address of the sender.
Pro	Protocol code. Code 1 indicates ICMP.

Continues

Table 19-15 *show ip rsvp request Field Descriptions (Continued)*

Field	Description
DPort	Destination port number.
Sport	Source port number.
Next Hop	IP address of the next hop.
I/F	Interface of the next hop.
Fi	Filter (Wild Card Filter, Shared Explicit Filter, or Fixed Filter).
Serv	Service (value can be **rate** or **load**).
BPS	Requested rate of the reservation in bits per second.
Bytes	Bytes of burst size requested.

show ip rsvp reservation

To display RSVP-related receiver information currently in the database, use the **show ip rsvp reservation** EXEC command.

> **show ip rsvp reservation** [*interface-type interface-number*]

Syntax	Description
interface-type	(Optional) The name of the interface.
interface-number	(Optional) The number of the interface.

Command Mode
EXEC

Usage Guidelines
This command first appeared in Cisco IOS Release 11.2.

Use this command to show the current receiver (RESV) information presently in the database for a specified interface or all interfaces. This information includes reservations aggregated and forwarded from other RSVP routers.

Sample Display

The following is sample output from the **show ip rsvp reservation** command:

```
Router# show ip rsvp reservation

To              From        Pro DPort Sport Next Hop      I/F   Fi Serv BPS Bytes
132.240.1.49  132.240.4.53  1   0     0     132.240.1.49  Se1   FF LOAD 30K 3K
```

Table 19-16 describes significant fields shown in this display.

Table 19-16 *show ip rsvp reservation Field Descriptions*

Field	Descriptions
To	IP address of the receiver.
From	IP address of the sender.
Pro	Protocol code. Code 1 indicates ICMP.
DPort	Destination port number.
Sport	Source port number.
Next Hop	IP address of the next hop.
I/F	Interface of the next hop.
Fi	Filter (Wild Card Filter, Shared Explicit Filter, or Fixed Filter).
Serv	Service (value can be **rate** or **load**).
BPS	Requested rate of the reservation in bits per second.
Bytes	Bytes of burst size.

show ip rsvp sender

To display RSVP PATH-related sender information currently in the database, use the **show ip rsvp sender** EXEC command.

> **show ip rsvp sender** [*interface-type interface-number*]

Syntax	Description
interface-type	(Optional) The name of the interface.
interface-number	(Optional) The number of the interface.

Command Mode

EXEC

Usage Guidelines

This command first appeared in Cisco IOS Release 11.2.

Use this command to show the RSVP sender (PATH) information currently in the database for a specified interface or all interfaces.

Sample Display

The following is sample output from the **show ip rsvp sender** command:

```
Router# show ip rsvp sender

To             From         Pro DPort Sport Prev Hop       I/F  BPS  Bytes
132.240.1.49   132.240.4.53  1   0     0    132.240.3.53   Et1  30K   3K
132.240.2.51   132.240.5.54  1   0     0    132.240.3.54   Et1  30K   3K
```

Table 19-17 describes the fields shown in this display.

Table 19-17 *show ip rsvp sender Field Descriptions*

Field	Description
To	IP address of the receiver.
From	IP address of the sender.
Pro	Protocol code. Code 1 indicates ICMP.
DPort	Destination port number.
Sport	Source port number.
Prev Hop	IP address of the previous hop.
I/F	Interface of the previous hop.
BPS	Reservation rate in bits per second the application is advertising it might achieve.
Bytes	Bytes of burst size the application is advertising it might achieve.

show queue

To list fair queuing configuration and statistics for a particular interface, use the **show queue** privileged EXEC command.

>   **show queue** *interface-type interface-number*

Syntax	Description
interface-type	The name of the interface.
interface-number	The number of the interface.

Command Mode

Privileged EXEC

Usage Guidelines

This command displays statistics for interfaces configured with the fair queuing strategy.

Sample Display

The following is sample output from the **show queue** command. There are two active conversations on the serial 1 interface. WFQ ensures that both of these IP data streams, one TCP and the other UDP, receive equal bandwidth on the interface while they have messages in the pipeline.

```
Router# show queue serial1

  Input queue: 0/75/0 (size/max/drops); Total output drops: 303628
  Queuing strategy: weighted fair
  Output queue: 64/1000/64/303628 (size/max total/threshold/drops)
     Conversations  2/2/256 (active/max active/max total)
     Reserved Conversations 0/0 (allocated/max allocated)

  (depth/weight/discards/tail drops/interleaves) 45/4096/1123/0/0
  Conversation 244, linktype: ip, length: 50
  source: 55.1.1.1, destination: 66.1.1.2, id: 0x0000, ttl: 59,
  TOS: 0 prot: 6, source port 55, destination port 55

  (depth/weight/discards/tail drops/interleaves) 19/4096/302541/0/0
  Conversation 185, linktype: ip, length: 118
  source: 55.1.1.1, destination: 66.1.1.2, id: 0x0000, ttl: 59,
  TOS: 0 prot: 17, source port 20, destination port 20
```

Table 19-18 describes the fields shown in this display.

Table 19-18 *show queue Field Descriptions*

Field	Description
Input Queue	Input queue size in packets.
Total output drops	Total output packet drops.
Queuing strategy	Type of queuing active on this interface.
Output queue	Output queue size in packets.
Conversations	WFQ conversation number.
Reserved Conversations	Total number of reserved WFQ conversations. Default is 256.
depth	Queue depth for the conversation in packets.
weight	Weight used in WFQ.
discards	Number of packet discards for the conversation.
tail drops	Number of tail drop packets for the conversation.
interleaves	Number of packets interleaved.
linktype	Protocol name.
length	Packet length.
source	Source IP address.
destination	Destination IP address.
id	Packet ID.
ttl	Time to live count.
TOS	IP type of service.
prot	Layer 4 protocol number.

show queuing

To list all or selected configured queuing strategies, use the **show queuing** privileged EXEC command.

show queuing [custom | fair | priority | red]

Syntax	Description
custom	(Optional) Status of the custom queuing list configuration.
fair	(Optional) Status of the fair queuing configuration.
priority	(Optional) Status of the priority queuing list configuration.
red	(Optional) Status of the WRED configuration.

Default

If no keyword is entered, this command shows the configuration of all interfaces.

Command Mode

Privileged EXEC

Usage Guidelines

This command first appeared in Cisco IOS Release 10.3.

Sample Displays

The following is sample output from the **show queuing custom** command:

```
Router# show queuing custom
Current custom queue configuration:

    List   Queue   Args
    3      10      default
    3      3       interface Tunnel3
    3      3       protocol ip
    3      3       byte-count 444 limit 3
```

The following is sample output from the **show queuing** command. There are two active conversations in the serial interface 0. Weighted fair queuing ensures that both of these IP data streams—both using TCP—receive equal bandwidth on the interface while they have messages in the pipeline, even though there is more FTP data in the queue than RCP data.

```
Router# show queuing

    Current fair queue configuration:

        Interface        Discard      Dynamic        Reserved
                         threshold    queue count    queue count
        Serial0          64           256            0
        Serial1          64           256            0
        Serial2          64           256            0
        Serial3          64           256            0

    Current priority queue configuration:
```

```
List   Queue  Args
1      high   protocol cdp
2      medium interface Ethernet1
Current custom queue configuration:
Current RED queue configuration:
  Interface: Ethernet3   Exp-weight-constant: 9
    Class   Min-th   Max-th   Mark-prob
    0       20       40       1/10
    1       22       40       1/10
    2       24       40       1/10
    3       26       40       1/10
    4       28       40       1/10
    5       31       40       1/10
    6       33       40       1/10
    7       35       40       1/10
    rsvp    37       40       1/10
```

Related Commands

To locate documentation of related commands, you can search online at www.cisco.com.

custom-queue-list
fair-queue
priority-group
priority-list interface
priority-list queue-limit
queue-list interface
queue-list queue byte-count
random-detect

show tech-support rsvp

To generate a report of all RSVP-related information, use the **show tech-support rsvp** command.

> **show tech-support rsvp**

Syntax Description

This command has no arguments or keywords.

Default

This command reports on all RSVP activity.

Part
VI

Command Reference

Command Mode

Privileged EXEC

Usage Guidelines

This command is not required for normal use of the operating system. This command is useful when contacting technical support personnel with questions regarding RSVP. The **show tech-support rsvp** command generates a series of reports that can be useful to technical support personnel attempting to solve problems.

Any issues or caveats that apply to the **show tech-support** command also apply to this command. For example, the enable password, if configured, is not displayed in the output of the **show running-config** command.

The **show tech-support rsvp** command is equivalent to issuing the following commands:

show ip rsvp installed
show ip rsvp interface
show ip rsvp neighbor
show ip rsvp request
show ip rsvp reservation
show ip rsvp sender
show running-config
show version

Refer to the displays and descriptions for these commands for information about the **show tech-support rsvp** command display.

show traffic-shape

To display the current traffic-shaping configuration, use the **show traffic-shape** EXEC command.

> **show traffic-shape** [*interface-type*]

Syntax   Description

interface-type   (Optional) The name of the interface.

Default

Traffic shaping details for all configured interfaces are shown.

Command Mode

EXEC

Usage Guidelines

This command first appeared in Cisco IOS Release 11.2.

You must have first enabled traffic shaping using the **traffic-shape rate**, **traffic-shape group**, or **frame-relay traffic-shaping** command to display traffic-shaping information.

Sample Display

The following is sample output from the **show traffic-shape** command:

```
Router# show traffic-shape

        access Target   Byte  Sustain   Excess    Interval  Increment Adapt
I/F     list   Rate     Limit bits/int  bits/int  (ms)      (bytes)   Active
Et0     101    1000000  23437 125000    125000    63        7813      -
Et1            5000000  87889 625000    625000    16        9766      -
```

Table 19-19 describes the fields shown in this display.

Table 19-19 *show traffic-shape Field Descriptions*

Field	Description
I/F	Interface.
access list	Number of the access list.
Target Rate	Rate that traffic is shaped to in bps.
Byte Limit	Maximum number of bytes transmitted per internal interval.
Sustain bits/int	Configured sustained bits per interval.
Excess bits/int	Configured excess bits in the first interval.
Interval (ms)	Interval being used internally, which may be smaller than the committed burst divided by the committed information rate if the router determines that traffic flow will be more stable with a smaller configured interval.
Increment (bytes)	Number of bytes that will be sustained per internal interval.
Adapt Active	Contains "BECN" if Frame Relay has backward explicit congestion notification (BECN) adaptation configured.

Related Commands

To locate documentation of related commands, you can search online at www.cisco.com.

frame-relay traffic-shaping
show traffic-shape statistics
traffic-shape adaptive
traffic-shape fecn-adapt
traffic-shape group
traffic-shape rate

show traffic-shape statistics

To display the current traffic-shaping statistics, use the **show traffic-shape statistics** EXEC command.

> **show traffic-shape statistics** [*interface-type*]

Syntax Description

Syntax	Description
interface-type	(Optional) The name of the interface.

Default

Traffic shaping statistics for all configured interfaces are shown.

Command Mode

EXEC

Usage Guidelines

This command first appeared in Cisco IOS Release 11.2.

You must have first enabled traffic shaping using the **traffic-shape rate**, **traffic-shape group**, or **frame-relay traffic-shaping** command to display traffic-shaping information.

Sample Display

The following is sample output from the **show traffic-shape statistics** command:

```
Router# show traffic-shape statistics

      Access Queue   Packets   Bytes   Packets   Bytes    Shaping
I/F   List   Depth                     Delayed   Delayed  Active
Et0   101    0       2         180     0         0        no
Et1          0       0         0       0         0        no
```

Table 19-20 describes the fields shown in this display.

Table 19-20 *show traffic-shape statistics Field Descriptions*

Field	Description
I/F	Interface.
Access List	Number of the access list.
Queue Depth	Number of messages in the queue.
Packets	Number of packets sent through the interface.
Bytes	Number of bytes sent through the interface.
Packets Delayed	Number of packets sent through the interface that were delayed in the traffic shaping queue.
Bytes Delayed	Number of bytes sent through the interface that were delayed in the traffic shaping queue.
Shaping Active	Contains "yes" when timers indicate that traffic shaping is occurring and "no" if traffic shaping is not occurring.

Related Commands

To locate documentation of related commands, you can search online at www.cisco.com.

frame-relay traffic-shaping
show interfaces
show ip rsvp interface
traffic-shape adaptive
traffic-shape group
traffic-shape rate

traffic-shape adaptive

To configure a Frame Relay subinterface to estimate the available bandwidth when backward explicit congestion notifications (BECNs) are received, use the **traffic-shape adaptive** interface configuration command. To stop adapting to congestion signals, use the **no** form of this command.

> **traffic-shape adaptive** [*bit-rate*]
> **no traffic-shape adaptive**

Syntax Description

bit-rate	(Optional) Lowest bit rate that traffic is shaped to in bits per second.

Default

The default is half the value specified for the **traffic-shape rate** or **traffic-shape group** command options.

Command Mode

Interface configuration

Usage Guidelines

This command first appeared in Cisco IOS Release 11.2.

This command specifies the boundaries in which traffic will be shaped when BECNs are received. You must enable traffic shaping on the interface with the **traffic-shape rate** or **traffic-shape group** command before you can use the **traffic-shape adaptive** command.

The bit rate specified for the **traffic-shape rate** command is the upper limit, and the bit rate specified for the **traffic-shape adaptive** command is the lower limit to which traffic is shaped when BECNs are received on the interface. The rate actually shaped to will be between these two bit rates.

You should configure this command and the **traffic-shape fecn-adapt** command on both ends of the connection to ensure adaptive traffic shaping over the connection, even when traffic is flowing primarily in one direction. The **traffic-shape fecn-adapt** command configures the router to reflect forward explicit congestion notification (FECN) signals as BECNs.

Example

The following example configures traffic shaping on serial interface 0.1 with an upper limit of 128 kbps and a lower limit of 64 kbps. This configuration allows the link to run from 64 to 128 kbps, depending on the congestion level.

```
router(config)# interface serial 0
router(config-if)# encapsulation-frame-relay
router(config)# interface serial 0.1
router(config-if)# traffic-shape rate 128000
router(config-if)# traffic-shape adaptive 64000
router(config-if)# traffic-shape fecn-adapt
```

Related Commands

To locate documentation of related commands, you can search online at www.cisco.com.

show traffic-shape
show traffic-shape statistics
traffic-shape fecn-adapt

traffic-shape group
traffic-shape rate

traffic-shape fecn-adapt

To reply to messages with the forward explicit congestion notification (FECN) bit, which is set with TEST RESPONSE messages with the BECN bit set, use the **traffic-shape fecn-adapt** interface configuration command. To stop backward explicit congestion notification (BECN) message generation, use the **no** form of this command.

> **traffic-shape fecn-adapt**
> **no traffic-shape fecn-adapt**

Syntax Description

This command has no arguments or keywords.

Default

Traffic shaping is disabled.

Command Mode

Interface configuration

Usage Guidelines

This command first appeared in Cisco IOS Release 11.2.

Enable traffic shaping on the interface with the **traffic-shape rate** or **traffic-shape group** command.

Use this command to reflect FECN bits as BECN bits to notify the other data terminal equipment (DTE) that it is transmitting too fast. Use the **traffic-shape adaptive** command to configure the router to adapt its transmission rate when it receives BECNs.

You should configure this command and the **traffic-shape adaptive** command on both ends of the connection to ensure adaptive traffic shaping over the connection, even when traffic is flowing primarily in one direction.

Example

The following example configures traffic shaping on serial interface 0.1 with an upper limit of 128 kbps and a lower limit of 64 kbps. This configuration allows the link to run from 64 to 128 kbps, depending on the congestion level. The router reflects FECNs as BECNs.

```
router(config)# interface serial 0
router(config-if)# encapsulation-frame-relay
router(config)# interface serial 0.1
router(config-if)# traffic-shape rate 128000
router(config-if)# traffic-shape adaptive 64000
router(config-if)# traffic-shape fecn-adapt
```

Related Commands

To locate documentation of related commands, you can search online at www.cisco.com.

show traffic-shape
show traffic-shape statistics
traffic-shape adaptive
traffic-shape group
traffic-shape rate

traffic-shape group

To enable traffic shaping based on a specific access list for outbound traffic on an interface, use the **traffic-shape group** interface configuration command. To disable traffic shaping on the interface for the access list, use the **no** form of this command.

> **traffic-shape group** *access-list bit-rate* [*burst-size* [*excess-burst-size*]]
> **no traffic-shape group** *access-list*

Syntax	Description
access-list	Number of the access list that controls the packets that traffic shaping is applied to on the interface.
bit-rate	Bit rate that traffic is shaped to in bits per second. This is the access bit rate that you contract with your service provider or the service levels you intend to maintain.
burst-size	(Optional) Sustained number of bits that can be transmitted per interval. On Frame Relay interfaces, this is the committed burst size contracted with your service provider.
excess-burst-size	(Optional) Maximum number of bits that can exceed the burst size in the first interval in a congestion event. On Frame Relay interfaces, this is the excess burst size contracted with your service provider. The default is equal to the burst-size.

Default

This command is not on by default.

Command Mode

Interface configuration

Usage Guidelines

This command first appeared in Cisco IOS Release 11.2.

NOTE	Traffic shaping is not supported with optimum, distributed, or flow switching. If you enable this command, all interfaces will revert to fast switching.

Traffic shaping uses queues to limit surges that can congest a network. Data is buffered and then sent into the network in regulated amounts to ensure that traffic will fit within the promised traffic envelope for the particular connection.

The **traffic-shape group** command allows you to specify one or more previously defined access lists to shape traffic to on the interface. You must specify one **traffic-shape group** command for each access list on the interface.

Use traffic shaping if you have a network with differing access rates or if you are offering a subrate service. You can configure the values according to your contract with your service provider or the service levels you intend to maintain.

An interval is calculated as follows:

- If the *burst-size* is not equal to zero, the interval is the *burst-size* divided by the *bit-rate*.

- If the *burst-size* is zero, the interval is the *excess-burst-size* divided by the *bit-rate*.

Traffic shaping is supported on all media and encapsulation types on the router. To perform traffic shaping on Frame Relay virtual circuits, you can also use the **frame-relay traffic-shaping** command.

If traffic shaping is performed on a Frame Relay network with the **traffic-shape rate** command, you can also use the **traffic-shape adaptive** command to specify the minimum bit rate the traffic is shaped to.

Part
VI

Command Reference

Example

The following example enables traffic that matches access list 101 to be shaped to a certain rate and traffic matching access list 102 to be shaped to another rate on the interface:

```
router(config)# interface serial 1
router(config-if)# traffic-shape group 101 128000 16000 8000
router(config-if)# traffic-shape group 102 130000 10000 1000
```

Related Commands

To locate documentation of related commands, you can search online at www.cisco.com.

access-list
show traffic-shape
show traffic-shape statistics
traffic-shape adaptive
traffic-shape fecn-adapt
traffic-shape rate

traffic-shape rate

To enable traffic shaping for outbound traffic on an interface, use the **traffic-shape rate** interface configuration command. To disable traffic shaping on the interface, use the **no** form of this command.

> **traffic-shape rate** *bit-rate* [*burst-size* [*excess-burst-size*]]
> **no traffic-shape rate**

Syntax	Description
bit-rate	Bit rate that traffic is shaped to in bits per second. This is the access bit rate that you contract with your service provider, or the service levels you intend to maintain.
burst-size	(Optional) Sustained number of bits that can be transmitted per interval. On Frame Relay interfaces, this is the committed burst size contracted with your service provider.
excess-burst-size	(Optional) Maximum number of bits that can exceed the burst size in the first interval in a congestion event. On Frame Relay interfaces, this is the excess burst size contracted with your service provider. The default is equal to the burst-size.

Default

Traffic shaping is disabled.

Command Mode

Interface configuration

Usage Guidelines

This command first appeared in Cisco IOS Release 11.2.

NOTE	Traffic shaping is not supported with optimum, distributed, or flow switching. If you enable this command, all interfaces will revert to fast switching.

Traffic shaping uses queues to limit surges that can congest a network. Data is buffered and then sent into the network in regulated amounts to ensure that traffic will fit within the promised traffic envelope for the particular connection.

Use traffic shaping if you have a network with differing access rates or if you are offering a subrate service. You can configure the values according to your contract with your service provider or the service levels you intend to maintain.

An interval is calculated as follows:

- If the *burst-size* is not equal to zero, the interval is the *burst-size* divided by the *bit-rate*.

- If the *burst-size* is zero, the interval is the *excess-burst-size* divided by the *bit-rate*.

Traffic shaping is supported on all media and encapsulation types on the router. To perform traffic shaping on Frame Relay virtual circuits, you can also use the **frame-relay traffic-shaping** command.

If traffic shaping is performed on a Frame Relay network with the **traffic-shape rate** command, you can also use the **traffic-shape adaptive** command to specify the minimum bit rate the traffic is shaped to.

Example

The following example enables traffic shaping on serial interface 0 using the bandwidth required by the service provider:

```
router(config)# interface serial 0
router(config-if)# traffic-shape rate 128000 16000 8000
```

Related Commands

To locate documentation of related commands, you can search online at www.cisco.com.

show traffic-shape
show traffic-shape statistics
traffic-shape adaptive
traffic-shape fecn-adapt
traffic-shape group

INDEX

Symbols

? command, xxxi

A

abbreviating commands (context-sensitive help), xxxi
access-list command
    access list policy propagation configurations, 18
    CAR (committed access rate), 26, 28
    configuring GTS, 100
access-list rate-limit command, 155–156
    CAR, 26
access lists
    GTS, configuring for, 100
    policy propagation via BGP, configuring, 18
addresses, IP precedence (signaling), 121
all IP traffic, configuring CAR and DCAR for, 24–25
AS path attributes, configuring policy propagation via BGP, 17
assigning
    packets
        to custom queue lists, 56
        to priority queues, 61–62
    priority queuing lists to interfaces, 63
average command, 73
avoid command, 50

B

backward explicit congestion notification, See BECN
bandwidth, saving (configuring CRTP), 151
BECN (backward explicit congestion notification)
    FRTS (Frame Relay Traffic Shaping), 97–98
    GTS (Generic Traffic Shaping), 96
    WFQ (weighted fair queuing), 43
benefits (QoS), xvi
best-effort service model, xvii
BGP (Border Gateway Protocol)
    classification, xxi
    policy propagation (packet classification), 7
bgp-policy command, 157

bgp-policy ip-prec-map command
    access list policy propagation configurations, 18
    AS path policy propagation configurations, 18
    community list policy propagation configurations, 17
bits (IP precedence packet classification), 4–5
broadcast queues, creating for FRTS interfaces, 111–112
byte counts (CQ)
    determining, 46–47
    values, 46

C

CAR (committed access rate), xx, 15, 23–24
    classification (policy examples), xx
    commands
        access-list, 26, 28
        access-list rate-limit, 26
        continue, 25
        drop, 25
        end, 25–26
        interface, 24, 26–27
        random-detect precedence, 27
        rate-limit, 25–27
        set-prec-continue, 25
        set-prec-transmit, 25
        show access-lists, 28
        show access-lists rate-limit, 28
        show interfaces, 28
        transmit, 25
    configuring
        examples, 28–31
        for all IP traffic, 24–25
        policies, 26–27
    IP precedence, 122
    monitoring, 28
    multiple rate policies, 92
    packet classification, 3, 8
    rate limiting, xxiv, 89
        average rate, 90
        excess burst size, 91
        matching criteria, 90
        normal burst size, 90
    restrictions, 93
    routers supported on, 89
caution (usage in text), xxix

H-J

K-L

Q

R

T